CRIME FICTION, 1800–2000

Related titles by Palgrave Macmillan

Warren Chernaik, *The Art of Detective Fiction* (2000)
Ed Christian, *The Postcolonial Detective* (2001)
Stephen Knight, *Form and Ideology in Crime Fiction* (1980)
Bruce F. Murphy, *Encyclopedia of Murder and Mystery* (2002)
Hans Bertens and Theo D'haen, *Contemporary American Crime Fiction*
   (2001)

Crime Fiction, 1800–2000

Detection, Death, Diversity

Stephen Knight

First published 2004 by
PALGRAVE MACMILLAN
Houndmills, Basingstoke, Hampshire RG21 6XS and
175 Fifth Avenue, New York, N.Y. 10010
Companies and representatives throughout the world

PALGRAVE MACMILLAN is the global academic imprint of the Palgrave Macmillan division of St. Martin's Press, LLC and of Palgrave Macmillan Ltd. Macmillan® is a registered trademark in the United States, United Kingdom and other countries. Palgrave is a registered trademark in the European Union and other countries.

ISBN 0–333–79178–9 hardback
ISBN 0–333–79179–7 paperback

This book is printed on paper suitable for recycling and made from fully managed and sustained forest sources.

A catalogue record for this book is available from the British Library.

Library of Congress Cataloging-in-Publication Data

Knight, Stephen Thomas.
    Crime fiction, 1800–2000 : detection, death, diversity / Stephen Knight.
        p. cm.
    Includes bibliographical references and index.
    ISBN 0–333–79178–9 (cloth)—ISBN 0–333–79179–7 (pbk.)
    1. Detective and mystery stories, English—History and criticism.
    2. Detective and mystery stories, American—History and criticism.
    3. Crime in literature. I. Title.

PR830.D4K59 2003
823'.'087209—dc21   2003051447

10 9 8 7 6 5 4 3 2 1
13 12 11 10 09 08 07 06 05 04

Printed in China

For Elizabeth

Contents

Preface

No detective is needed to identify the vigorous life and remarkable diversity of crime fiction. The statistics are dramatic – over a billion Agatha Christie novels sold, American feminist detectives expanding from 40 to 400 between 1980 and 2000, even a global estimate that a third of the fiction published in English belongs to the genre. Visual evidence is obvious in the large and heavily patronised crime and mystery sections in bookshops and public libraries, and the massive output of crime stories in film, television and computer games seems to have enhanced rather than reduced the interest in literary fictions of crime.

But the study of the genre is harder to detect. Remarkably, there is now, since the recent demise of *Clues*, no academic journal devoted to crime fiction and there are none of the regular international scholarly conferences or conference-sections that seem routine in other literary fields, including science fiction. The books that have appeared in the past tended to be directed at a general readership rather than academic research or teaching, such as Barnard on Christie, Durham on Chandler and Symons on the whole genre, like the output of the Popular Press at Bowling Green and the recent encyclopaedias edited by Reilly, Pederson, Herbert and Winks. No doubt this is partly because of the unprestigious nature of the form, parallel to the round-up reviews of new crime novels that are positioned late in the review pages of magazines and newspapers. The shortage of depth analysis in the past seems caused also by the fact that traditional literary criticism has found little to say about a genre whose effects and successes do not depend much on profundities of style and insight but rather draws its massive popularity from dynamic variations on compulsive patterns and from its own rapid responses to changing sociocultural concerns. On the relatively rare occasions in the past when a critic has brought a strong analytic technique to the genre – usually a non-literary one – there have been highly positive results, as in Messac's scholarly exploration of origins, the structural accounts of genre and sub-genre by Todorov, Cawelti and Priestman, Porter's development of 1970s critical theory to explore the ideologies of crime fiction, Kayman's deployment of legal theory and history, or Miller's use of Foucault to unfold the subtleties of the nineteenth-century classics.

In recent years work of this kind has been expanding, apparently because of the growth of theory-informed approaches in literary criticism and the world-wide move of English studies towards a broader curriculum – not only are there now hundreds of courses on crime fiction in universities and colleges, but the impact of feminism, cultural studies, postcolonial and ethnic studies is clear in the important books produced by scholars like Klein, Munt, Reddy, Malmgren, Pepper, Soitos and Walton and Jones, and also in the recent Palgrave series edited by Clive Bloom and a regular flow of cutting-edge essay collections. The new range of sophisticated analysis has substantially enlightened this book – it is striking how many of the references to critics are dated in the last ten years – as I have sought to combine the insights of crime fiction critics with my own experience as a reader, reviewer, teacher and researcher in crime fiction for over 40 years to produce an account of the whole genre from its obscure and tentative origins to its highly diverse present.

This book does not claim a complete coverage – even the largest of the encyclopaedias cannot do that. Rather, it traces the changing patterns of crime fiction over the last two centuries while it has been developing as a separate genre, with its own structures and responses to disorder. I have tried to treat authors and texts according to their importance and impact, and so, unsurprisingly, there are fairly full discussions of well-known major authors from Poe to Paretsky. But I have also dealt with authors from the past whose work and significance has often been overlooked, like William Russell, G. W. M. Reynolds, Metta Fuller, Emile Gaboriau, J. S. Fletcher, Carolyn Wells, Gladys Mitchell and Margaret Millar. I have also tried to select from the modern period writers who are shaping, rather than merely repeating, the modern patterns in the genre.

Description always involves evaluation, and some readers may well disagree with my emphases and my omissions – but that kind of engaged and refining reading is the purpose of a book like this. There are also ways of treating the material that might well cause dissent and stimulate development: others may see differently the relations of the disciplinary amateurs and the police detectives of the early to mid-nineteenth century, or the treatment of the psychothriller as being essentially separate from the crime novel and the gangster story, or the final arguments that the postmodern mystery is a form of dissenting diversity and that there is now a new sub-genre in the thriller of violence. I recall how valuable for its coverage and how provocative in its assertions I found Julian Symons's *Bloody Murder* as I was starting to work seriously on crime fiction, and how my own book of 1980 was in a real way an attempt to rewrite his account. If this new analytic survey has similar productive results I will feel that the dusty days in libraries, the painful poring over plots, dates and details, have been fully worth while.

One of the major issues facing the author of an account of crime fiction is which terms to use to describe, and so sort, its varying forms. Some people use the term 'detective fiction' for the whole genre, others call it 'mystery fiction'. But as a reader soon discovers, there are plenty of novels (including some by Christie) without a detective and nearly as many without even a mystery (like most of Patricia Highsmith's work). There is, though, always a crime (or very occasionally just the appearance of one) and that is why I have used the generally descriptive term 'crime fiction' for the whole genre. The sub-genres are as elusive to name. The name 'thriller' is sometimes used for all crime fiction, but sometimes just for the detective-free mystery adventure and at other times for the excitements of the private-eye pattern. In addition to this uncertainty, 'thriller' is too simply emotive for useful employment except in the special case of the psychothriller, where the psychological emphasis justifies the sense of disturbing excitement in the term.

Sub-generic definitions must interrelate as parts of the whole genre. In his recent book Malmgren has divided the genre into three types: 'the mystery' – the Christie approach; the 'detective story' – Chandler-style writing; and 'crime fiction' – work in the James M. Cain tradition and including gangster stories. Valuable though Malmgren's analysis often is, this seems potentially confusing: in fact mysteries, detectives and crimes interweave among the sub-genres, and I have preferred here to use terms which depend on centrally structural, even technical, features of the texts which do not overlap like Malmgren's categories. I call the Christie approach the 'clue-puzzle' and the American variation the 'private-eye' story. Such neutrality seems advisable: it is surprising how many authors who claim objectivity still use the highly emotive terms 'golden age', 'hard-boiled' or 'tough-guy' to describe the sub-genres, without noting, let alone challenging, the attitudes and values that trail behind such terms. With less difficulty, for the important sub-genre à la Cain and Highsmith where the writer tells the story of a crime and a criminal (whether the protagonist is a professional gangster or suddenly turns to crime), I, like Tony Hilfer in his study, use the neutral term 'crime novel'.

Even with clear, structurally based and unemotive terms, there will be overlaps, like the Californian Perry Mason puzzles or the private-eye-like adventures in detection by the very English Albert Campion, but the clear definitions expose such hybrids. There have been other classifications: Symons felt that most crime fiction after the Second World War was essentially the 'crime novel', by which he meant a mystery with augmented characterisation, and Priestman has in his 1998 book also argued for a major compounding of the formal puzzle and the adventurous detective in the modern period. I feel that these overlaps and condensations are better understood if the three major sub-genres are still recognised; and in the modern period I would add as sub-genres the police procedural, the psychothriller, the postmodern crime novel and the mystery of violence. It seems then possible to recognise – as in the case of Thomas Harris (and indeed Wilkie Collins) – how an author skilfully combines elements of sub-genres for a special impact.

The other question that must be resolved about an overview of a huge genre is how to handle it as a whole. This study, like most except that of a serious formalist like Cawelti or a true connoisseur like Irwin, is essentially chronological, but because I have laid emphasis throughout on both the content of the material and its social connections, I have argued in the structure of the book itself that there are three major stages. The first is how the detective become central to the genre, essentially the nineteenth-century material leading up to Doyle. The second is how death become the focus of the author's concerns in both the clue-puzzle and the private-eye story: I have taken this up to the Second World War with, especially in the crime novel, some overlap into the following decade. Thirdly, I have not identified a single structural or contentual focus for the modern period but have called it a time of diversity, in that the variations that occur, especially in terms of gender and race, all in some way move away from the now established and consciously recognised patterns. The separations of these three stages are not perfect: the cosy clue-puzzle survives to the present and so does the macho private-eye story; because of its essentially modern and diversifying character I have discussed the psychothriller here even though Millar began them during the war. The threefold structure of this book responds to my experience and understanding of the evolution of crime fiction, whatever reservations and cross-references need to be made along the way.

Those three sections and their inherently developed themes provide the sub-title for this book: *Detection, Death and Diversity*; in using as the main title *Crime Fiction, 1800–2000* I suggest both the chronological range of the genre and the book and within that framework it is important to note that this is a more interwoven and international body of writing than has often been recognised. While the bulk of the early material is British – and now the Americans have much more than caught up – it is striking how simplistic are attempts to give national value to elements of crime fiction (or perhaps anything else). As a Welshman who long worked in Australia, I assume the right to comment on Americans who seem to feel tough and hard-boiled as they write about their favourite guys, or English who ruminate about the golden age as if it is all their own to play with. Much in the genre contradicts such naiveties: American crime writing developed in many ways early and independently – Gaboriau's novels were translated in America before Britain and Anna Katherine Green domesticated the form well before Doyle transmuted it. If that is forgotten, or was never known, in England, Americans themselves seem to overlook the fact that they too produced English-style clue puzzles in New York, every bit as elaborate and artificial as those that Chandler belittled. Yet not all is shared: there are major differences between countries and even regions in who the detective is and how he or she operates, and these are world-wide as well as transatlantic – I have at times commented on crime fiction in English outside America and Britain. But there is still an advantage in thinking of the genre as an Anglo-American entity, and then seeing how it differs structurally, thematically, locally rather than approaching it in nationalist blinkers and finding no more than long-standing prejudices.

As well as large decisions about terms and treatments, authors have to decide on technique. To simplify the approach to all this material I have not used footnotes but have in the text given brief details, amplified in the References printed at the end of the book. In the quest to be as fully informative as possible, I have tried to give in the text accurate dates of the first appearance of a work, and also the variant titles that occur surprisingly often between England and America. When an author writes under a pseudonym I have given a first reference in inverted commas and noted the real name parenthetically, but have from then on used the pseudonym itself; similarly the date and other information only appears when a text is cited for the first time in each part.

A book covering so much detail requires not only long labour but generous assistance. I have consistently been aware how much I have gained from colleagues around the world, and would like to thank warmly my colleagues at Cardiff: Martin Coyle, Claire Gorrara, Dawn Harrington, Martin Kayman and David Skilton; my graduate students Mary Fallon, Struan Sinclair, Heather Worthington and the incomparably informative Lucy Sussex; I also owe debts for data, thoughts and contacts to Ian Bell, Gavin Edwards, H. Gustav Klaus, Andy Kelly, David Matthews, Helen Phillips and Martin Priestman. Research over some time that has contributed to this book has been financially supported by the Department of English at Melbourne University and the School of English, Communication and Philosophy at Cardiff University and also by grants from the Australian Research Council and the British Academy. I have received both academic input and memorable hospitality from Barbara and Seymour Chatman at Berkeley, while at Rochester, New York, Bette London and Tom Hahn have been much more than generous in housing, advising and entertaining me on my travelling inquiries.

As in a Poirot revelation, the family comes last, but they really did it. For putting up with piles of books, heaps of papers, amounts of domestic absence and absent-mindedness that even Holmes never inflicted, I am still indebted to Margaret; I remain grateful to David for his skills in the posthuman world of electronics; and, in return for our daughter Elizabeth's enthusiasm, interest and interrogation, this book is hers.

Part I
Detection

1
Beginnings

I BEFORE DETECTION

This summer's holiday reading included detectives of very diverse kinds: a neurotic Edinburgh detective inspector, a feisty native Alaskan tour-guide-cum-detective, a British black investigative journalist, a postmodern and lesbian translator-investigator in modern Barcelona. Places and peoples of the modern world are richly represented in crime fiction through the focal figure who detects the crime, and these modern authors – Ian Rankin, Dana Stabenow, Mike Phillips and Barbara Wilson – will all be discussed in Part III as part of modern diversity.

But the detective was not always there: he, and sometimes she, emerged through the nineteenth century, as this Part will explore, and the immensely popular collections of crime stories usually called *The Newgate Calendar*, which appeared in the eighteenth century, can be taken as the archetype of pre-detective crime stories. But the pattern found in the *Calendar* is not itself new. *Sundry strange and inhumaine Murthers, lately committed*, proclaims a pamphlet published in London in 1591: a woodcut shows a crazy-eyed man axing three children to death. The anthology *Blood and Knavery* (Marshburn and Velie, 1973) offers access to crime stories, including this one, from around 1600. They can be very grisly: the axe-murderer was hired by the children's father, and in other stories Mr Page is murdered by the wife and her hired assistants, while Mr Trat, a curate, is killed on the highway, brought to his house, cut up, boiled and salted.

Not all Elizabethan and Jacobean crime stories dealt with murder. A popular form was the 'cony-catching pamphlet', describing neat ways of picking pockets or cheating at dice, even the elaborate instruments used for stealing goods through windows. The threats to property explored in these pamphlets were taken very seriously and carried increasingly heavy penalties: through into the

nineteenth century, more and more minor crimes were punished
with hanging under what become known as the 'Bloody Code'.
Highly successful versions of 'cony-catching' pamphlets appeared
as late as George Barrington's *New London Spy* (1805), but as the versions of *The Newgate Calendar* developed, with a major edition in
1773, they tended to emphasise murder. This interest in a range of
crimes, fatal or not, continued right through nineteenth-century
crime fiction, but the crucial feature of these early stories is that none
of them includes anyone who could be described as a detective.

A sub-title to the Elizabethan murder pamphlets suggests a major
reason for this: 'Wherein is described the odiousenesse of murther
with the vengeance which God inflicteth on murtherers.' Divine
guidance lies behind the revealing of guilt. It can operate through
human agency, as when after the murder of Mr Page of Plymouth his
sister observes his torn nails, his broken neck and bloody knees, and
knows he has not died quietly in his bed, as his wife insists. Similarly,
to identify the killers of Mr Trat the local people collect evidence.
But the stories are not presented as mysteries, needing a solution –
rather, they are parables of shocking aberration. Either the person's
guilt is obvious from the start, like the family axe-murderer, or can
be worked out by a few telling details that are generally observed.
Sometimes the criminals are the human agents of avenging providence and a sense of Christian guilt brings them to confess, as with
Mrs Page's lover and accomplice. Both the narrative voice and the
circumstances are heavily weighted towards punishment, not discovery, and execution is always the climax of these stories. Murder
will out, they insist, for both moral and religious reasons, and all
the stories operate in a world drenched in Christian belief: the axe-
murderer is shown with an elderly devil dressed in black suit and
smart hat, urging him towards murder with an extended claw.

This makes the stories seem simple in ideological terms, as if all
threats are thoroughly dismissed, and Christian and humane values
are unproblematically demonstrated in action. But while it is a
world of powerful morality, with heavy assertions about sin and
crime made by the narrators, the effect of the narratives is not so
simple. Each story indicates how easy it is for ordinary respectable
people suddenly to become monsters of crime – the devil, the sins,
human anger and malice can so easily disrupt everyday social order.
These early stories show how ordinary human resentments – at
being evicted, or at being married against one's will – can cause
horrific crimes. And if it is unnervingly easy for crime to develop, it

is not quite as simple as it sometimes seems to identify the criminals. There is no problem about the axe-murderer or Mrs Page and her accomplice, though modern justice might not feel that her lover, absent from the murder scene and more a motive than a criminal, should hang as well. But more curious – and something that will recur – is the fact that in the Trat case none of the four accused agrees to confess. They are pressured 'in the bowels of Christ' to cleanse their souls; they are separated for further pressure. There is some sign that the woman is yielding, but in the end she and the three men 'died obstinate and unrepenting sinners' (1973: 56–7). The evidence connecting guilt to any particular one of the four is not at all clear. The author of the text is clearly bothered by this, and gives three different explanations: they had sworn not to confess; they feared worse punishment, presumably death by fire; and, most significantly, they hoped for 'reprieval at the last, since they thought the proofs were not sufficient against them' (1973: 57).

In the absence of sure knowledge about a crime – and that is not rare through the eighteenth century in the *Newgate Calendar* stories – the local magistrates accept more or less what the public thinks and act on it, and the jury does the same in most cases. Unlike under French law, it is not possible to use torture to verify guilt (or create the appearance of it), and so there remain these puzzling cases that require difficult explanations for the confident surface of the text to remain untroubled. This absence of certainty about who committed a crime – occasional, but still telling – becomes a more important and disturbing problem and will in time lead to the presence of the detective who can, in fiction at least, provide clear and complete answers.

Just as God and the Devil play a major role in the 1591 pamphlet, the development of eighteenth-century stories about crime has a religious context. The *Newgate Calendar* was originally produced by the chaplain of Newgate prison in London, where criminals were lodged before trial and execution. This figure, the 'Ordinary of Newgate', published reports about the criminals, heavily laced with Christian sentiments, showing how they came to confession and a devout end on the scaffold. The stories offered a moral warning to others and publishing them seems to have been one of the income-generating perquisites of the chaplain: they appeared both in cheap pamphlets and also in more expensive small collections. It was later in the century that publishers undertook the major, and expensive, anthologies now thought of as *Newgate Calendars*: there was a medium-sized one in 1728, another small one in 1748, then a large and purposefully collected five-volume version in 1773 which must have done very well, as there was another in 1779 with the grand name *The Malefactor's Register or the Newgate and Tyburn Calendar*, re-issued in each of the two succeeding years. The publisher William Jackson produced a *New and Complete Calendar* in six volumes in 1795, which was reprinted in 1800. Then a heavily revised version, edited by the lawyers Andrew Knapp and William Baldwin, appeared in 1809, was reprinted several times and revised, finally appearing as *The New Newgate Calendar* in 1826. *Calendars* kept appearing well into the nineteenth century; Camden Pelham – probably a pseudonym – produced one called *The Chronicles of Crime* in 1841, which was itself reissued several times.

All the *Calendars* claim to be fact. But they are often substantially rewritten in the process of republishing, and the stories have no stability. An account can change not only its moral significance but its actions in a new edition, and in some cases may simply be invented and then repeated: the popular story of George Cadell murdering his pregnant girlfriend which appears first in the *Calendar* of 1773, appears in rewritten form in both 1779 and 1826 and then re-emerges in a single-page broadside in the 1820s and 1830s. This story is always undated and suspiciously formulaic – it is probably an invention that found its way into the quasi-factual collections (what ballad-publishers called a 'cock', because it would crow often). But fiction itself often imitates the *Calendar* form. Daniel Defoe, the great chronicler and interpreter of English geography, trade, social events and adventures, also wrote some semi-fictions and complete inventions about crime. He published a factual, though also strongly moralised, *Life of Jonathan Wild* (1725), interviewing the famous, deeply corrupt and for a while terrifyingly powerful thief-taker cum fence before his execution; in 1723 he produced a largely fictional biography of *Colonel Jaque* (also known as Colonel Jack), a criminal turned soldier; and entirely fictitious is the famous criminal autobiography *Moll Flanders* (1722), for many commentators the first major novel in English.

Moll's story – growing up, going wrong, but always avoiding the gallows – is in its pattern and its realistic detail just like the criminal lives and deaths beloved of the *Calendar* editors and readers, except that Defoe gives it a scope and a compelling life that converts the criminal figure from a stereotype of dangerous aberrance to an intriguing representation of the charm of social outlawry. Moll's story is a happily ending version of the fascination people had with the great rogues – Dick Turpin, Captain Kidd, Jack Sheppard and Jonathan Wild himself.

Ian Bell comments that 'the Augustan press was infatuated with the representation of criminals' (1991: 64), and it is not easy to tell whether there was, as was thought at the time, a genuine rise in criminal activity, or whether the growth of reporting of events made this seem the case. It certainly seems clear that the dramatic growth of mercantile prosperity in this period, so much celebrated and charted by Defoe and his colleagues, itself generated the physical and social mobility in which crime thrived, and where people felt uncertain of their surroundings.

The eighteenth-century novel, as Bell has shown (1991), is rich with crime, and this is no longer mythic and grandiose as in Elizabethan tragedy, but the everyday misdeeds of an ebullient ordinary world. Swindlers, pickpockets, procurers, burglars throng in the margins of the work of Richardson, Fielding and Smollett, and it seems highly appropriate that Fielding, seeking a secure income, became a magistrate and attempted, with his brother, the famous 'blind beak' Sir John Fielding, to improve the systems of justice. Imposing the law then depended on the local magistrate (usually a landowner with no legal training) and local constables (often ex-soldiers with very limited training, equipment or interest): constables frequently employed a deputy to do the actual work, as if they were clergymen. The early *Calendar* stories show this system in operation: a crime occurs; local people make observations; they either arrest someone and call for the constable, or provide information that leads to arrest. Very soon there is a trial and an execution. It is as if the community, in the light of God's commands, is protecting itself with the help of a few deputed specialists. That was the conception of justice: that is what most of the *Calendar* stories show in action, and in doing so they realise a specific ideology about crime, its threats, and the values that will – hopefully – contain it.

The *Calendar* stories are not about wicked oppressive lords – almost no trace of the Gothic is present – or dangerous foreigners. Though the occasional overseas villain or corrupt gentleman is found, this is a world without challenges to the certainties of class or race. The personnel are very ordinary, ranging socially from servants to lower gentry, many of them being farmers, town tradesmen, their daughters, wives and, often the cause of trouble, sons. Set usually in and around small towns, the normal story will tell about a young man or woman who falls into bad company, becomes influenced by gamblers, soldiers, drinkers, idle apprentices or loose women, and so develops bad habits which will lead eventually to theft or murder. There are variations: a couple of lovers might combine to kill a wife or husband; an aspiring man may kill a girl who is holding him back, especially a pregnant one; a servant can murder for money or jewels. Among these stories are scattered a few exploits and deaths of professional criminals, often highwaymen, sometimes pirates, and there is the occasional aristocrat who goes bad: his story is related regretfully and with much satisfaction about the social neutrality of English law. But the solid thrust of the *Calendar* is to insist that most crime comes from sudden and unstructured social aberrance. The early Elizabethan stories showed that too, but no devils prompt the killers now; yet still the criminals are caught by the old methods of social observation or, occasionally, Christian guilt, as Knight has argued (1980: 11–13).

Though the devil has retired, and the clergyman is no longer making the profits now commercial editors and publishers have taken over these narratives of crime, there is still a final confession from the criminal and words of Christian cheer to the reader at the end: these stories, from as late as 1800, are still inherently in touch with the Elizabethan shock pamphlets. They all belong essentially to a pre-urban, pre-capitalist, pre-detective world. But things are not as simple as the values in the text proclaim. The *Calendar* texts themselves show the strain of believing in communal detection and Christian guilt in an age that is, socially and economically, a long way from the religious rural feudalism where those views originated.

There remain stories where people do not confess: Mary Edmondson is accused of murdering her aunt; she says burglars did it, and there is a cut on her arm. Only limited circumstantial evidence exists against Mary, but she is found guilty, though she still refuses to confess, even as she is hanged. The narrator is baffled and assumes she must have been one of those rare people prepared to die lying. But there is a gentleman, Mr Holloway, who has made inquiries and satisfied himself of Mary's guilt. So the narrator can be content: in this case, it seems, there is someone who functions more to resolve the threat of doubt than the threat of crime, though there is no generic or conventional way of naming him as such.

Struan Sinclair's close analysis of the varied *Newgate Calendars* reveals that it is not, as has previously been thought, a uniform tradition. He sees the *Calendars* from 1809 to 1826, edited by the lawyers Knapp and Baldwin, as representing a major 'shift from a theological to a mainly legal frame of reference' (2000: 150) and he shows that in these later stages there are more investigations, more clues, more emphasis on trials and their complexities than in the earlier, simply hopeful stories, and also more doubt. A typical case (which in fact precedes Knapp and Baldwin) is that of Christopher Slaughterford. A businessman, he is quickly cleared by the magistrates when his fiancée is found murdered. Neighbours press for his trial; he is acquitted. But the neighbours and the dead girl's family insist he did it, and he is tried again, and this time, on the same thin evidence, found guilty. Slaughterford – the name is ill-fortuned – denies the crime, and even evades execution: when the noose is placed around his neck, he throws himself down from the scaffold, to die as a suicide. The *Calendar* presents the circumstantial evidence and the dubious witnesses sceptically, and concludes in a distinctly agnostic moment that he is one of 'the many instances of innocent people suffering on circumstantial evidence' (1779: 122).

With such evidence recognised as a potentially very unreliable source of certainty, with confidence in divine providence as an insurer of justice substantially reduced, and with many people feeling that the ferocious 'Bloody Code' was in part savage and in part inefficient – juries were unlikely to convict for petty theft in the knowledge that it meant death – there was a serious problem both for the law and for the narratives which set out to persuade people that the threats of crime were being confronted by credible forces. In the limited factuality of the *Calendar* the problem was occasionally explored, especially in the later versions of that multi-form text, and some sense that suitable investigations would bring greater assurance had been envisaged. But the detective, the person to fill this gap in both law and ideology, was not easily brought into existence.

II   ENTER THE DETECTIVE

The reforms brought about by the Fieldings and their colleagues had two main foci. One was the exchange of information: they realised that magistrates and constables would be in a much better position to arrest criminals if they knew who they were, so they arranged for facts and descriptions to be circulated (Emsley, 1996: 221). The Fieldings' other major reform was to have specialists in criminal-catching – and the lack of central concern with murder at this time was revealed in calling them 'thief-takers'. Established in 1749, they became known as 'Bow Street Runners' because they were mobile police attached to the Bow Street court in central London; later they came to have patrols, both in day- and night-time, and there was a separate branch on horseback to counter highwaymen, but their origin was as mobile specialists to investigate reported crimes and pursue identified criminals. They operated until 1839, after the 'New Police', the modern police constables, were established by Sir Robert Peel in London in 1829, but they never had a very high profile, and never gained much credence as icons of security; they tended to be better at recovering property than catching criminals, and were often assumed to be in league with the thieves themselves, as Jonathan Wild had notoriously been in the early eighteenth century.

If the Bow Street Runners did not credibly resolve the problems of identifying criminals and securing justice, the idea of a self-sufficient individual inquirer was no more popular. This was in part because in England the whole idea of inquiries into people's behaviour was unattractive: even before, but especially during and after the French Revolution, government-funded inquirers were regarded as spies – the word was used long into the nineteenth century as a synonym for detective. Neither the gentry with their peculiar private practices nor the ordinary people with their substantial suspicion of the authorities liked the idea of investigations, and the reformist plans of the late eighteenth-century Utilitarians to improve policing received a largely cool reception. The sheer difficulty of conceiving of someone who, on his own, could inquire into crime and justice is powerfully developed in William Godwin's novel of 1794. This was originally entitled, with a political edge, *Things As They Are*, but from its 1831 edition on was known by its original sub-title *Caleb Williams* – so sounding more like a novel and less like *An Enquiry Concerning Political Justice*, the important sociopolitical text Godwin published in 1793 just before turning to this fiction of crime and the problems of detection.

Godwin, still better known on the continent of Europe than in Britain, was the first serious theoretical anarchist, arguing for a world of 'reasonable anarchism' where people expressed to each other clearly their thoughts and feelings and came to mutual judgements and plans of action without the need of governmental intervention or traditional hierarchies of power – a position closer to what was later known as syndicalism than the bomb-stained image of anarchism familiar in the late nineteenth century. Part of a brilliantly innovative family – his wife was Mary Wollstonecraft, the still potent proto-feminist, and their daughter was Mary Shelley, author of *Frankenstein* – in his novel he probed the possibilities of social and criminal inquiry.

Falkland, a northern landowner and sophisticate, despises Tyrrel, a neighbouring landowner, and tries to moderate his brutishness. But after Tyrrel assaults and humiliates Falkland in public – and honour and reputation are all to Falkland – he is found murdered. The blame is fixed on a farmer and his son, whom Tyrrel has turned off their land. But Caleb Williams, the poor, clever youth whom Falkland has favoured as his secretary, begins to suspect his master. This all sounds familiar, easy to imagine as an effective, even moving, novel, or perhaps especially a film, where the brave young man will expose the older, decadent authority figure.

It does not work like that. Caleb is an inefficient inquirer, watching his master uncertainly, trying in vain to discover the mystery of the trunk Falkland has in the attic – we never discover what it contains. In several confrontations, including in court, Falkland's authority as master proves more powerful than Caleb's curiosity, and Caleb himself becomes Falkland's victim, a fugitive falsely accused of theft, and he never exposes the crime successfully. This pattern might in itself seem familiar, with Caleb cast as the brave but finally impotent inquirer, a tragic victim of power. But it does not work like that either: the striking fact is that the novel shows there is something evaluatively wrong with Caleb's desire to inquire. Finally, face to face with Falkland, he recognises he should not have been so privately, sneakily, inquisitive, but should have appealed to Falkland's better nature – indeed, he should have practised 'reasonable anarchism'. Caleb's curiosity destroys himself as well as Falkland: Falkland dies, and Caleb feels a criminal. Godwin never means to justify the aristocratic life – he says that Falkland has 'swallowed the poison of chivalry' ([1794] 1970: 326). But he does not offer revolution as an alternative, nor even the morally based criticism of the aristocracy that will be so common in the nineteenth century, including in crime fiction, with its corrupt lords and ladies and its basis of moral judgement focused by the single authoritative character who reveals the criminal. Godwin presents different values: he sees a better system than aristocratic power as one of affectionate debate – Caleb is finally certain that Falkland could not have resisted his 'frank and fervent expostulation' ([1794] 1970: 323). Even this, now perhaps improbable, idea about resisting power was itself an optimistic compromise for Godwin: in his original ending Falkland faces Caleb down once more, Caleb is dismissed by the magistrate as an accuser and becomes permanently and fatally deranged.

However much Godwin's revised ending offered the possibility of reasonable reform, it had no real confidence: as Gavin Edwards has commented (2000: 542), Godwin, like Swift, attacks conservative power without having sufficiently radical tools to make a real impact. Godwin cannot imagine his inquirer as a bearer of truth and liberty, a heroic detective, because he would be merely an individual (for a fuller discussion of this see Knight, 1980: 26–8). Though historians have seen Caleb as a prototype detective, Julian Symons has a sceptical discussion of this reading (1992: 35–6) and the only real detective in the story is an unappealing character called Gines, a low-level thief-taker of a semi-criminal kind, who dogs Caleb's footsteps.

Where the *Newgate Calendar* showed simply the need for a detective to identify the real facts of a puzzling case, *Caleb Williams* indicates that the figure of a hero who bears values powerful enough to defeat the threats of the text is not yet possible in crime fiction. Godwin's own commitment to anarchism and hatred of the aristocracy prevents him from using a gentleman for such a role, but later, in a different context and from a different position, a gentleman was shaped as a recognisable quasi-detective, in the hands of Edward Bulwer.

A young man seeking to get on in the world through his writing, and with social and political ambitions – he would become a Member of Parliament and eventually Lord Lytton – Bulwer took up the fashionable and successful form of the 'silver fork' novel, an ironic name for detailed and admiring stories of aristocratic life. *Pelham*, published in 1828, starts in that way, with a young aristocrat, who expects to inherit an earldom, lounging around the noble salons of Paris. There are some suspicious characters about, and there is something mysterious, even threatening, in the background of his friend Glanville, but these are for the moment loose threads, at most sub-plot to the young man's development. He returns to London, and becomes a Member of Parliament, but then the story starts to change in plot and tone. He loses his seat; his relative the earl marries late and has a son. As Pelham is himself removed from the aristocratic world and needs to earn a living, the crime element of the story begins to develop. Pelham's friend Glanville becomes increasingly mysterious; more is seen of the decidedly dubious English visitors to Paris – one called Tyrrell, a slightly different spelling from Godwin's but surely a gesture towards the earlier novel. Pelham has contact with the London criminal world and the aura of mystery and criminality comes to dominate the novel. Pelham himself finds Tyrrell murdered, and Glanville is suspected, on circumstantial evidence. Pelham acts now like the 'gentleman' who verified the guilt of Mary Edmondson, but he is operating on behalf of an innocent victim of circumstantial evidence like Christopher Slaughterford. Detection itself is fairly limited: there are 'officers', presumably Bow Street Runners, involved and some physical evidence – a broken knife with a part left in the body. The explanation comes not through detection but as a result of active pursuit, with an exciting final sequence in one of London's criminal strongholds. It turns out that Tyrrell was murdered by Thornton, one of his evil friends, who had previously raped Glanville's lover and driven her to a deranged death. Glanville had indeed chased him with evil intent, but he was dead before Glanville could kill him – a moment predicting Agatha Christie's intricate complications around the corpse.

A nobleman maddened by a thug called Tyrrell; deep suspicion of his actions; inquiries by a well-educated young man who is close to the aristocratic world; rumour, dubious evidence, complications in the underworld and doubtful characters: in these respects *Pelham* is the same as *Caleb Williams*. But Bulwer's novel is also the structural reverse of Godwin's: here the inquirer is himself an aristocrat as well as being clever and persevering, and the suspect nobleman is exculpated; the unsavoury types that Falkland employed to hunt Caleb are now the cause of the crime. Bulwer has straightened out the difficulties that Godwin encountered and explored, and created a story where the values of friendship, perseverance, organisation, courage and, within limits, rational inquiry are seen to triumph over the threats of violent disorder.

Pelham simplifies and reorganises the patterns implicit and complex in *Caleb Williams*, but it does not do this in a vacuum. The thirty years between the two texts had seen not only the Napoleonic wars and the post-war political oppressions in England, but also the steady growth of the Utilitarian movement for reform in many areas of British life, and this powerful and wide-ranging pressure is strongly to be associated with the development and significance of the detective. Michel Foucault has argued in *Discipline and Punish* (1977) for the existence of two different structures of power in society, and in this period one is giving way to the other. Sovereign power and disciplinary power take many forms – politics, education and medicine are major versions – but in the context of crime the difference between them is of central importance to Foucault, as discussed by During (1992, Chapter 6, 'Discipline'). Sovereign power is realised in seeing the criminal personally resisting the power of the sovereign and so being publicly revealed as aberrant – in the pillory, by branding or maiming, and in many cases by public and often torture-based execution. The body of the criminal is marked with retribution for his, and occasionally her, offence against the king's peace. This is basically the situation in *The Newgate Calendar*: forgery is a capital crime not for economic reasons (though in reality they are powerful) but because the sovereign's head has been falsely imitated; wives who kill their husbands are burnt at the stake (and there are instances of this) because their crime is 'petty treason': the husband is the king of the family and so the wives suffer like those who attack the king in high treason. Criminals are at times executed at the place of their crime, and symbols may state their offence against royal order: Norman Ross, a servant who murdered his mistress for money, had his right hand cut off before execution, and it was nailed on the gallows above his body as he was hanged. Such sights, like the bodies of highwaymen left in chains beside the roads they prowled, bespeak in unmediated form the terrible and direct power of the sovereign, ratified, as consistently expressed in the *Calendar*, by the God in whose name the sovereign rules by divine right.

But, as the Fieldings knew, public displays of power and vengeance did not appear to deter criminals, and certainly did not effectively catch them in the way the *Calendar* mostly imagines is possible. It was an ideological system more than a factual legal process. The mechanisms the Fieldings put in place – professional thief-catchers, disseminating information – were in their simple way the first moves toward disciplinary policing. By 'discipline' Foucault, as During outlines, does not suggest that people behave according to orders. He refers to a central rational intellectual discipline of the mind, and its constraining effects: he refers to studying things, finding out how they work, what in detail can be done about them, bringing enlightenment, reason and scholarship to bear on perceiving and re-handling the patterns and problems of society. The work of the *philosophes* in France and the Utilitarians in Britain is to collect information, consider policy and recommend new practices, design institutions, undertake new professional activities, all in the spirit of rational reform.

The detective will also operate in this disciplinary way. The Utilitarians in Britain recommended changes in many areas – electoral reform, industrial and mercantile development, medical innovations, sociological study and data-gathering – but they also approached crime and criminals in new ways. They saw the need for a new kind of police, not just men like the Runners earning commissions for arrests and tips for recovering property, but a semi-military organised force: as Martin Kayman shows (1982: 87–8) plans for this were in place in England by 1796, expressed by Patrick Colquhoun in his book *A Treatise on the Police of the Metropolis* (1796), but the English suspicion of 'spies' made the process slow, and it is striking that the first such police worked in the Thames dockland, structurally central to London's economic activities and a hotbed of mercantile theft, but not in fact affecting directly the everyday life of the bulk of its people.

The idea of rational inquiry leading to the containment of crime is an occasional shadow of the future in the *Newgate Calendar* and there are, as Sinclair has indicated (2000), increasing elements of such inquiries in the later versions of the *Calendar*. This approach seemed improper in *Caleb Williams* – although Caleb has the intelligence, the skills and the determination to be a disciplinary detective, he has no institutional place from which to operate: he is Falkland's servant and owes him total personal loyalty, whether to serve or to advise. But Pelham, gentleman as well as literary and parliamentary figure, has a position from which he can investigate. Perhaps largely because of his higher social status and the less socially embarrassing nature of the crime, he has a location for disciplinary detection – of a fairly simple sort, admittedly – and can operate in that way. *Pelham* was not a particularly influential novel – the model of the gentleman detective takes much longer to develop, but Pelham is the first who can be called a disciplinary detective at the rational level, and that model is going to be, especially through Poe, Gaboriau and Doyle, immensely influential.

But that is not all that Foucault's work can suggest about crime and its treatment in fiction. Very important for his argument about power and crime is a change of response to criminals. Instead of being, as it were, mere bearers of a crime, and so to be marked or destroyed in rejection of that crime, the criminal becomes seen himself, and herself, as an individual capable of going astray or attaining social salvation through disciplinary processes. Under sovereign power people did not stay in gaol: they were acquitted, physically punished, executed, transported. After trial, only debtors stayed in gaol, until their debts were paid off. But disciplinary power believes that criminals can be reformed, just as bodies can be healed or society improved: therefore criminals are imprisoned, made to work, suffer, listen to lectures and prayers, so they can rejoin society. The gaol becomes called, as it still is in North America, the penitentiary, because the criminal does penance there, both physical and psychic, and will in theory learn a better, penitent way to live.

This new practice in itself concerns crime fiction very little – a remarkably small amount of it occurs in gaol, among real criminals – but what is highly influential is the notion that the criminal's own feelings and thoughts are of interest. Again, Godwin is an innovator, charting the inner thoughts of both Caleb and to some degree Falkland as well. This idea was to remain important in crime fiction: it flourished in the twentieth century as the psychothriller, but was a matter of possible interest from the start, and produced some striking early texts like *Wieland* (1798), by the innovative American novelist Charles Brockden Brown, where the mind of the murderer is powerfully, and self-consciously, explored. It may well be that the greater inherent individualism of the new, self-made, American society stimulated this element more quickly than in Britain, but *Pelham* has some aspects of this, as, drawing like Brown on *Caleb Williams*, Glanville's own dark possibilities are revealed.

The idea that criminals were not just social failures, but humans who had chosen a dangerous, but somehow also exciting, path also draws on the period's Romantic fascination with flawed heroes – Schiller's *Die Räuber*, 'The Robbers' (1781), is a Robin Hood-like story in which, because he has committed real crimes, the noble outlaw does not return in honour to his former social status, but dies in violent tragic grandeur. This was very well known in English – a fourth edition of the 1795 translation was in print by 1800; both Falkland in the second draft of *Caleb Williams* and Caleb in the first go the same way as Schiller's noble Charles, such *Sturm und Drang* is central to Brown, while Glanville's life at the end of *Pelham* is consumed by grief and illness. The hero of Bulwer's other major crime novel, *Eugene Aram* (1832), is another kind of classic heroic criminal, a genius who is finally tried for a casual money-seeking murder long ago. This is a true story, a *Newgate Calendar* favourite, and in reality

Aram died on the gallows in 1759, but Bulwer's flawed hero dies in gaol as part of his tragic downfall.

The partly tragic self-consumption of the criminal will remain one path for crime fiction, to be powerfully realised in the twentieth-century American 'crime novel', and it is remarkably strong in the early period. In 1827, *Blackwood's Edinburgh Magazine* printed a story by Henry Thomson called 'Le Revenant', which was so popular it also appeared as a prose broadside in drastically shortened and not very comprehensible form. It is not the ghost story it sounds like: rather it is about a man who has been hanged, and survived. His viewpoint is central, the story is in the first person, and so we are able to shudder at the experience, watching the morning dawn, hearing the scaffold being erected, waiting for the end. The story creates the idea that the criminal, though guilty of the antisocial crime of forgery – fairly minor and forgivable, though still punished by death – also has an identity and a right to human feeling. And he escapes the gallows that the Bloody Code imposed for even minor crimes: it is clear that his girlfriend has somehow persuaded, or bribed, the authorities to get him cut down in time for revival. Though it does provide a sense of what it is like to be condemned to death, this is not primarily a socially significant or reformist story. Those did exist: Victor Hugo in 1829 wrote *La Dernière Journée d'un Condamné a Mort* specifically as propaganda against executions, and for the same purpose it would be translated into English in 1840, as *The Last Days of a Condemned Man*, by an M.P., Sir P. Hesketh Fleetwood. More simply, 'Le Revenant' is exploring criminal feelings, for the reader's excitement, in a low-level form of Romantic individualism.

This was a common theme in a number of stories in *Blackwood's Edinburgh Magazine* in the early nineteenth century, which brought the Gothic interest in sensational feelings and insights into close contact with domestic crime. Usually called 'Tales of Terror', they have been anthologised by Robert Morrison and Chris Baldick with a full introduction (1995), and are discussed at some length by Heather Worthington (2003: 66–92). The *Blackwood's* writers deal with stark sensation like being buried alive or being hanged, and they offer grisly and sometimes sexist forensic investigations and explorations of evil human potential by authors including James Hogg, John Gault, Charles Lamb and John Wilson, the editor of *Blackwood's*. As Wilson's authorship indicates, the stories are structural to the magazine: the taste for grisly and aberrant sensation is the darker side of the rational individualism of Enlightenment Edinburgh that officially guides *Blackwood's*.

An inherently similar but better-known condensation of Romantic Gothic and domestic crime appears in the remarkable essay by Thomas De Quincey, 'On Murder Considered as One of the Fine Arts'. This appeared in *Blackwood's* in 1827: it was so successful that De Quincey went back to the topic twice, in 1839 and 1854, but it is his first effort that has the major impact. In the form of a mock speech to a learned assembly he praises as a fine Romantic artist John Williams, the notorious Ratcliffe Highway killer in East London, who used a hammer to kill seven people from two families, on two separate occasions. Or so it seemed: he hanged himself in gaol before trial, and his guilt is doubted by P. D. James and T. A. Critchley (1971). De Quincey was fascinated with crime: when he was editor of the *Westmorland Gazette* in rural north-west England he filled the paper with factual but also sensational crime reports (Worthington gives details, 2003: 50–3), and what he does here is to aestheticise violent murder. He is not writing as a reporter – in fact, as Thomas Burke points out (1928), he has altered almost all the details, including the date: the killings happened in 1811 but he always calls it 1812. Taking his lead from the Romantic fascination with the sublime, and, as Duncan Campbell indicates, drawing consciously on Kant's idea of the sublime (1998), De Quincey ironically asserts that the mass excitements of crime – ballads and broadsides were everywhere at the time – are in fact functionally the same as elite admiration of stupendous Alpine views and staggering feats by Byronic heroes. Deliberately shocking as he liked to be – as in the title of his *Confessions of an Opium-Eater* (1823) – De Quincey is exploring the public fascination with crime and its sudden, startling eruption in the East End of London.

The location is important: the *Calendar* stories were mostly set in small towns, and though increasingly they occur in London, there is little sense in them of the danger of the city itself. Both *Caleb Williams* and *Pelham* see the city as a place to hide, but as crime fiction develops through the nineteenth century, around the world, it is clear that it is to a large degree centred on the growing, mysterious, threatening cities – London, Paris, New York (and some less predictable like Philadelphia and Melbourne) – where no one knows anybody else, where anyone could be an enemy, and where, more than ever before, there is the need for some expert to navigate this mysterious world, identify these strange people, and bring order both in the hoped-for reality of the new policing systems and also in the patterns of threat and value of crime fiction.

De Quincey's East End, full of transients and immigrants, is a place of social mysteries and Romantic horrors as sublime in their way as Wordsworth's Lake District. Here, as in later psychothrillers, there is no detective to focus the process, but the probing intelligence of the writer acts as proxy for the curious, sympathetic and even sadomasochistic interests of the audience. De Quincey, in his wickedly ironic way, makes a brutal and sordid murder in East London into a story of Gothic grandeur, and in doing this he is touching on a major strand in the development of crime fiction. The Gothic novel, which seized so much attention in Europe and America in the late eighteenth century, has powerful appeal as a genre speaking about – and validating – individual feeling, including fear and horror, and so it is a part of the whole Romantic movement against classicism and rationalism. It also makes central the female experience of powerlessness and oppression and links these emotive forces to places redolent of the past, the obscure, the mysterious: Landrum notes that 70 novels between 1794 and 1854 use 'mystery' in their titles (1999: 3), a code word that will later belong to crime fiction.

Some would see the Gothic as a direct source for crime fiction. Messac has argued (1929: 142–57) that Schiller, with his criminal hero in *Die Räuber* and his unfinished novel *Der Geisterseher* (1786–7), in which an aristocrat inquires into alarming mysteries, was an initiator of the genre. But there is very little actual detection involved in *Der Geisterseher*, and *Die Räuber* is no more than pure Gothic excitement. The other text identified as proto-detective from this period is E. T. A. Hoffmann's *Das Fräulein von Scuderi* (1820), usually translated as *Mademoiselle de Scudéry*, in which an elderly lady supervises the explanation of some mysterious crimes in Paris, and saves the suspected innocent who is victim to circumstantial evidence. Both Messac (1929: 306) and Richard Alewyn (1983: 71–3) see it as an archetype of crime fiction, but here too there is no real detection; as in so many early stories the narrative manipulates events so that the appropriate people confess to what has happened – as well as the equally common device of a crucial witness just turning up out of the blue. Though there is a locked house, rather than a locked room, and alibis and characters' movements are traced in some detail, Mademoiselle de Scudéry supervises the unravelling of the mystery by the plot itself: she does not share Pelham's active and fairly involved organisation of data, looking towards the focused inquiries of the real disciplinary detective. In fact, the world of Hoffmann's story, in which the elderly *Fräulein* appeals directly to the king to save the suspect, is an example of sovereign power in full-blown action.

Yet although Romantic Gothic fiction and, as in De Quincey's case, essay writing do not generate the operating detective, they realise the ambient mood of fear and doubt which the detective will exorcise. It is also notably international. Symons stresses the achievement of Doyle; Alewyn sees German Romanticism as a source; Messac makes much – not unfairly – of the French tradition. In recent years American scholars have begun to disinter the powerful early moves towards crime fiction that were made soon after their country became independent. It is clear there were narratives of crime in America before then: even if they first appeared embedded in sermons, these, as Karen Halttunen has shown, were 'gradually replaced by a variety of secular accounts' (1998: 2) which merged with the allegedly factual pamphlets of the eighteenth century, which Daniel A. Cohen has discussed (1993). A major development into the fiction of disciplinary detection in the nineteenth century will become clear below in authors like Edgar Allan Poe, Anna Katharine Green and early professional detectives like Jem Brampton and Allan Pinkerton (the last being also the author's name). But America had its own Gothic treatment of crime and resistance to it, and there were both some uniquely national features and also some signs of very early development. The name usually associated with this is Charles Brockden Brown, the prolific but short-lived author of novels of mystery and emotional adventure set in cities and vast expanses, themselves mysterious and Gothic, of the newly independent country. *Arthur Mervyn* goes beyond *Caleb Williams* in making the inquirer both confident and eventually successful, though the novel lays more emphasis on the picaresque self-establishment of Arthur Mervyn than on the crimes, mostly mercantile, which he encounters and is sometimes alleged to have committed. It also, as usual in Brown's work, makes great and sometimes clumsy structural use of long personal narratives rather than dramatic action, though, as in the yellow-fever sequences, Brown's realistic action can be very powerful. Larry Landrum refers to *Edgar Huntly* (1799) as 'America's first detective novel' (1999: 1) and this is a fair account of Huntly's pursuit of Clithero Edny, whom he believes to have murdered his friend Waldegrave, to whose sister

Mary he addresses his first-person account. But Brown, who was strongly influenced by Godwin, takes much further the psychic disturbances of Falkland and Caleb Williams: Clithero – who did not, it turns out, kill Waldegrave – is a deranged sleepwalker who eventually commits suicide. But the novel's full title is *Edgar Huntly or The Memoirs of a Sleep-Walker*, and Huntly finds himself remarkably like Edny, to the point of his own derangement, and even wonders if he might have done the murder himself while sleep-walking. The very elaborate plot includes inheritance puzzles and sudden reappearances of characters, but while there are some mystery and detection elements throughout, the emphasis is on psychic disturbance, with a particularly impressive use of the wild American setting and the 'savage' natives as projections of the dark possibilities of the respectable individual's mind and behaviour.

The influence on Poe and Hawthorne is clear, and Romantics like Shelley and Hazlitt admired Brown a good deal, but his main importance is as a powerful, sometimes hypnotic, creator of the first examples of American Gothic, not as a stage in the development of the generic possibilities of crime fiction. A greater impact in this context was that of the slightly later American pioneer novelist James Fenimore Cooper. It is not easy to see any of his novels as being in themselves generically crime fiction – they are primarily stories of adventure, setting the potent world of nature against the corruptions of civilised culture. But Cooper's use of a skilled, independent hero who confronted, tracked and frustrated his enemies with skills equal to a native American was very influential, especially in France: Alexandre Dumas (the father) wrote a sprawling narrative called *Les Mohicans de Paris* (1856–7) and, as Messac indicates in his chapter 'Pathfinders' (1929, Part III, Chapter 2), the early American authors, especially Cooper, influenced the many French writers and their English followers, who made use of brave, tough policemen as pioneers for law and order in what seemed the wild new worlds of the growing cities.

III   REALISTIC POLICE

While the concept of an intelligent, heroic, even romantic detective inquirer was slowly and uncertainly developing and Gothic crime stories were exciting readers by concentrating on the criminal, not the explanation of the crime, the Bow Street Runners were still in action – though not always admired or very important in the texts. Dickens in *Oliver Twist* (1838) gives them the comic names Blathers and Duff, and the narrative itself, not them, causes Bill Sykes's dramatic end. With a similar elision of the Runners as detective agents, G. P. R. James in his socially elevated romance *Delaware* depicts a Runner of 'solid strength' (1833: 248), but he does not do very much detecting in the story: it is Delaware's officer-class friend who clears him of suspected crime, much like Pelham.

However, there is one substantial text devoted to the Runners. In 1827 a fictional account of their activities appeared as *Richmond: Scenes from the Life of a Bow Street Runner* – the author is just given as 'Richmond'. The most commonly cited candidate is the journalist and popular author Thomas Gaspey; E. F. Bleiler is sceptical about this in his introduction to the reprint (1976: x–xi), but the lurching zest of the story certainly reads like Gaspey's picaresque story (which includes convict material from Australia), *The History of George Godfrey* (1828). Before that there is a temporal gap in Gaspey's publications which would fit his authorship of *Richmond*, and its topic does match his other crime-focused work such as *The Mystery* (1820) and *The Witch-Finder* (1824).

Tom Richmond has respectable parents, but the first part of the story tells how, rather than go into a profession, as his father wishes, he has adventures with gypsies, in the theatre, several brushes with the law and an affair which ends in his lover's death. Only then does he, by coincidence, meet an old friend who invites him to join the Runners. After this slow approach to crime and detection, the first long episode, the best-focused in the book, engages the young law officer with a child's body on London's Putney Heath. He investigates in a sequence of active if not very detailed detection, and identifies behind the crime the hand of a low-level master criminal named Jones. But only minor offenders are traced, and Richmond moves on to a second story, set in the country, involving small-time criminals, smugglers, body-snatchers (a recurrent theme in this early period) and a suspected but innocent gang of Irish navvies. This story is never resolved and Tom moves on again to be engaged with racecourse crime and aristocratic fraudsters, with the egregious Jones still behind things (as he apparently was in the rural mystery). The wicked aristocrats are frustrated, Richmond gains another girlfriend (she is rescued from a life of crime); and then follow two distinctly cobbled-together stories, one a highly improbable tale of a husband who bullies his wife and servants by impersonating

Petruchio from Shakespeare's *The Taming of the Shrew* – he is scared by the Runners back into order – and finally a long sequence, typical of the early period of urban crime stories, about a wealthy but foolish young man who is taken up by fraudulent gamblers and forgers.

Richmond shows himself capable of disguise and watchfulness, and exhibits a consistently moralistic sentimentality. The book is a simple and loosely assembled narrative of occasional detection that apparently was never very successful: though it was pirated in America, it did not sell well in Britain, and was reissued with the original sheets rebound in 1845, when criminal sagas, which Keith Hollingworth (1963) discusses as 'Newgate novels', had been popular, such as Bulwer's *Paul Clifford* (1830) and *Eugene Aram* (1832) and Ainsworth's *Jack Sheppard* (1839), not to mention Dickens's *Oliver Twist* (1838) and *Martin Chuzzlewit* (1844). Richmond's lively, rambling yarns about criminal activity are not far from the 'cony-catching' tradition, but such popular material seems ill-matched to a three-volume novel at one and a half guineas, and the lack of intensity, either criminal or Romantic, of the Bow Street Runner's adventures seems to have made this a false start in detective-focused crime fiction.

A stronger contender, in veracity, plotting and the strength of the detective's character, was the almost contemporaneous *Mémoires* of Eugène François Vidocq, published in France in 1828–9 and almost immediately translated into English, according to Messac (1929: 278), by the distinguished all-round man of letters George Borrow (though the British Library catalogue attributes it to William Maginn). Vidocq was a real detective, and before that a real criminal, condemned to the galleys. He, like other criminals, was brought into the Napoleonic policing system, rose to be head of the Sûreté, and after retiring in 1827 produced his memoirs, with the aid of ghost-writers, whose efforts became so imaginative that Vidocq personally disavowed their fourth volume, as is discussed by Ascari (2000).

Not only in book form was Vidocq famous; in 1829 there were two plays derived from the memoirs on the London stage, and they made much of his famous capacity for disguise – he could even, it seems, make his height seem different. The memoirs were frequently reprinted in the nineteenth century, often in curtailed form, and fragments from the memoirs and invented versions recur in the periodicals, in English and French, for many decades. Vidocq is certainly a detective: a plain-clothes investigator, he pursues known criminals into the mysterious environs of Paris and country towns, interviews people who know them, watches and waits. He is highly ingenious and will often pose as a criminal to gain information, and he is brave and active, risking his life if his disguise were penetrated. He is something of a trickster – he enjoys discussing Vidocq with his apparent fellow criminals, and his unveiling as himself is often a major feature of a capture.

Apart from disguise, bribery, energy and patience, his strongest weapon is his knowledge: he can recognise many criminals, or identify their practices – he is internal to criminal activity, not a rationally operating outsider. Only occasionally does empirical detection occur. In one lengthy story in Volume 3 (reprinted by Cassiday, 1983), a butcher has been robbed and murdered; a fragment of an address is discovered and reproduced in the text, like so many scraps of letters and notes in later crime fiction. In Holmesian mode Vidocq works out the full address, but then his knowledge takes over: he knows who lives at the address, masquerades as a friendly criminal, and eventually sends the pair of villains to the gallows. It is breathless, thrilling stuff, both more operatic and more intense than Richmond's rather thin and rambling adventures. Much of the plain-style detection that was to be a major part of crime fiction until the 1860s ultimately derives from Vidocq stories. In France especially he cast a long shadow: Balzac knew him personally, and he is the basis for the powerful figure who appears in *Père Goriot* (1835) as Vautrin and then returns as Collin in *Illusions Perdues* (1843): Ernest Mandel has gone so far as to say that this figure is 'the hero of the Comédie Humaine', Balzac's immense series of novels (1984: 7).

Powerful as Vidocq's memoirs are, they are not so much a cause as a symptom of the growing interest in detection in the period. As well as Pelham's detective efforts there is a quite well-developed amateur detective in *Eugene Aram*, the young Walter Lester, who tracks his suspicions of Aram down in the style of a Caleb Williams without problems – an apparent model for Walter Hartright in Wilkie Collins's *The Woman in White* (1860). Related to the developing detective and his role are regular essays in the periodicals about the weakness of circumstantial evidence: Drexler lists ten essays appearing on this topic in *Chambers's Edinburgh Journal* from 1832 to 1842 (1991: 128, n. 70).

Throughout this material there is evident a widespread awareness that some form of expert police work is needed in order to have any security in identifying the mysterious criminals abroad in the modern world. But the efforts of these emerging figures are far from authoritative in the early stories: the criminals are caught through red-handed action, or, very often, by being persuaded into confession, and this work can often be done by the narrative itself rather than an agent of inquiry.

A good example is in a series of unnoticed stories that appeared in the American *Gentleman's Magazine*, starting in 1838. The series is entitled 'The Diary of a Philadelphia Lawyer' and the most memorable is 'The Murderess': in a wordy introduction the lawyer says that women make the best of citizens and the worst of criminals and then, changing from its lofty tone, the story launches into a direct report of a woman accused of child murder – the lawyer is engaged to defend her. The body is examined for its injuries; the mother claims it was an accident; in a vigorous courtroom scene she is acquitted because the evidence against her is inconclusive; she disappears. There has been no real inquiry: the defending lawyer has just observed events. The mystery is only explained through the narrative. A few years later the lawyer receives a letter from the woman, confessing all: she had, like a *Calendar* criminal, been led astray by a man, connived in a murder for money, then had his baby. But next she fell in love with his best friend, and they murdered her previous lover. Eventually she had indeed killed the child, smashing its head against the wall in deranged despair. Finally – providence takes a resolving hand – at her dying request her confession has, somewhat improbably, been forwarded to the lawyer. Melodramatic, sexist, even prurient, this is a powerful story, but its narrative method is decidedly clumsy. The disciplinary detective is absent, and only a set of creaking narrative devices, more literary but also clumsier than the coincidences of the *Calendar*, bring the story to a resolution.

But that is not all that is of interest about 'The Diary of a Philadelphia Lawyer'. It shows how crime fiction was developing outside England, and also has contact with the major early American creator of the genre. The editor of the *Gentleman's Magazine* in 1839 was to be Edgar Allan Poe and he certainly knew the magazine before that: the combination of wordy intellectual opening, subsequent reportage, sensational crime and a remarkable resolution was obviously noted by that multi-talented writer, because in 1841 he published the first of his detective stories, which were to bring together for the first time the Gothic melodrama that had been a major element in early crime fiction with the concept of a clever explanatory figure who had not appeared before (the suggestion that

Voltaire's Zadig or even Sophocles' Oedipus is the first detective, made by Messac (1929) and Sayers (1928) among others, is merely elaborate self-validation, not source study). Many writers have felt that Poe founded the crime story as we know it; but in fact there were some elements already, if uncertainly, in place, and his influence did not operate properly until a good deal later, when it was mediated by Gaboriau and exploited by Doyle. It is more accurate to say that Poe saw the possibilities that others were only half grasping, and, as he did with the horror story and the melodramatic poem, constructed a form strong enough to predict the possibilities of the genre that was not yet in being.

IV   EDGAR ALLAN POE'S INITIATIVE

Only three of Poe's stories feature his famous detective, the Chevalier C. Auguste Dupin (he is given the aristocratic title only in the second of them): 'The Murders in the Rue Morgue' (1841), 'The Mystery of Marie Rogêt' (1842–3) and 'The Purloined Letter' (1845). They are remarkably different in tone and even structure, and many commentators would add to them two non-Dupin stories, 'Thou Art the Man' (1844) which contains a murder, detection and a surprise revelation of the killer, and, less convincingly, 'The Gold Bug' (1843) which involves finding a treasure through solving a cryptogram – but it really only relates to crime fiction because Conan Doyle and many others later worked cryptograms into their criminal mysteries.

A collection of Poe's stories published in 1840, before he created Dupin, was called 'Tales of the Arabesque and Grotesque', a title borrowed from Hoffmann, and stressing the Gothic elements so powerful in Poe's many stories of horror and non-detective mystery. Poe himself named the three Dupin stories 'tales of ratiocination', stressing the intellectual process he added to the aura of Gothic mystery, creating the mix central to the Dupin stories and so much later crime fiction. A later anthology title, still used, is 'Tales of Mystery and Imagination', which catches well the balance between an investigated enigma and the highly imaginative methodology that Dupin claims to operate, insisting he has the power of a poet to see solutions as a whole, while also offering detailed and empirical explanations for his insights.

For the first time the detective is highly literary: the narrator and Dupin meet in an ancient library; Dupin is very widely read, has a richly literary style, can match D., the villain of 'The Purloined Letter', for poetic ability, and ends that story with a telling classical quotation. By these means literary readers can project themselves into Dupin: the values he brings against the bizarre and varied threats of the stories are imaginative and intellectual, even passive – though he does examine the scene of the crime in two stories (in 'The Mystery of Marie Rogêt' he works entirely from his armchair, reading the newspapers and thinking), this is off-stage and he merely reports his activity to the narrator. The stories do not create his activity, he is never in danger, nor does he have Vidocq's exhaustive knowledge of the criminal world. Indeed none of the Dupin stories actually involves a crime as such – one is a killing by a rogue animal, another, apparently, an abortion gone wrong, the third a piece of royal court intrigue. The intellectuality of the detective and the presentation has itself permeated the type of crime, distancing it as far from everyday reality as the Paris setting displaces the story from Poe's first American readers. This unreality is not quite so true of the second story, 'The Mystery of Marie Rogêt', as there Poe deliberately set out to solve in fiction a mysterious death that had just occurred in New York. The genuine newspaper reports are reprinted in Gallicised form; Dupin ponders them; and he comes up with a solution – which was in fact wrong. Developments in the case while Poe was writing the serialised publication forced him to rewrite and produce a clumsy and quite unconvincing ending (Walsh, 1968): crime fiction, it is clear, needs to be fictional to achieve proper resolutions.

The first Dupin story has a very lengthy opening, like the Philadelphia lawyer getting out of hand, then a long factual sequence derived from newspaper reports, and no action. Dupin tells the baffled narrator all that he has achieved just before the final meeting with the seaman whose orang-utan has caused the chaos in the rue Morgue. What Dupin reports as his method is part intellectual, part empirical. Someone (he already suspects it is an ape from the tufts of hair) must have left the room: people were on the stairs; the chimney is blocked by a body. So, the evidently locked window cannot be locked, and he finds by close, quasi-scientific scrutiny the broken nail and works out how the window accidentally slammed shut. In the same analytical way, in 'The Purloined Letter' he knows the letter must be hidden somewhere obvious, as no one has been able to find it: and there it is, above the fireplace, masquerading as nothing but a letter. Dupin's method combines apparent subtlety with an inner simplicity, as does his famous feat of mind-reading in 'The Murders in the Rue Morgue' – he has actually watched the narrator's glances, gestures and reactions as he has walked through the streets, and, having followed this series of minute points, knows where they must have led in terms of opinions and responses. The aura of genius combines with the actuality of simple explanation – a very skilful piece of characterisation (Doyle will imitate it carefully), which gives the story both a surface complication and an actual simplicity: the audience can admire and also understand.

This is what is lacking in what is in other respects more fully a detective story, 'Thou Art the Man', written after Dupin was established in two cases. The structure of the story is rich in crime fiction motifs: there is an innocent suspect, likely, in *Calendar* style, to be condemned on circumstantial evidence; there is an investigation by a detective figure, but it is curiously, and ineffectively, off-stage; there is a fine revelation of the least likely suspect – apparently the first of all – and a genuinely startling dénouement: the dead body sits up and, through the inquirer's ventriloquist skills, announces to the killer 'Thou art the man' – he faints in obvious guilt. Dorothy Sayers felt this was 'unpleasantly flippant in treatment' (1928: 19), and it clearly has a parodic element, mocking the *Blackwood's* writers, and also Brown's interest in ventriloquism, displayed in *Wieland* and elsewhere in his work. It also creates features that later writers, notably in the 'golden age', would reproduce without a sense of irony; though it does describe the effects of detection, it does not foreground the detective.

Yet for all their differences, and the sense that Poe was innovating more than even he fully grasped, the stories have a collective importance. Primarily, they condense the idea of Gothic thrill and rational inquiry: where the classic Gothic novel would make a character exhibit some rational courage in the face of overwhelming sensual and sensational excitement, here the order is reversed: these are stories that impose the mastery of a mind on the unusual and stimulating. They also have an important location. Paris, for English-speaking readers, was a city of excitement, and for Americans more exotically foreign than London, though it is also in some ways a displacement of wealthy, volatile New York and Philadelphia. Poe is one of many major crime writers who to some degree make a character out of a city – and they always seem to be writing about a city in which they were not brought up: there is a sense of thrill, of danger, or even shaping the self, in Doyle's London, Chandler's

Los Angeles, Paretsky's Chicago: the urban experience runs deep in crime fiction.

Commentators have seen other profundities in Poe's work. The Freudian Marie Bonaparte has written about Oedipal features of the stories – the daughter is not so much stuffed up a chimney as returned to the womb, the letter above the fireplace stands in for a clitoris (1949). Jacques Lacan has, today even more famously, seen in 'The Purloined Letter' a fable of the way in which letters, signs, are the basis for our consciousness and sense of identity (1966) – and two other modern gurus, Derrida (1975) and Barbara Johnson (1980), have spoken in similar ways in a debate discussed by John Muller and Will Richardson (1988) and John T. Irwin (1994, Chapter 1). Theorists as these are, generators of what Irwin calls 'intellectual vertigo' (1994: 11), they have had little interest in the complex forces of urban life, mass communication and gender that seethe beneath the surface of 'The Mystery of Marie Rogêt' but some social analysis of the stories has been offered: Dupin, as John Rignall has argued (1998), can be taken as the archetype of the *flâneur*, the alienated urban onlooker, outlined in Water Benjamin's subtle essay focusing on another Poe story, 'The Man of the Crowd' (1973).

Poe did not suddenly change the course of crime writing: his impact was felt much sooner in France than England – Baudelaire translated him, Gaboriau and others raided his stories for ideas. As Messac shows, his influence there was considerable (1929: 348–78), but in England, while Wilkie Collins in 1854 brought Poe's subtle idea back to the world of English lawyers and financial fraud in 'A Stolen Letter', and one of the 1860s police writers showed knowledge of his work (Andrew Forrester Jr, to be discussed below – see pp. 34–5), it was not until Gaboriau's reworking of Poe's idea sparked off Conan Doyle's creation of the ultimate hero-detective that his brilliance began to have its deserved effect. But before that, there was much detective activity. In France, for the most part crime fiction continued to be a rambling representation of aristocratic crimes and urban fears; in England, and increasingly in America and elsewhere, the plain detective of the 1850s and 1860s plied an unimaginative but clearly popular trade, largely separate from the Gothic tradition which would, in modified form, thrive again in the sensational movement of the 1860s.

2
The Development of Detection

I   PLAIN ENGLISH DETECTION

When the 'New Police', essentially the modern English police force, were formed in London in 1829, soon to be paralleled in American cities, much stress was laid on the fact that they were to be 'preventive': they were not to be undercover, plain-clothes detectives – or spies, according to English opinion. As Kayman explains (1992: Chapter 3, 61–80), the 'New Police' were to be highly visible – especially with their tall helmets and quasi-military uniforms: the idea was that they would walk about the city and act as visible indicators of the power of the state, a constant threat to wrong-doers that they would be apprehended and punished. A reform project as they were, and a public body of skilled men as they were meant to be, they were nevertheless in a major way a continuation of sovereign power – now delegated through commissioners and inspectors, but for all that a living visible arm of the national law.

There were some operations in plain clothes of a detective sort – or at least some of the later fictions imagine such activities in the 1830s – but it was not until 1842 that the police formally established a plain-clothes detective unit, and then it was tiny, just two inspectors and six sergeants when there were 4000 uniformed police in London. This slowness in moving towards real detection may help to explain how long it took for English fiction to develop its own imitations of Vidocq. The first clear step in the direction of a new police-based fiction was the appearance in July 1849, in the middle-of-the-road *Chambers's Edinburgh Journal*, of 'Recollections of a Police Officer' by William Russell. Nothing is known of this prolific author, and some have thought the name a pseudonym. The series title also changed when the stories came out in book form in 1856 as *Recollections of a Detective Police-Officer*; the simpler *Recollections of a Policeman* was used for the rarely noted (especially in England) earlier book publication in America in 1852, another striking instance of the vigour of crime fiction across the Atlantic.

Russell's Thomas Waters is, like Tom Richmond, a gentleman fallen on hard times, humble as his activities are. He engages himself in the first story, again like Richmond, with a gentleman drawn into a corrupt gambling circle, but the stories soon settle into an urban and mercantile context. In the classic story 'X.Y.Z.' (named for the signature on a personal advertisement in the newspapers – the world is that of literary-minded readers), Waters watches, follows, listens at windows like Vidocq and eventually manages to clear the honest clerical worker who is wrongly suspected as a result of the cunning schemes of hardened criminals. Coincidence, surveillance and persistence are, also as in Vidocq, the key methods of Waters's success. Plain and rather banal as he is, less exotic and errant than Tom Richmond among his gypsies, theatricals and dubious aristocrats, Waters was nevertheless a great success as a detective who countered credible threats of sudden disgrace and disaster in respectable middle-class life, lower as well as upper, and countered them by the methods of patient attention and naive persistence that were themselves key values in the nineteenth-century litany of self-improvement.

Waters was, as Philip Collins notes, 'so hugely popular that it led to an immediate vogue for yellow-back detective stories' (1962: 211). The context was now propitious for success, unlike in the time of Richmond. The development of new, cheaper printing processes and the steady lowering of stamp duty, which was finally abolished in 1861, as well as the growing literacy of ordinary working people, helped construct an audience for these popular forms of plain detection, especially in the 1860s, and mostly in the cheap 'yellow-back' fiction, which sold well at low prices, especially on railway bookstalls. And not accidentally there: in his social history of railways, Wolfgang Schivelbusch has written, in a chapter called 'The Compartment' (1977: Chapter 5), about the ways in which on the new trains, shut in carriages from which they could neither escape nor ask the driver to stop, as on the stage-coach, people greatly feared those with whom they might be immured. It was a fine location for a fiction of social anxiety, and the simple operations of the street-level detectives appeared to have had a calming effect, much as the depiction, and defeat, of random international violence in the spy novels of Ian Fleming and his kind eased the nerves of air-travellers in the 1960s and 1970s.

Among the new fictional police, detection seems a steady, slow development of a limited disciplinary response to crime, but there were in fact earlier movements made in amateur detecting. The bulk of the very early detection was amateur, though it was also of a more purely professional and disciplinary kind than was available or credible among the plain police. The earliest of these detection-oriented and discipline-based stories were produced by Samuel Warren, a barrister with medical training. From 1830 on *Blackwood's* was printing his series called 'Passages from the Diary of a Late Physician', published in two-volume form in 1832, with a third volume to follow in 1838: Worthington sees them as the first genuinely disciplinary stories to be produced as a project and a series (2003: 99–133). Warren's stories were very popular, and appear to give rise to many more in the same vein. Peter Drexler lists no less than 17 separate stories and series in the journals from 1831 to 1847, with ten different named authors and seven anonymous texts, which all have a disciplinary and professional approach to explaining crime and identifying criminals (1991: 124, n.20).

Detection in detail is occasionally present in these disciplinary amateur investigators, but it emerges as a central feature in a later series attributed to Warren: 'The Experiences of a Barrister', which first appeared, before 'Waters', in *Chambers's Edinburgh Journal* in March 1849. The opening story, 'The Contested Marriage', deals with a mother trying to win for her son the estate of her now dead husband, who married her against his father's wishes and under an assumed name, then left for a respectable aristocratic life and another marriage. The estate has now passed to another branch of the family, so the story combines the theme of rights to inherited property, an obsessively common topic in the period, with that distaste for the aristocracy that is endemic to bourgeois Victorian fiction. The case is resolved by the energetic action of an 'Attorney-at-Law' (an appointed legal officer, close to a solicitor in function, but not of high status). He is vigorous, very keen on his fees, named Samuel Ferret (could there be a play on the author's name, Samuel Warren?). He rushes about the country and eventually traces the clergyman who performed the secret marriage – he too has a colourful name, the Revd Zachariah Zimmerman.

Quite sharply written, with some of the verbal energy of his contemporary, Charles Dickens (some thought them equals), Warren's stories give everyday detection an element of disciplinary power with their interest in the law and the data of the modern state: it is through church registers that Mr Ferret finds his clergyman. The same is true of a slightly later series called *Leaves from the Diary of a Law Clerk* (1857), written by the untiring William Russell. The unnamed clerk here is involved in cases less than Gothic or grandiose: jewel theft, burglary, inheritance-jumping, insurance fraud and forgery – those favourites of simple detection at this time – are all present, but there are also several murders, an abduction and arson to give a slightly more Gothic flavour. A few stories involve careful and quite searching detection, but in others the narrator merely gives a legally focused account of what happened around a crime. The detective genre is not yet fully and firmly established and the later stories are drawn from *Chambers's* 'Confessions of an Attorney series', involving lawyers called Flint and Sharp. These collections often blur their focus late on as material is being gathered to fill a volume: the last story is a grim tale of innocents executed in the old days, as if generally justifying the mildly disciplinary approach of these stories.

The disciplinary amateurs were the first to be published in numbers in the 1830s and 1840s. In the 1850s it seems that police like Waters and civil figures like Mr Ferret interweave, but by the 1860s the standard focus of popular crime stories has become a police detective. Some of these new fictions were barely of a professional standard: in 1860 'Charles Martel', a pseudonym for the literary hack Thomas Delf, produced *The Detective's Notebook* (1860). It started with the cases of Sergeant Bolter, dealing with unmelodramatic instances of burglary, jewel theft, forgery, debt. In one story an important clue is a button left at the scene of crime, and the Sergeant plods through the clothes emporia of London before spotting it by chance on a waistcoat. The collection degenerates from this procedural policing into a set of Delf's off-cuts – sketches of crime, a mildly pornographic novella called 'The Libertine's Victim', and a few vignettes without the Sergeant at all, including a barrister's reminiscences.

Nevertheless the collection did well enough to stimulate a follow-up, *The Diary of an Ex-Detective* (also 1860, but the British Library copy is dated 9 November – the first Martel was accessioned on 23 May). This is a much more competent production, focused on the exploits of Inspector F. – presumably meant to be the well-known Inspector Field, previously honoured by Dickens in his factual stories about the detective department in *Household Words* (starting in 1850; reprinted in *Hunted Down*, 1996). As was customary, the stories in the second collection by Martel involved mostly non-violent crimes, but there are some definite advances in detection, including in one of the two murder cases the examination of bloodstains and an appendix to explain the details. Gambling, burglary, mail-robbery and blackmail are the everyday crimes detected, with substantial attention to detail and a steady, if unexciting, level of plotting. This collection also fades structurally at the end, as the last two stories do not deal with Inspector F. at all and the previous one is just a story told to the Inspector, but clearly the second volume was successful because in 1862 Inspector F. appeared again, but this time in *The Experiences of a Real Detective* by the ever-industrious William Russell.

A writer called Andrew Forrester Jun. was active in this mode. Nothing is known about him, and it could be a pseudonym referring to the Forrester brothers John and Daniel, who were active in private inquiry work – the second Martel volume was dedicated to them, as the first was to Field. Under Forrester's name appeared a set of detective stories from 1861 on, exploiting the same reasonably credible, moderately unexciting vein as Russell and Martel, with collections like *Revelations of a Private Detective* (1863) and *Secret Service* (1864). An innovative move was made when in 1864, with *The Female Detective*, Forrester invented a woman inquirer, who gives her name as Mrs G— (which may be Mrs Gladden, or that may be one of her aliases) and is working as detective for the police – at a time when no women at all worked for the detective service. In fact there were no actual women detectives until the twentieth century: those who were appointed in the 1880s to the detective department were merely there to search and guard women prisoners. Though the Gothic heroine had often been a brave inquirer into disorder and threat, the idea of a woman actually being a detective had not occurred – though sometimes writers came close, as in Catherine Crowe's *Susan Hopley* (1841), where, as Sussex argues (2003), the leading figure, a servant, plays a major role in identifying the real criminal in a welter of confusing circumstantial evidence. The boldness of Forrester's move is indicated when the female detective starts by discussing the surprise caused by her role, but also the professionally effective potential of her gender:

> if there is a demand for men detectives, there must also be one
> for female detective police ... the reader will comprehend that
> the woman detective has far greater opportunities than a man of

intimate watching, and of keeping her eyes on matters near which
a man could not conveniently play the eavesdropper.   (1864: 3–4)

This first volume is, not unusually, uneven. There is a novella about,
as is so common, inheritance problems called 'Tenant for Life' in
which Mrs G— plays a calm and intelligent role in bringing order, if
not exactly justice, to a disrupted family in a complex legal situation;
then follows a short wry story about 'Georgy', a charming and eventually successful young embezzler who escapes justice. Later comes
what E. F. Bleiler, in his 'Introduction' to the reprint in *Three
Nineteenth-Century Detective Novels* (1977), rates as a very successful
long crime story, 'The Unknown Weapon'. This novella deals with
the strange death of the rough-mannered son of a miserly squire. He
is found outside his father's house, stabbed by a strange harpoon-
like weapon which someone has tried, unsuccessfully, to remove.
The female detective insinuates herself into the housekeeper's
friendship and interviews a maid with very limited intelligence,
who is terrified about a strange large box. A well-developed and
interesting investigation reveals a grisly secret: in order to steal his
father's valuables, the son had himself concealed in a box sent to the
house. Hearing a noise from it, the housekeeper stabbed the box
with an archaic weapon. As often happens in later work, the detective makes an ethical judgement, and the housekeeper is not
pursued by the law. It is Mrs G—'s finest case, combining the investigations of Waters with a moral critique and narrative control not
unlike that of Elizabeth Gaskell.

Success breeds imitation when there is a public demand for a particular genre, and later in 1864 (the British Library copy is dated
January 1865) there appeared *Revelations of a Lady Detective* – the
author has been identified, without certainty, as the prolific William
Stephens Hayward. The detective, Mrs Paschal, is a well-born and
well-educated widow who works for the official police, is deputed
cases in an orderly way, takes on disguises and tracks her villains
with some courage. As Kayman comments, while she is 'institution-
ally still a public servant, she operates like an independent professional' (1992: 124). There is more melodrama than in Forrester: in the
opening story, 'The Mysterious Countess', Mrs Paschal, having infil-
trated herself as the Countess's maid, tracks the villainess through a
dark and fearful labyrinth into a bank vault where she has been
helping herself to gold bars. Even this seems tame beside the second
story, 'The Secret Band', where an Italian gang vendetta is going on

in London: in a staggering conclusion, Mrs Paschal is bound and gagged and about to be drowned a riverside hideaway when the villainous gang-leader is struck dead by a bolt of lightning, and justice miraculously prevails.

This extreme note is not often struck; Mrs Paschal is usually successful through being skilled, sensible and brave. Her techniques of disguise, patience and courageous encounters with criminals hark back to Vidocq, as well as to Mrs G—. The presence of these women detectives suggests that publishers knew there was a substantial female audience for crime fiction by this time – as of course there had been for Gothic fiction, and indeed all fiction. It is probable that Mrs Paschal was produced by a man, but the Forrester stories present Mrs G—'s attitudes and interests, and the women characters in general, so convincingly that it seems quite possible they were written by a woman. There may be a candidate for female authorship. It is noticeable that the Forrester detective stories stop after 1864, with only reprints appearing until 1868, then nothing. That is the year when an unidentified Mrs Forrester starts to produce her three novels, *Fair Women* (dated 1868 but the British Library copy is stamped 8 November 1867), *From Olympus to Hades* (1868) and *My Hero* (1870). These are standard three-decker gentry romances, but it is notable that the first involves a man shot while poaching – the first explanation of the death in 'The Unknown Weapon' – and later has a chapter title 'Drawing the Arrow Head'. It is easy to suspect that a woman writer, perhaps connected to the Forresters, worked first in one lucrative and popular literary genre and then turned to another.

There seems no reason why the competent imitations of Waters's male policing that 'Forrester' produced before *The Female Detective* might not also have been produced in a cross-gender mode. In fact there is a clear parallel for this: in early 1866 the new Melbourne-based *Australian Journal* began to publish the first of a very long-lasting series of crime stories by a writer called 'W.W.', which was a version of 'Waif Wander', a pseudonym used for poetry and more general prose by Mary Fortune. She appears to have first taken up a detective series written by J. S. Borlase, then produced her own detective, Mark Sinclair, in 'Dead Witness', a confidently structured and well-written story about a body in a bush waterhole in the goldfield region of Victoria (see Knight, 1997: 113–16; Sussex and Burrows, 1997). Fortune, only recently unearthed by Lucy Sussex (1989), wrote crime fiction into the twentieth century, and clearly was familiar with the stories appearing in the London magazines – the *Australian Journal* was a close but vigorously localised imitation of the *London Journal*.

Another major figure outside London appears at the same time in *Leaves from the Note-book of the New York Detective* (1865). No author is named, but the 'editor' is John B. Williams, M.D. (a possible source for Dr Watson), who met on a train James Brampton, also known as Jem, heard the story of his first case, and was then given his case-book to write up. Jem's father was 'a respectable merchant' (the social level is again a common feature) and the son trained as a doctor (discipline again), but when an old schoolfriend asked for advice, he turned into a consulting detective after a while spent as a detective police officer (1865: 4–5). Poe was a rich source. Jem 'possessed to an eminent degree the power of analysis' and he operates 'by educating the powers of observation' (1865: 3, 4). But Brampton is more direct than Dupin. The stories are short (about 4000–5000 words on average), vigorous, and told in the first person; they exhibit mystery (a locked room), clues (a left-handed murderer), and reveal Jem's clarity of mind, speed of action and that decisive moral judgement that is a feature of private detection. Though he is often enigmatically called a 'private detective officer', he does not get his cases through an office like Waters or the female police detectives: the major role of chance and his own decision to investigate indicate that he is an early stage in the massive development of the private detective in North America.

Australia and America were not the only other countries to develop detectives. In Ireland Robert Curtis produced a series of stories for the *Dublin University Magazine* (then owned by Sheridan Le Fanu) about *The Irish Police Officer* (1861), and James M'Levy wrote several collections about an Edinburgh police inspector – which he himself was – with his own name, starting with *The Curiosities of Crime in Edinburgh*, also in 1861. All these case-books of crime have local features, of language, attitude and even crime – more business-oriented in America, more rural in Australia and Ireland – but the basic pattern recurs, insisting that patient, courageous, low-level policing is a credible value to place against the threats, some of them murder, to be found in these varied but essentially modern contexts.

Moments of melodrama occur through the plain detectives of the 1850s and 1860s, though few were as remarkable as Mrs Paschal's avenging lightening bolt. In general this material is not close to the Gothic, and has a low-temperature approach to both the threats

and the values embodied in the texts. But there were more exotic
fictions: G. W. M. Reynolds, a prolific writer, publisher, and radical
sympathiser – he spoke at some of the major Chartist meetings in
1848 – imitated in English the sweeping melodramatic romances of
crime that Eugène Sue published in 1842–3 under the general title
Les Mystères de Paris. Reynolds could read French and his *Mysteries
of London* started appearing before Sue was published in English in
1845. They were at the simplest and liveliest level, appearing first as
penny weeklies and then in book form from 1846–1850, containing
nearly a million words.

It is hard to think of any form of melodrama which does not
appear in Reynolds's saga. It concerns a pair of noble twins, one our
hero, one to be the central villain; there is also a fiendish professional
criminal and body-snatcher, 'The Resurrection Man', a brave
woman who is threatened with all kinds of indignities, appears
illustrated in flimsy clothing, cross-dresses, marries the villain and
has his child. Her brother-in-law, the good twin and hero, marries
the daughter of an Italian prince and eventually succeeds him as
ruler. Amazingly exotic stuff, with vivid if clumsy writing and vigorous, sometimes semi-pornographic illustrations, this material
reveals that the spirit of Gothic melodrama, so strong early in the
century, does not disappear, but continues, and will in less shapeless
form play a major part in the development of crime fiction in the
novel of sensation.

II SENSATION

Literary histories tend to relate sensationalism to the 1860s, and
conveniently find that Wilkie Collins's *The Woman in White* (1860)
was the first example of the form. But Bulwer and Ainsworth, not
to mention the early Dickens, had used crime and excitement as
a central mechanism; there were others who did this, like Catherine
Crowe in *Susan Hopley* (1841) and Caroline Clive with a powerful
study of a respectable man who slipped into criminality in *Paul
Ferroll* (1855). The approach was treated more excitably in
Reynolds's *Mysteries* and the whole school of heavily breathing fiction that came from the cheap publishers of Salisbury Square, from
three-decker novels down to the 'penny dreadfuls', which include
Reynolds's productions and celebrate popular monsters like
Sweeney Todd, the demon barber or Sawney Bean, the cannibal. But

there was also the powerfully sensational impact of theatre. The major crime stories, famous murder cases like those focused on Eugene Aram and Maria Marten, and the feats of Vidocq, were sensations – in every sense – on the stage; Wilkie Collins himself, like his friend Dickens, was fascinated by popular theatre, wrote for it and even performed in it. What the sensation novel did was bring both Gothic sensibility and that popular energy into the domain of conventional respectable fiction – and so achieve a greater effect by suggesting that strange and terrible events could occur right within the respectable home, that shrine of Victorian values. Henry James, who might seem far from such vulgarities, could see and partly admire that Collins had:

> introduced those most mysterious of mysteries, the mysteries which are at our own doors ... instead of the terrors of 'Udolpho', we were treated to the terrors of the cheerful country-house and the busy London lodgings. And there is no doubt that these were infinitely the more terrible. (1921: 110)

The threats of passion and crime could thrive not just in the mysterious romantic foreignness of the Gothic novel nor the pullulating streets and lower social orders of popular melodrama, but within the walls of respectability.

The Woman in White caused a sensation in modern terms – readers besieged the shops, there were 'Woman in White' fashions, tea-rooms, merchandise of all kinds. But it is important to note that 'sensation' also has a literal meaning: the novels were meant to stir, shock, excite the reader's senses. From its shudder-inducing opening in night-time north London, through the cold pines of Blackwater Park, the drenching, chilling rain that Marian suffers as she listens at night to the criminals plotting, the consuming fires at the church where Sir Percival dies, to the cold humiliation of the slab on which Count Fosco's naked body eventually lies, *The Woman in White* is an intensely physical book, with a visceral impact all the more effective because the reader is respectable, intelligent, invited to analyse as well as respond to all these different stimuli. Collins has the power to internalise the Gothic element, in part somatically through the physical oddities of his characters – Marian's moustache, Laura's pallor, Glyde's cough, Fosco's huge but nimble body – but also through the way in which they are all involved in a genuinely complex mystery, much more elaborate than the simple puzzles faced by Pelham or Caleb Williams: Collins presents a set of enigmas that consistently shake certainties about rank, gender, class, body, even consciousness.

He did not come to this immediately with *The Woman in White*, as is often suggested by commentators. He had worked in forms of crime fiction before, with startling variety and effect. His second novel, *Basil* (1852), was an excitable melodrama without detection, but he took a intriguing step in his first crime-focused novel, *Hide and Seek* (1854). The plot concerns the usual family mysteries, faced in part by a young white-collar worker, but also by Matthew Marksman, who has returned from America: he was scalped there, and that, as well as his name and his rough manners, his brave, patient and even cunning dedication to his detective quest, indicate that he too is a descendant of Cooper's frontier pathfinders, translated to the London mystery novel.

Equally innovative was the story Collins published in *Household Words* in 1856, 'The Diary of Anne Rodway', in which a poor dressmaker investigates the death of her friend Mary. There is coincidence in her finding the rest of the cravat that her dead friend held in her hand, but detailed detection is the thrust of the story, and the police are not very helpful. Anne is a genuine amateur detective, but it is noticeable that she does not resolve the case; her boyfriend returns from America to provide a masculine resolution.

In *The Woman in White* Collins has no professional or even full-time detective: he uses a naive young man, Walter Hartright, as the central inquirer, but only after a woman, Marian Halcombe, a much more confident and capable version of Anne Rodway, has made considerable strides towards uncovering the mysterious plotting of Glyde and Fosco. She is suddenly removed from the plot by an illness caught in the rain – like Anne Rodway, a woman cannot be allowed to go through to the end – and in the later part of the novel Marian is a strange third in the fugitive London domesticity of Walter and Laura, while the man races around detecting and frustrating these fearsome enemies. Walter has returned from his South American adventures stronger-minded, capable of the intensity and rigorous activity of detection; Collins's consistent use, in his early mysteries, of transatlantic detectives suggests that for him, at least, the genre has a non-English, even American, dynamic.

The crimes are, as is common, those of aristocrats, though somewhat displaced, as Sir Percival is really an impostor and Fosco is Italian; Laura's uncle is an enfeebled member of the wealthy gentry and Walter, a drawing master, represents in an aesthetic way both the disciplinary world and upward social mobility. If crime is dastardly and anti-woman, detection is never really a thematic element – sensation and bourgeois take-over are the major themes. But what detection there is, like the cravat Anne found, is bracingly mundane, straight out of the Waters and Ferret tradition. It focuses on letters, witnesses, church ledgers and especially realistic is Laura's railway ticket: the date on which she travelled to London is the crucial clue by which Walter can destabilise the villainous quasi-gentry.

Collins's success led to many imitators, and to some resistance to sensation fiction. The Archbishop of York attacked the new phenomenon in 1864, and many journalists and reviewers wrote, mostly with some deprecation, about this innovative force in publishing, as Patrick Brantlinger has shown (1982). Confirming the notion of a substantial female readership for this material, Mary Elizabeth Braddon's *Lady Audley's Secret* appeared in 1862. If Collins had stirred people and their senses, this novel excited them at a deeper level. Lady Audley, diminutive, lovely, sweet and skilled, mistress of a beautiful rustic aristocratic house, is represented subtly, but incrementally, as a crazed killer. Braddon has reversed Collins: it is as if Laura Fairlie imbibes the virulence of Glyde, the cunning of Fosco and the unsettling female power of Marian Halcombe.

Braddon, always a fluent plotter, combines two mysteries – what has Lady Audley really done, and what will she do next ? It transpires that she meant to murder her husband, but in one of the great escapes – and plot devices – of the nineteenth century he climbed out of the well, fled to Liverpool and took a ship to America. Later, haunted by the thought that her husband's nephew is getting close to the secret, she burns down an inn to kill him – and fails again. Finally tucked away in a French asylum because of the madness that taints her family – this is her real 'secret' – she is a figure who seems to be presented in a partly understanding, even sympathetic way: she can charm the male readers while alarming them, and also make women feel that in some way she has fought her corner well, and is a type of female, if not quite feminist, noble outlaw.

Her only opponent is Robert Audley, an idle, almost spineless, lawyer: with the largely off-stage exception of her first husband, there are no macho men in this story, indeed very few in the whole of sensationalism. Robert Audley becomes a conscious amateur detective, tracing carefully Lady Audley's past, but he is her cousin, not an outsider coming in to cleanse a dirty world, as will later become the norm. His own love-life is an intermittent theme, and the least convincing element in the novel is his romance with Lady Audley's first husband's sister, ignoring as he does the robust, direct, hard-riding cousin who loves him dearly. As with Marian Halcombe, sensationalism does not have much of a positive position for a strong women, though Collins, in his nervous way the most radical, later makes detectives of Magdalene Vanstone, on her own behalf, in *No Name* (1862) and the accused man's wife in *The Law and the Lady* (1875). Braddon swept on to many more novels, never catching again quite the mix of thrillingly gendered crime and sexually exciting beauty of her first novel, but always confirming the switchback ride of sensual stimulation and alarming thrills that made sensationalism a major force of the period. A key feature, as Elaine Showalter has noted (1978), is secrecy. All is not what it seems in respectable life: the apparently gentlemanly Sir Percival is a scrounging crook; the exquisite hostess of Audley End is a mad would-be killer. Part of the power of sensationalism, its inherent threat, is the alarming distance between the apparent and the real, the depth of the abyss into which the evil, greedy, or simply mad, characters fall.

Before Braddon published *Lady Audley's Secret* and shortly after the book publication of *The Woman in White*, another major force in the popular Victorian novel had launched into full sensationalism. Ellen Wood, traditionally called Mrs Henry Wood, started publishing *East Lynne* in January 1861 in a magazine edited by W. Harrison Ainsworth, the veteran novelist who produced several criminal heroes, like *Jack Sheppard*. *East Lynne* may have itself given Braddon the idea for a criminal heroine. Wood had lived in France for 20 years and she has the confident, complicated narrative drive of the *feuilleton* writers, and something of their limited characterisation as well. Isabel Vane, beautiful and nobly born but alone in the world, marries a respectable provincial lawyer, Archibald Carlyle: a blissful life is possible, but she just gets things wrong. Feeling her husband has lost interest in her, she is seduced into adulterous elopement by the distinctly theatrical villain Captain Francis Levison.

Murder is about: a mysterious killing in the past is linked with Richard Hare, brother of Barbara, the detecting friend and future bigamous wife of Isabel's husband; suspicions, identities, possibilities are steadily worked through. Unlike *Lady Audley's Secret*, but like *The Woman in White*, this is based on male villainy, and Levison turns out to be the murderer as well as the seducer. Combining detailed, George Eliot-like, domestic realism with an intricate set of mysteries, suggesting that plain bourgeois honesty and methodical morality are the keys to defeating deceit and temptation, this is a powerful story that was immensely successful in book form and on the stage. To an extent it is an exploration of the difficulties of inno-cent married women and the ease with which they could fall into error, but Wood lacks the emotive tension of Braddon or the socially symbolic power of Collins: this is melodrama, richly laid on, and developed at full length. Some of the detection that occurs is inher-ently disciplinary, from lawyer Carlyle, though it is only occasional and hardly made central, and more interesting is the effect of the doggedly inquiring nature of Barbara Hare: finally given more scope than Marian Halcombe, she is perhaps even a source for the soon-to-appear lady detectives, Mrs G— and Mrs Paschal.

Detection was a recurrent element in these first major sensational novels, and in some others it can dominate, so that it is as easy to call it a detective novel. In *The Notting Hill Mystery* (serialised in *Once a Week* in 1862–3 and published as a novel in 1865) by the pseudonymous 'Charles Felix', an insurance investigator puzzles over the recent death of a woman insured for the very large sum of £25,000. Her husband the Baron (himself dubious, being both noble and foreign) is able to show there was no trace of poison, as had been suspected. A very complicated plot develops, with twins separated very young, one taken by gypsies and the circus (dim resonances of *Richmond* can be heard); much forensic detail is offered about antimony poisoning and mesmerism, and there is a splendidly sensational quasi-scientific explanation to it all: the Baron has poisoned his wife's twin sister and his powers of mes-merism have transferred the effect to kill his wife for the insurance money.

Sensation stories are in one sense realistic novels, foregrounding letters, descriptions and banal details – in *The Notting Hill Mystery* one twin has very broad feet because she was a tightrope walker – but they also tend to have deeply improbable lurches in the plot that suggest there are strange forces in the world beyond mere realism. Mesmeric transference between twins is a classic example, but there are many others. In *The Woman in White* Walter returns from South America and arrives, by quasi-providential agency, at Laura's mother's tomb just at the moment Laura and Marian have arrived there from London; equally strained and just as structurally impor-tant is the dream in Collins's *Armadale* (1866). George Talbot's escape from the well or the polyvalent villainies of Fosco and Levison are other examples of this bold hyper-realism that seems central to sensational fiction.

A classic example occurs in an American novel that matches Braddon for early major work by a woman, Metta Fuller's *The Dead Letter*. Published in book form under the gender-obscuring name 'Seeley Regester' in 1867, having been serialised by the popular dime-novel producing firm of Beadles, this uses an energetic detective, Mr Burton, who comes from the office of the detective police to solve a family murder. Like Waters with higher skills, he telegraphs and hurries about the country, decodes a cypher, analyses handwriting, and consistently keeps the multiple suspects under investigation. With a family at odds and a final explanation and revelation scene, the structure is much like the future pattern of the clue-puzzle, and, as B. J. Rahn comments, Fuller uses many of the techniques that Poe had already deployed (1988). This is less literary and elaborate than Collins and Braddon, but it offers both a vigorous narrative and a well-constructed puzzle. Not all is likely – Burton has a new lead when, on a trip to California, he accidentally overhears people talking about the case, but this is just a typically sen-sational strained use of coincidence, like the opening where a postal worker encounters a dead letter relevant to himself and the case that develops. The sudden piece of improbable plotting that characterises the sensation novel comes when the detective employs his clairvoyant daughter to give him the precise details of a suspect's whereabouts. Presumably this is why Bleiler said this was 'a very bad novel' (1977: x), because otherwise *The Dead Letter* is effective and confident, with a reasonably surprising final revelation, and this must define the novel more as a detective novel than a sensational thriller.

Many commentators have felt that Collins's *The Moonstone* (1868) similarly moves towards the mainstream of detective fiction: T. S. Eliot called it 'the first and greatest of English detective novels' ([1927] 1932: 412) and Dorothy Sayers said it was 'probably the very finest detective story ever written' (1928: 25). It is certainly more formally like a detective story than the earlier sensational novels, though it is based on jewel theft and there is no one masterful and all-organising unraveller of the crime. There are in fact several detectives, including two professionals, a great deal of evidence, investigation, and finally both amazing revelation and just retribution.

The first detective is the uniformed and sombrely-named Inspector Seegrave: he makes no headway in pursuit of the missing diamond, but insists on searches, and shows special suspicion of the servants: he exposes the limits of the visible and authoritarian style of sovereign-power policing. A disciplinary specialist is brought in from London, a dry, sharp-eyed lower-middle-class man with a name suggesting ordinariness, Sergeant Cuff. He makes some empirical advances: he spots the smeared paint in the room where the Moonstone was stolen, he checks everybody's washing for paint traces, and like a modern Vidocq identifies and suspects a servant who is a reformed thief. Focusing on the case and on an unsophisticated interpretation of human behaviour as he does, he decides that the hostile silence of Rachel Verinder, the eighteen-year-old who received the fateful jewel on her birthday, must be behind the robbery. But Cuff is misled and enrages Rachel's mother, Lady Verinder. Anthea Trodd (1989: Chapter 12, 'The Policeman and the Lady') has drawn attention to the conflict between male police and higher-class women in the world of sensation fiction, which presumably charts a conflict over gender-related power: there is often a lack of a powerful senior male figure in the household. As a result Cuff is dismissed and the story moves on through various narrators, all baffled both by the circumstantial evidence and the absence of any credible interpretation of it. The multiple-witness style that Collins developed for *The Woman in White* powerfully expresses the idea of a community that observes, ponders, but, without a disciplinary expert, cannot achieve the simple certainties of the *Newgate Calendar* kind of community.

The truth will eventually be brought out by a different sort of detective, who has disciplinary skills but curiously – it would seem compulsively – limited authority. This is a seriously ill, of mixed (but uncertain) race, socially and personally enfeebled doctor's assistant who dabbles in mental science, and is able, in a cross between a mesmeric seance and a psychoanalytic session, to gain access to the illness-damaged memory of Dr Candy, who played a crucial part in the mystery. Ezra Jennings seems like a combination of the medico-legal men of the 1840s and 1850s with the obsessive personality and powerful, though limited, insights of Dupin – and he is another of Collins's detectives from overseas. It is he who persuades the central characters to re-enact the night of the theft, and he who has perceived that – here is the flamboyant sensationalist element – a laudanum-sodden, anxiety-ridden, sleepwalking Franklin Blake has taken the jewel for its greater safety. With his interest in American sources for the investigation of mysterious crimes, Collins may well have

known Charles Brockden Brown's use of somnambulism as the key
to strange events in *Edgar Huntly*. Splendid though the idea of sleep-
walking crime may be – classically sensational in both its physical
realisation and its daring improbability – this is not the whole
story. The jewel was then taken by the apparently very respectable
professional man Godrey Ablewhite, to support his secret immoral
lifestyle. A well-hidden version of Percival Glyde, he dies not as
a white man, and certainly not an able one, but disguised as a
dark-skinned sailor: and he dies at the hands of some very able non-
whites, the Brahmins who have followed the Moonstone across the
world and at all costs to themselves, to restore it to their temple.
Throughout the story, and released by its fine, brisk ending, are two
fables about appearance and reality: the respectable sanctimonious
upper bourgeoisie, to whom Godfrey belongs, can be deadlier enemies than the more facile foreign threats of figures like Fosco, and –
the more searching of the two evaluative conclusions – the Indian
people who have recently been so widely vilified in the English
response to the 'Mutiny' of 1857 are in fact capable of a level of
fidelity and faith, not to mention skill and intelligence, that deserve
our admiration.

Collins here, as in all his work, has thematic concerns deeper and
wider than the usual range of crime writers, and many commentators on the novel treat it, like Poe's stories, as a source of potent
symbolism. Hutter (1975) reads the Moonstone itself and the smear
on the nightdress as bearing sexual symbolism; Rachel's silence, her
mother's early death, the absence of an effective father figure (a
common lack in sensational fiction) all suggest a thematic exploration of issues relating to gender and power, while among the
servants especially the subject of class is questioningly explored,
and Jennings's enigmatic ethnic origin returns to the racial theme
connected to the stone and its origins. *The Moonstone* is the most
multiple and powerful work of the sensational tradition, and shows
Collins at his most radically inquiring, but it still, finally, re-establishes
order. Franklin and Rachel marry, Verinder House and its essentially
noble line are restored, just as at the end of *The Woman in White*
another semi-disciplinary individual (Walter's art skills are matched
by Franklin's being a philosopher of a sort) is socially elevated.
English society can trundle on, having exorcised some demons,
physical and emotional, along the way.

The best of the sensational writers have an exciting way of
bringing to the surface issues that much Victorian writing and

thinking – and feeling – represses: but the overall domain of their work remains politically conservative, however personally liberating some of its excitements might seem to be. As a whole it recognises threats to order, including ones based on gender, sexuality, race and class, but it will find in sound moral responses, varying amounts of thoughtful detection, and a great deal of well-organised and some-times vertiginous plotting a set of consoling values – calm, watchful masculinity, for the most part, but also female fidelity. These will be supported by other more exotic powers, like Ezra Jennings's wayward genius or even, at a stretch, clairvoyance and coincidence, in order to recreate an order very much like the stasis which was disturbed at the start of the story.

That inherent stasis underlying the sensational form – and indeed the patterns of crime fiction as a whole – may explain why Charles Dickens, who seems to have circled around crime fiction a great deal and for all of his career, never wrote a text that could fairly be allotted to the genre: he always sought movement, reform, not stasis restored. Elements of crime fiction recur, however. He used Bow Street Runners in *Oliver Twist* (1838) but the ending is like *The Newgate Calendar* brought to new and dramatic life. *Barnaby Rudge* (1841) starts with a *Calendar*-style murder but, as Peterson comments (1984: 82), Dickens loses interest in this in favour of his historical theme of the Gordon riots. In *Martin Chuzzlewit* (1844) Nadgett is a Ferret-like street-level inquirer who plays a significant role in bringing Jonas Chuzzlewit to a kind of justice. After the *Household Words* articles praising the new detective police, in *Bleak House* (1853) Dickens made a major figure of Inspector Bucket, the powerful, enigmatic, all-seeing investigator – supported strongly by his wife, and using information from several other quasi-detectives in the novel. It is he who identifies, in mystery mode, the real crim-inal as Madame Hortense, not the long-suspected Lady Deadlock, but the power of detection is restricted to mechanics and, as D. A. Miller notes, all the amateur detectives in the story fail (1988: 70–1). The novel's mysteries are greater than mere puzzles and even Bucket's detection is not as important as, nor key to, the exposition of social crimes that permeate this massive account of nationally perceived threats and values. There is a police inspector in *Our Mutual Friend* (1865), but he is a minor character; the criminal emphasis is on the psychic self-revelations made by the sensation-ally named Bradley Headstone. This pattern continues in Dickens's last work, the unfinished *The Mystery of Edwin Drood* (1870). Here he is clearly in some way following Collins in a story focused on crime and sensation, and there appears to be a disguised figure who is potentially a detective, but the fact that the final scene was evidently to combine physical and psychic action involving the villainous Jasper and the allegedly dead Drood was probably going to return (like George Talboys) indicates that this would have been an emotional melodrama, like so many of the plays Dickens and Collins enjoyed, and not as close to the crime-focused, detective-resolved form as *The Moonstone* had come.

But even without Dickens's real support, the position of crime fiction by the end of the 1860s was a strong one. The police detectives had continued – there were reprints right through the decade; the sensational had become a standard form for fiction writers. But though detectives operated in both, none of them had created the special power of Poe or acted as a model for what was later to happen. For all the excitement of 1860s English crime writing, the nursery of the future was not there, but across the Channel: the hero detective was already alive in Paris.

III GABORIAU AND THE 1870s–1880s

Émile Gaboriau gained his literary experience in working as secretary to Paul Féval who, like Alexandre Dumas the elder, Ponson du Terail and Fortune du Boisgobey, continued the French passion (found in its most melodramatic form earlier in Eugène Sue and its most condensed and powerful version in Balzac) for long, interwoven, sometimes rambling narratives about crime, deception and the melodramatic sensualities of mid-century Paris. These stories usually appeared as newspaper serials – the famous *feuilletons* – and would then usually be published in book form. When he started to write his own novels, in a short but intense period from 1865 to 1873 (when he died), Gaboriau showed that he had also looked carefully at Poe, as Schutt discusses (1998). Some of his stories, like *La Corde au Cou* (1873, translated as *In Peril of His Life*, 1881) and *L'Argent des Autres* (1871, translated as *Other People's Money*, 1874) are basically sensational crime adventures with a little police work, but the best-known and most influential of them develop at novel length Poe's idea of careful, rational detection, both empirical and inspired. *L'Affaire Lerouge* (1866), often translated as 'The Widow Lerouge' but also known as 'The Lerouge Case' (and once, in America, as

'Crimson Crime') starts with the ugly murder of an old woman in a provincial town not far from Paris. Gévrol, a Parisian police inspector, distributes both searches and suspicion (just like Seegrave in the slightly later *The Moonstone*), but then an elderly amateur of crime, Tabaret, inspects the scene and famously declares from crucial clues just what the killer looked like, what he smoked, how he was dressed: the techniques of Dupin, later to be those of Holmes, fall crisply onto the page.

Tabaret, who earns the nickname 'Tir-au-clair' – 'Bring-into-the light' – from his capacity to penetrate mysteries, is a plump retired pawnbroker's clerk, who loved to read about crime and suddenly realised his *métier* was to be a detective. But for all his clarity of mind, the story is far from simple. His first conclusion about the murderer is quite wrong, and only at the end, in a dramatic sequence of action and revelation, is the villain revealed. It is not the long-suspected Viscount (who has been thought to be in reality the son of the murdered widow), but in fact Tabaret's fellow-lodger, the lawyer Noel Gerdy, who in his turn has been wrongly thought – and has posed as – the heir of the Comte de Commarin. To moderate further Tabaret's detective genius, it is, by a late irony, the plodding methods of the unimaginative Gévrol that eventually discover the widow's long-disappeared husband. He reveals the remarkable facts about the birth of the two young men, and so the motive for the murder.

While Poe seems to have inspired Tabaret, Gaboriau appears to be not fully convinced. The imaginative method starts well, but does not deliver much in the end, and Tabaret switches to a more mechanical and productive method with an alibi at the theatre to break, train times to be checked. As well as this complicated representation and critique of detection, Gaboriau offers the reader the voyeuristic pleasures and corrupt delights of Parisian society and aristocratic love-life. There is also an intense sub-plot, focusing on the *juge d'instruction*, the official in charge of the case, and his own failed love for the Vicomtesse. This type of complicity is a powerful element of later crime fiction, especially the American private-eye tradition, but is not seen much in the early period even though detectives like Vidocq and Richmond have been on the wrong side of the law: it is, though – another sign of Poe's prescience – clearly foreshadowed in the resemblance between Dupin and D. in 'The Purloined Letter'. There may be other symbolic depths to Gaboriau's story: Martin Priestman (1990: 57) has analysed it in terms of a

Freudian conflict between fathers and sons – including Tabaret as a
proxy father for the ultimately criminal lawyer – suggesting again
that detectives can be drawn into the evaluative quagmires of the
mystery. Complex, wordy, at times rambling, but always returning
to the mysterious and dreadful death, *L'Affaire Lerouge* is a much
overlooked major work, plainly recognisable as a novel of crime and
detection and providing a structural plan for so much that was to
follow.

But Gaboriau had more to offer: his most influential detective
does not operate in *L'Affaire Lerouge*. There is a policeman called
Lecoq in the opening scene, but he is just a spear-carrier. Gaboriau
recreated him as a man of good birth fallen on hard times, socially
like Waters but showing much more flair. He first appears in this
form in *Le Crime d'Orcival* (1867) and *Le Dossier no. 113* (1867), but it
is the two-volume *Monsieur Lecoq* (1868) which made his name. In
the first volume, 'L'Enquête' ('The Inquiry'), a ghastly crime has
occurred in a seedy bar in the Paris outskirts. Gévrol is there again,
getting most things wrong, and now a new-style, young and eager
Lecoq scrutinises the scene. He makes brilliant deductions from
stains, scraps of clothing and above all footprints, then rushes
around Paris in quest of the men and women he has traced at
the scene.

An arrest is made: but the prisoner will not speak. Lecoq keeps
him under just the kind of surveillance that Foucault saw as central
to disciplinary power in a prison – at one stage Lecoq lies in the attic
above his cell for days, watching for a revealing move; but none
comes. Finally the prisoner escapes, and vanishes over the wall of a
noble house. This clearly suggests he has grand connections, but
there the first volume ends, and that is all that was printed by
Hodder and Stoughton in the 1920 English translation under the
title *Monsieur Lecoq* – the 1881 and 1885 translations used, like the
French, two volumes with part titles 'L'Enquête' and 'L'Honneur du
Nom'. Many of Hodder's 1920 customers must have been puzzled
why Lecoq had became so famous for his brilliant conclusions, faced
with this indecisive ending. Had they bought Volume 2, separately
published as *The Honour of the Name* (1920), they would have been
able to trace the whole long story of treason and violence back to just
after 1815, when many political scores were settled and a chain of
events begun which – with multiple excitements, complications,
changes of identity and crucially revealing letters – led to the Duc de
Sairmeuse's presence in the fatal bar, to his arrest, and his obsessive

silence to preserve the honour of his name. This is all told in a lavish historical-novel style, and only at the end does Lecoq reappear to identify the real criminal and, understandingly, absolve the duke.

A roller-coaster of French class politics and sordid activity, the novel has its oddities – Lecoq's absence from Volume 2 seems to weaken his authority, and there is plenty of coincidence, confession and improbable discovery, not to mention the many over-convenient letters. But in its somewhat indigestible way it creates with great confidence the crime fiction pattern of murder, mystery, investigation, confusion and explanatory resolution. Though there is, compared with later stories, a substantial imbalance in favour of the past over the present, there is finally, as in *L'Affaire Lerouge*, a central focus on a mysterious and fatal event, suggesting that the explanation of what has happened, whether by persistent rational detection or by elaborate narratorial explanation, is a sufficient rationale for the elaborate structural core of a substantial novel.

Gaboriau, like the equally influential Dashiell Hammett, never really repeated himself. The major novels had great international impact and his pattern of closely involved detection among clues, mysterious twists, and with a final amazing revelation, became a powerful model for the emerging book-length crime-focused story. His novels were quickly translated in America, and clearly influenced Anna Katherine Green, to be discussed shortly. But Gaboriau novels, in the French, were reviewed on appearance in England and, as R. F. Stewart shows (1980: Chapter 12), 'the Gaboriau novel' became a brand-name for an increasingly identifiable genre. *The Moonstone* itself, and by extension *Edwin Drood*, for all their reticence about a hero-detective, their greater sophistication of narrative method and deeper symbolic and socially critical power, appear to draw on Gaboriau's tradition of astonishing dénouement and the involvement of a respected central figure in the crime. E. F. Bleiler sums up Gaboriau: 'He wrote the first novels in which the nature of the crime, the introduction and role of the detective, the extenders, the misdirections, the reader participation, and the solution are all carried through in their modern manner' (in Reilly, 1980: 1540).

The influence went further. From 1881 the London publisher Vizetelly issued a series of translations of Gaboriau's novels at one shilling a volume, and the young Fergus Hume, a New Zealand-born lawyer living in Melbourne and looking for something lucrative to write, was advised by a bookseller that Gaboriau was just the thing: he produced *The Mystery of a Hansom Cab*, set and first published in 1886 in Melbourne. (The title suggests Hume also knew one of the Fortune du Boisgobey novels that Vizetelly also published in English, *The Mystery of an Omnibus*.) A not particularly mysterious mystery, though it has a final twist written when Hume realised his first ending was too obvious (see Knight, 1986), it uses a strong-willed and somewhat unpleasant detective, Kilsip, sharing the detection with a smooth Melbourne lawyer. The 1887 London reprint became the first best-selling crime fiction mystery novel in English, with sales rapidly rising to something like half a million copies; though Anna Katherine Green's *The Leavenworth Case* sold very well, it was over a longer period: Hume, via Gaboriau, made the crime novel a major force in the market.

It is important to re-establish Gaboriau in the chain of influence and development of nineteenth-century crime fiction, but overlooking his work has not been the only gap in discussions of the tradition. The 1870s and 1880s have, when noticed at all, been seen as barren years – Ousby calls them 'something of an interregnum' (1976: 136) while Howard Haycraft sees them only as 'In Between Years', killing time between Collins and Doyle (1942: Chapter 2, title). In fact, as Drexler has argued (1998), a substantial number of crime novels and short stories were produced in this period. The magazines kept republishing material from the past, and in the collection of nineteenth-century crime novels assembled by Graham Greene and Dorothy Glover, described in a bibliography edited by Eric Osborne (1966), some 70 titles come from these years – and Greene and Glover were the first to say that this was a far from exhaustive collection. While it is not always easy to assign a story to a category, some revealing patterns can still be observed. Only five of the Greene–Glover novels use professionals as the investigators, mostly lawyers but one doctor, a pattern that looks back to the disciplinary amateurs of the 1830s and after. Nine of the stories involve private detectives but, very revealingly, eight of those originated and were set in America in the tradition of Brampton and Pinkerton. Amateurs – a surprise for many commentators who think Holmes was the first – dominate 13 of the novels: all but four of them are gentlemen. Another surprise is that 11 of the texts locate the authority of detection in a police officer, though now they are mostly senior figures, not street-level police like Waters and Sergeant Bolter. So detection is both common, and widely spread across the types, with a notable lack in England of professional private eyes – in fact Sherlock Holmes's professional and private status may well be the most innovative single feature of Conan Doyle's stories.

Few of these texts are now well known. Some show established sensation writers moving towards detection – Sheridan Le Fanu's *Checkmate* (1871) uses a foolish policeman and a clever lawyer in a fairly lacklustre way, compared with the genuinely alarming detective-free *frisson* of his earlier masterpieces like *Uncle Silas* (1864) and *Wylder's Hand* (1869). Mary Braddon kept turning out fluent mysteries and is still faithful to her amateur disciplinary detectives like Robert Audley, but usually uses a police detective as well. New writers like Fergus Hume and the Australian Basil Farjeon come into the genre, relying on clever and usually senior police detectives. But the most striking and influential developments are, as is not uncommon in the crime fiction genre, outside England.

Anna Katharine Green's *The Leavenworth Case* (1878) focuses on a murder, interweaves romance, manipulates the reader's expectations, and manages a surprise ending just like Gaboriau, but does it without so much detached exploration of the characters' past: there is a secret, but it is close in time, and known to dangerously many people present in the story. If she handles her own influences with confidence, Green shapes much for the future: a locked-room fake-suicide murder of a millionaire, with movements to be plotted, letters to be rescued, and the use of the post, the telegraph, an assistant overseas. Many of the later 'whodunit' techniques are first found in a coherent sequence in Green. She uses an official detective of a less than heroic sort: Ebenezer Gryce on first appearance is noted as 'a portly, comfortable, personage' ([1878] 1981: 5) – more like Tabaret than Lecoq, as Patricia Maida comments (1989: 7). Later he is incapacitated with rheumatism – or perhaps pretends to be, to stimulate the intervention of the young New York lawyer, and would-be lover of a Leavenworth girl, Everett Raymond, who tells the story and conducts a good deal of the investigation through the middle of the novel. But Gryce returns at the end and stages a classic and very early version of the final confrontation scene, which leads to the confession of a murderer who is very well concealed, if also perhaps a little improbable.

The romance detail, the narrator's breathless anxiety and the vapourish behaviour of the two Leavenworth beauties does not please everybody: Michele Slung, though speaking up for Green's pioneer status, felt that her novels are 'tainted and slowed down by pathos and sentimentality' (in Reilly, 1980: 696). But read in the context of the sensational novels, Green adds a major amount of detective work and makes it central to the value system of the novel; she also avoids the improbable events that Collins, 'Felix' and

'Regester' had relied on in their approaches to the novel of detection. There seems in fact to be little between Green's highly proper but also passionate New York world and the strains, in behaviour and in fiction, of the classic 'golden age' writers. In *The Leavenworth Case* and the many novels that followed it (which would include an older lone woman detective, Amelia Butterworth, and by 1915 a bright young woman, Violet Strange), Green effectively shaped a model that 40 years later Agatha Christie and others would use and in some ways refine: Green overdoes confession and the long informative speech, and the real detecting by Gryce tends to be off-stage, but the later writers would not inherently or structurally vary the pattern Green established.

Her first novel was very successful in America, but was not published in London until 1884, a sign that the English, then as now, regarded crime fiction as their own invention. But this was boom time in North American criminography. Equally successful and just as predictive of what was to come was the flood of dime novels in the period. As Gary Hoppenstand has shown (1982), a series like 'The New York Detective Library' – with a new novella for a dime every week – produced 801 titles between 1882 and 1899, and there were several other series of similar size. They starred an enormous range of heroes, from 'Old King Brady' who was 'a rugged and durable American' (Hoppenstand, 1982: 5) to the well-known star of popular theatre around the world, 'Hawkshaw, the Yankee detective'. The stories tended to be routine sub-Vidocq, or sub-Brampton, escapades relying on fist and gun rather than detective intelligence, but much more measured and intricate versions of detecting were also popular in America. Allan Pinkerton, son of a Glasgow police sergeant, both led and wrote about the activities of a public agency. As Lavine (1967) records, Pinkerton wrote 18 accounts of his crimes, more or less based on real experience, starting with *The Expressman and the Detective* (1874). In the highly coloured *The Gypsies and the Detective* (1879), a crime is reported – a gypsy girl has tricked a man out of a large amount of gold. Pinkerton, as 'Chief of the US Secret Service', is informed, and sends a selected operative. He is no tough guy: the 'young Englishman named Blake' (1879: 71) is handsome, gentlemanly and skilled, speaking several languages, including Romany, and able to pose as a newspaper reporter. After an enquiry at novel length, and with Pinkerton's intervention, the case is successfully resolved. The novels are somewhat stilted compared with the exploits of Jem Brampton and the dime-novel detectives, and, again unlike both, they represent threats coming mostly from out-side respectable American society. Their greatest significance is as an index of just how strong was the growing audience for reasonably realistic crime fiction at novel length.

Far from an interregnum, the 1870s and 1880s were a period of rapid expansion in both the numbers and the kinds of crime fiction published, as ongoing traditions – including the Waters approach and the sensationalists – operated side by side with the strengthen-ing of intellectual police work and a growth in the presence of ama-teur detectives, especially of the higher social classes. Not everybody admired what Stewart (1980) has shown is the new con-scious identification of the detective story as a genre. Robert Louis Stevenson and his son-in-law Lloyd Osbourne, in the Epilogue to *The Wrecker* (1892), spoke slightingly of a genre where 'the mind of the reader, always bent to pick up clues, receives no impression of reality or life, but rather of an airless, elaborate mechanics' (1892: 426). It was a complaint that would recur in the mouths of Dorothy Sayers and Anthony Berkeley Cox, as will be discussed in Part II, but neither publishers nor most popular writers shared their concern. It was certainly not a worry for Stevenson's acquaintance and fellow-Scot, Arthur Conan Doyle, who, after a modest beginning as a published writer, turned his mind early in 1886 to writing something in the new and expansive genre of crime fiction.

IV DETECTIVE APOTHEOSIS: SHERLOCK HOLMES

Intriguing and memorable as some of the nineteenth-century detec-tives were, there is only one great detective. Ousby went so far as to say Sherlock Holmes is 'the most famous character in English litera-ture' (1976: 3). That might be disputed by Hamlet, Jane Eyre and Frankenstein's monster, but Doyle's creation is unquestionably an apotheosis, a conveying of quasi-divine status on the figure that had slowly emerged through the nineteenth century: a detective who is highly intelligent, essentially moral, somewhat elitist, all-knowing, disciplinary in knowledge and skills, energetic, eccentric, yet also in touch with the ordinary people who populate the stories. These people fall consistently into error and danger and represent the anx-ieties of the readers who flocked to buy, enjoy and believe in the fables of protection created by Arthur Conan Doyle. Holmes com-bines features of many detectives – the aloof stance of a Dupin, the acuteness and when necessary the courage of Lecoq, the scientism of Ezra Jennings, the urban setting and ironic understanding of Gryce and Kilsip, the languidity of Robert Audley with a new trace of *fin de siècle* bohemianism in his interest in music, his taste for huge quantities of pipe tobacco and, in the early days at least, injections of cocaine solution.

Doyle was trained as a doctor, but being a Scot and a Catholic he was essentially outside the English middle class that he wrote about and whose values he so comprehensively shored up through Holmes, and in other writing, such as the 'Professor Challenger' stories and the patriotic history of the Boer War, for which he was knighted. Creativity was in the family: his uncle and father were illustrators – the father with little success, partly caused by his mental derangement, a family tragedy of which there seems no overt trace in Doyle's writing. His uncle Dickie Doyle worked for *Punch*, and with that awareness of the literary world and the model of Sir Walter Scott before him, the young Doyle aimed for a career in writing, as well as medicine. He had already published energetic stories of adventure when, according to his memoirs, he decided to try a type of detective story that would be less subject to coincidence and where the detective's methodology would be 'something nearer to an exact science' (1924: 75).

He was aware of predecessors – he mentions Gaboriau's 'dove-tailing of his plots' and Poe's 'masterful detective, M. Dupin' and shows a wider knowledge of the genre when he refers to clumsy inquirers as 'Mr Sharps and Mr Ferrets' (1924: 74, 75). In Doyle's claim to innovation and credibility, science was to be important: Watson first meets Holmes beating a corpse to ascertain the details of bruising, and there is a strong scientific aura, with test tubes and other equipment, monographs on ash and newsprint. But if the romance of science is part of Holmes's modern methods, he also practises in other disciplinary modes – he keeps very good records of criminals and is expert in the use of reference works: a teachers' directory gives him the key clue in *The Hound of the Baskervilles*.

Like Dupin, Holmes can engage in arias of interpretation and mind-reading – many of the stories begin with this interpretative magic as Holmes decodes a hat, a watch, a stick, even just the appearance or clothing of a visitor. These sequences create a famous brand-image, but it is striking that, as with Dupin, they never in fact reveal the mystery of the story: they are only detective flourishes, used for characterisation and aura alone. Holmes's actual methods of discovery are a good deal more banal – and so with some relief the reader can actually understand the crucial manoeuvre in the exposing of the criminal and imaginatively participate in it. In 'Silver Blaze' what he calls, in his often-quoted enigmatic statement, 'the curious incident of the dog in the night-time' is a matter of plain common sense: the dog did not bark because it knew the murderer. He amazes the police, in the first story of all, *A Study in Scarlet* (1887), with an apparently obscure deduction about the villain's height based simply on knowing that you write on a wall at your own eye height.

Inside the scientific mumbo-jumbo, the learned baggage, the mystique of all-night pipe-smoking and austerely distant behaviour is someone who can apply the common knowledge of the human tribe. It is both exciting and consoling to have a hero so grand who is also so familiar, like a Beowulf whose princely courage and sense of duty matches that of the humblest soldier, a Lancelot whose chivalric grandeur is riven by the banal division between passion and duty. The essential power of Sherlock Holmes is that his substantial disciplinary authority is in fact enacted in a publicly accessible way: the ultimate methods of solving a crime are usually as simple as any used by the mid-century detective foot-soldiers.

Doyle effectively established this powerful mix of the subtle and the simple by grafting the image of Dupin, along with his naive narrator, onto the active urban dedication of Gaboriau. Stewart has described the strong resemblances between *L'Affaire Lerouge* and *A Study in Scarlet*, from the title and generalisations about crime through to specific details like reading footprints and cart-tracks while lying flat on the ground (1980: Chapter 13). Doyle, with an engaging mock-naivety, has Holmes in the first story say 'Lecoq was a miserable bungler' and 'Dupin was a very inferior fellow' ([1887], 1929: 18); he does, in a sort of reparation, give Holmes a French grandmother, sister to an artist (mentioned in 'The Greek Interpreter'). But if the approach is basically French, from Dupin and Gaboriau, the transatlantic plot draws on Doyle's own early writing on the model of the American master of moralised adventure stories, Brett Harte, though there is also a model closer to home. In *A Study in Scarlet*, the violent historical origin of the crime among the Mormons, though told historically in Gaboriau-style, draws directly on the work of Robert Louis Stevenson in *The Dynamiter* (1885, written with the help of his wife Fanny), which also provides the idea of young men about town deciding for excitement to become private detectives – though the Stevensons were decidedly ironic about the idea.

In part because it was, again like sections of *The Dynamiter*, at the awkward novella length, and no doubt also because he had little reputation yet, Doyle found *A Study in Scarlet* difficult to sell in 1886 and eventually settled for £20 and later publication, in Ward Lock's undistinguished *Beeton's Christmas Annual* for 1887. But somebody noticed: perhaps because of the American context, an editor from Lippincott's commissioned another novella, and this became *The Sign of Four* (1890: published in the US as *The Sign of the Four*, which is the phrase used in the text). Doyle remained a borrower: here he drew on Wilkie Collins for his story, making it another tale of the aftermath of an English theft of an Indian treasure. The story is in some ways more exotic than *The Moonstone* – it includes a militant pygmy rather than admired Brahmins, and a returned colonial official more languid than the European traveller Franklin Blake at his worst – but also more simple: the climax is a boat chase, with a western-style gun-battle, down the Thames, and Doyle offers little of Collins's implied criticism of English attitudes to race, class and conventional morality.

It is structurally more successful than *A Study in Scarlet* – the historical material is, with Collins's guidance, integrated better and there is much more action and mystery, though neither novella makes much of a puzzle of the culprits – Doyle is still working primarily in an adventure mode and the criminal-revealing denouement, already present in Gaboriau and Collins, is not yet part of his armoury. But *The Sign of Four* is an exciting, confident piece of writing, and it attracted the attention of another transatlantic godfather of Sherlock Holmes: George Newnes, the Canadian owner of the new magazine *The Strand*, commissioned Doyle for six short stories.

The form seemed to suit his work very well. They were not that short – 12,000 words is the norm, so there is plenty of plot: Doyle said in his *Memoirs*, justifiably, that each story contained enough for a novel (1924: 97). There is also no need for a sub-plot (never one of Doyle's strengths, unlike Collins), but there is room for bold characterisation of detective and narrator. Perhaps most important of all, the tradition that the short story ends with a twist meant that Doyle started to use the 'revelation' ending – though not, it is interesting to note, in the very first story, 'A Scandal in Bohemia', where the twist is Irene Adler's cheeky treatment of the detective who thinks he has just defeated her (she is very like one of Stevenson's enchanting women of mystery, and Florizel, in his *The Suicide Club*, is also a Prince of Bohemia). But from the second story, 'A Case of Identity', onwards some form of plot revelation is usually used to give the stories a strong and surprising finish.

Newnes must have been delighted with the stories he received, and the public certainly were. Doyle tried to back out by raising his price – he still wanted to be Sir Walter Scott, and his historical novels, like *Micah Clarke* (1889) and *The White Company* (1891) are richly detailed, though somewhat two-dimensional. But Newnes's money brought more stories, some of them Doyle's finest work, like 'The Speckled Band' and 'The Man with the Twisted Lip'. The first dozen stories were published as *The Adventures of Sherlock Holmes* (1892), and they are a powerful set, with some surprises. There are no murders: even crime itself is rare and obscure – possible blackmail in 'A Scandal in Bohemia', impersonation of a daughter's imaginary fiancé in 'A Case of Identity', self-concealment as a beggar in 'The Man with the Twisted Lip'. These are not so much about the threat of crime as the disturbing disruptions of respectable lives by human error, sometimes seeming like crime – as when the father in 'The Beryl Coronet' thinks his son has stolen and broken the treasure, when he is in fact trying to retrieve and repair the villainy of his sister's alleged lover. The stories as a whole trace the possible torments of respectable life through its dangerous desires – for love, for money, above all for respectability. Even the high social level of 'A Scandal in Bohemia' deals, in Irene Adler's case, with those concerns as she is leaving the high life of royal mistress to become a respectable professional wife – the apparent villain becomes the heroine of the story.

As noticeable as the unexotic, and therefore all the more telling, nature of the crimes is the absence of the notorious Professor Moriarty. The master criminal, the sort of device used in *The Woman in White* and *East Lynne* to bring simplicity to the plotting and sympathy to everybody else, was resorted to by Doyle finally as he put an end to the second series of stories, published as *The Memoirs of Sherlock Holmes* (1894) and wrung out of him by Newnes's increasing payments. With the tellingly named 'The Final Problem' he felt he escaped the albatross Holmes had become by killing him as he himself killed Professor Moriarty. In his memoirs Doyle offers the excuse that he was 'weary of inventing plots', but a little later he more openly admits that he felt the stories were on 'a lower strata of literary achievement' (1924: 98 and 99). The *Memoirs* stories are still well done – Doyle was always a fine tale-teller, and an expert at quickly sketched characterisation – but the Moriarty-focused stories he went on to tell when Holmes was brought back to life lack the socially anxious involvement and the moral explorations of the best early work. Even before the final simplification of Moriarty, the second series of stories become more like mechanical expositions of Holmes's mastery, though there are still some highly effective ones like 'The Cardboard Box', notable partly because Holmes appears in the *Strand* illustration sporting a natty striped jacket and straw boater, but also because it was judged too grisly – the box contains a severed ear – to be reprinted in the volume and only turned up years later in *The Case-Book of Sherlock Holmes* (1927). 'The Yellow Face' is a fine story in which Holmes is completely mistaken because he underestimates the moral power of the American characters. But in general, Doyle's imagination grew more strained and his effects less subtle towards the end of the stories that become the *Memoirs*, so it was perhaps no very great fictional loss when Doyle decided he must resist the money by killing Holmes off at the end of the second series in 1893.

But in the world of publishing and substantial royalty payments, nothing is forever, and in 1901 Newnes tempted Doyle to write a Holmes novella, to be serialised in *The Strand*. Doyle did not exactly revive his hero – he set the narrative back in time, when Watson and Holmes still shared their friendly, homosocial life together in Baker Street. *The Hound of the Baskervilles* (1902) has all the qualities of Doyle's best work: a vivid characterising opening, with Holmes deducing from a walking stick and identifying at a glance both the type-face of a newspaper and the date of a manuscript, as well as some urban enigmas like the boot missing in a hotel and the falsely bearded man who shadows Sir Henry Baskerville from a hansom cab. These details will all be tracked down by Holmes in his various detective modes, including the use of a boy for assistance, isolated inquiry in difficult circumstances, and final brave action. That would make the shape of a short story. But this is a novella and, as in some of the early stories, the scene moves to the country, to Dartmoor apparently haunted by a spectral dog. Here the story develops, and a sub-plot is necessary for length and complexity, involving an escaped convict. Holmes is apparently absent from the moor – both a resemblance to Gaboriau's detective-less middle sequences, and perhaps a residual effect of Doyle's distaste for his hero, but Watson keeps notes to inform Holmes, and eventually the master reappears.

As in Doyle's own career, Holmes was not easily disposed of: he has been secretly present on the moor, the brooding, even Byronic, figure Watson and Sir Henry glimpse at night. This melodramatic scene, as well as the moor, the title, the whole story of the spectral Hound, all bring back into detective fiction in full power that element of the Gothic which was so strong in the early years of crime fiction – overshadowing detection in Bulwer and most of the sensationalists – but much reduced in the mid-century police fiction and the world-wide detective development. The outcome of the novella will, however, be to rationalise and disempower the Gothic. The old ghostly story is not true now, if it ever was: the modern hound is just a big dog daubed with phosphorus; the real threat is not in fact the supernatural but the dark desires of apparently respectable people. Stapleton wants to gain the title and money of the Baskervilles to whom he is related. It may be that here, as in Collins and sometimes Gaboriau, the narrative and imagery are potent enough to touch deeper themes – the bog, the ancient huts seem to represent the atavistic abyss into which modern, respectable people can fall, as Stapleton finally, literally, does; Holmes as the master of this world seems also like the superego mastering the ancient morass of the human id. At the same time the story realises some of the id-like prejudices of the English: Stapleton, like the doctor in 'The Speckled Band' and many other villains of the imperial period, has come back from overseas somehow tainted with foreignness, unlike Sir Henry who has the bracing strength of white North America to add to his sterling English blood – Doyle often reworks imperial themes, as Hennessy and Mohan have shown in the case of 'The Speckled Band' (1989). Throughout *The Hound of the Baskervilles* women are treated as chattels, like Mrs Stapleton, or nuisances, as the voluptuous and much gazed-at Laura Lyons or the trying, embarrassing butler's wife. The treatment of gender is consistent with that outlined for the Holmes short stories in general by Catherine Belsey (1980: 107–16).

If the text speaks its ideology both in an aggressive racist and gendered voice and also in anxious terms about what apparently respectable men can do, it also indicates its own interests, and the special concerns of crime fiction as a whole, in the way it handles the escaped convict. Out on the moor, parallel to Holmes in isolation, and eventually mauled to death in mistake for Sir Henry, is Selden, the Notting Hill murderer. A real criminal, representing not elaborate games to frighten relatives to death, but the kind of

street violence that genuinely did concern the police throughout nineteenth- and indeed twentieth-century London. Crime is a
formation of the modern cities, with their alienation and mystery,
but the fiction does not represent the most real and most common
villainies of the new conurbations. In the early nineteenth century
the major concern was young criminals (Dickens dealt with it in
Oliver Twist) and in the later part of the century the statistical threat,
and public concern, was baby-farming – overfilled and undersuper-
vised crèches, where children often died (who ever wrote about
that?), and violent mugging, the world from which Selden comes,
but a world with which the story has no concern at all. He is the
focus of the complicating sub-plot, simply dispensed with when
the text-extending work is over: he does not challenge the aberrant
bourgeois Stapleton as a threat.

The new Holmes story lifted the circulation of *The Strand* substantially, and Newnes offered Doyle more than he could resist, with a
knighthood and a new wife to support: for £100 per thousand words
he immediately resurrected Holmes in the stories that became *The
Return of Sherlock Holmes* (1905). They are still witty, dense with detail,
and full of interesting ideas, but lack the street-level anxiety of the
first stories. They often reuse the master criminal as an enemy and,
as Ousby has noted, they tend to take on 'a grossly macabre tone'
(1976: 171); on this development see also Knight (1981). These
excesses show how Doyle was squeezing his imagination, and none
of the future stories, nor the last novella, *The Valley of Fear* (1914),
which returns in rather mechanical mode to American material, were
to match the impact of the work that made Holmes, as entertainment,
object of admiration, and fantasy protection, a household name.

Sherlock Holmes and the crimes he encounters are fictions: but
the imaginative and ideological forces realised in the stories are real;
in that respect Holmes is an archetype of the whole century's crime
fiction. It is through the techniques of fiction and writing that this
massive body of literature has been assembled to speculate about
social disorder, threats to property and body, and to imagine
responses to them. Detectives were a realistic enough need, though
in factual terms they only slowly came into being and then initially
in small numbers: fiction created them more liberally and, as in the
case of women detectives and scientific analysis, sometimes far
ahead of the reality. But, as Foucault indicates, the key move was to
understand and imagine the disciplinary nature of the modern
world, in law and education, railway trains and prison buildings.

The authors created models of such discipline in various ways, ranging from limited plodding police who were only just separated from the sovereign model of their servile helmet-wearing colleagues, through the restricted activities of the lawyers and clerks who observed the law in its mysterious operation, to the highly intelligent analyst who, remarkably anticipated by Poe with Dupin, offers various forms of intellectual activity as a shield against criminal disruption – yet, as is so clear with Lecoq and Holmes, also keeps in touch with the simple reality of common sense and the audience's actual capacities.

But the other move of disciplinary society was to be interested in the criminal as a person capable of reform, not just a physical instrument of crime who must be ineffaceably branded as aberrant. The concern with the criminal's feelings, and the possible criminality of the readers, is also an element that recurs among the earliest texts – notably in Godwin and Brown – but also in the less restrained stories in the periodicals, like Reynolds's *Mysteries of London* and many other penny dreadfuls, and it is this interest in the human and emotive reality of criminality that surfaces in the sensationalists, as everything is made available to the senses of the characters and readers. That was what Stevenson saw as the real path for a writer; even when he was writing lightly – or perhaps euphemistically – as in *The Dynamiter*, there was always an edge of sentient identification with the criminals. His friend and compatriot Arthur Conan Doyle, though, was quite happy with the clues, conventions and limited characterisation of crime fiction. Yet through locating his early mysteries in the ordinary lives of baffled people – the quivering daughters, the outraged fathers, the down-at-heel despairing clerks who populate his *Adventures* stories – he, like Poe before him, brought sensations about crime into contact with a detective who was both an elite genius and a thoroughly humanised person, Watson's fellow-lodger. At the end of *The Hound of the Baskervilles* the two oddly assorted friends go off to enjoy a concert, to stimulate their senses in a legitimate, respectable way: the ultimate detective, who brings together so many of the strands that had developed throughout over a century of crime fiction, and the average man, the doctor, who also represents the discipline of writing.

Part II
Death

Part II
Death

3
After Sherlock Holmes

I ENTER DEATH

Doyle established on a world-wide basis the figure of the detective as central to crime fiction. However many successful detectives there had been before Sherlock Holmes, their successes were subsumed into and superseded by that archetypal presentation of the somewhat aloof, infinitely clever, quite active, but always reliable hero who helped a baffled and threatened populace symbolised by Dr Watson.

But if Holmes in that way represented the full development of the detective, Doyle's work by no means established that other major stage in crime fiction, the insistence on death as the major crime. The two first novellas, *A Study in Scarlet* (1887) and *The Sign of Four* (1890), did involve gruesome murders, but many of the short stories focused on crimes against property or frauds of some kind. As Doyle wrote on, and squeezed his imagination for material, the stories became at times more blood-curdling, but his third novella, *The Hound of the Baskervilles* (1902), did not include a murder – a malice-induced heart attack and a mistaken dog-mauling were as far as the villainy actually went. Other short stories of the period also usually deal with theft and fraud, but it is noticeable that the novels of the later nineteenth century, from *Lady Audley's Secret* (1862) on, often deal with murder. It may be that the novel's extended plot needed a more serious crime than jewel theft, and mysterious murder could allow the involvement of more characters and so fill more space.

Other factors privileged death in crime fiction. Late nineteenth-century literature shows an increased interest in the grisly and the sensational, in authors like Robert Louis Stevenson, Bram Stoker, even Herman Melville, and it seems that the mid-century obsession with property as the core of respectable life had shifted towards a central importance of the identity of the self, and threats towards it. Reading a novel is a different function from reading a magazine.

The magazine is inherently a communal form, implying social and cultural interaction; the novel creates an experience more likely to be individualist and identity-conscious – identity-anxious. It is also notable that the novel, at the turn of the nineteenth century as before, was a genre substantially read by women – and soon to be substantially written by them too, especially in crime fiction. There appears to be some gender factor in the shift from bloodless and money-linked crime to murder as the main focus, in the sense that the focus on property which came over crime fiction in the mid-nineteenth century is not only a bourgeois concern but also a male obsession. The causes are no doubt multiple, but it is in the period between the rise of Sherlock Holmes and the early 1920s that death becomes the central theme of crime fiction; in general that development is clear in novels, and slower to emerge in short stories, though they show a tendency to be more fatally concerned as the period passes.

II   SCIENTIFIC DETECTIVES

Though in the early twentieth century the novel was gaining ground as a form for crime fiction, much of the immediate impact of and response to Sherlock Holmes was still found in short stories. One approach was to take him seriously as a rational superman and to generate even more intensified versions of his skills in intensely scientific detectives, discussed by Kayman (2003). The most extreme example was Professor S. F. X. Van Dusen, invented by Jacques Futrelle, and known as 'The Thinking Machine', whose triumphs appeared in book form in *The Thinking Machine* (1907) and *The Thinking Machine on the Case* (1908). The stories are varied in both length and method but typically depend on the professor penetrating the mystery of some technically complicated crime, such as murder via a gas pipe in 'The Scarlet Thread'. The best-known 'Thinking Machine' triumph was 'The Problem of Cell 13', serialised in 1905, in which the detective insists he can escape from prison through thinking alone. In spite of this rational bravura the solution is highly mechanical and deeply improbable, relying on both rats and passers-by as reliable forms of communication. Futrelle was not restricted to Van Dusen: E. F. Bleiler feels *The Diamond Master* (1909), using Mr Czenki, a diamond expert, as the central investigator, is in some ways his best work (1973: ix). Futrelle was capable of creating both the highly artificial puzzles and, as in 'His Perfect Alibi', the elaborated explanations that were to be very important in the clue-puzzle; had he not died on the Titanic in 1912 at the age of 38 he probably would have been an even more important contributor to crime fiction.

A more limited scientific follow-up to Sherlock Holmes was pro-duced by Arthur B. Reeve in Craig Kennedy, a professor of chem-istry who at the start of *The Silent Bullet* (1912; in England *The Black Hand*) argues that 'there is a distinct place for science in the detection of crime' (1912: 1). These stories are based simply on a scientific or technical solution to a mystery, without much in the way of colour or complication. Set in New York, and rather ploddingly developed, Reeve's work had a substantial audience, but the lack of Futrelle's flair or Doyle's complexity makes them seem today like lifeless exhibits from the past. Reeve developed his interests in *The Dream Doctor* (1914), where the influence of Freud is clear and Kennedy engages in what he calls 'soul analysis'. In the title story, 'The Dream Doctor', part of the evidence is that a woman is sexually frigid, but the outcome still depends on mechanical matters, here typewriter evidence: as J. Randolph Cox comments, Reeve 'depends more on lie-detectors, ballistic, voice-prints and wire-tapping to solve crimes than observation and detection' (in Herbert, 1999: 378).

These mechanical limitations are transcended in the work of R. Austin Freeman. A medical man who early on co-wrote the imag-inative 'Romney Pringle' stories (see p. 71), Freeman became famous as the creator of Dr Thorndyke, the archetype of forensic experts. A scientist and lawyer who practises in London's legal district of the Inner Temple, Thorndyke brings genuine if sometimes over-detailed authority to scientific detection. Doyle had just guessed you could separate tobacco ashes on sight or tell which way bicycle tracks were going (wrongly, as critics showed): Freeman gives the specifics. In his first story, the novel *The Red Thumb Mark* (1907), he explains carefully how a fingerprint can be forged; a particular duck-weed is central to 'The Naturalist at Large', and later stories were some-times illustrated by photographs of equipment that Freeman actu-ally constructed, as for 'The Aluminium Dagger', where the fatal weapon has been fired from a rifle. Though there are some suc-cessful Thorndyke novels – T. S. Eliot thought *The D'Arblay Mystery* (1926) was 'perfect in form' ([1927] 1932: 143) – Freeman is best remembered for fairly long short stories, first appearing in *Pearson's Magazine* in 1908 and published as *John Thorndyke's Cases* (1909), which seemed to suit the narrow-focus approach better. After the first few the crime was usually murder, or sometimes apparent murder, and the emphasis was on the scientific inquiry, not on multiple suspects or local colour. Freeman specialised so much in methods of inquiry that he invented the 'inverted detective story', first appearing in *The Singing Bone* (1912), where the first section tells what actually happened and then the narrative simply charts the detective's finally successful struggle to share the reader's knowledge.

The emphasis on method and the lack of humour and colour make Thorndyke seem flatter and drier than Sherlock Holmes, though the structure is similar, including a Watson-like friend Jarvis and a laboratory assistant to provide both the meals and the assistance that Holmes derives from varied sources. Often cleverly thought out, more intricate and action-oriented than the Professor Kennedy stories, Thorndyke was much admired and still has his adherents, though, as with the other scientists, there is an almost complete lack of the symbolic subtleties that made the Holmes stories so powerful.

III   IRONIC ANTI-HEROES

Other writers responded to the impact of the great detective by deliberate reversal. One of the most striking examples was provided by Doyle's own brother-in-law, E. W. Hornung. After spending two years in Australia for his health, and writing several antipodean romances, including the energetic convict saga *The Rogue's March* (1896) in the spirit of Thomas Gaspey, he wrote stories for *Cassell's Magazine*, published together in 1899 as *The Amateur Cracksman*, about A. J. Raffles, a gentleman and fine cricketer who found himself short of funds and turned to crime. These are adventures, not mysteries, focused on theft, not murder. Written with both pace and flair, they have a wit that consistently questions the assumption that crime fiction must always be respectable in its ethic. Having been fortuitously introduced to robbery when touring Australia as a cricketer, as told in the retrospective story 'Le Premier Pas', Raffles, with his initially nervous helper Bunny, uses his place in society to steal jewels and cash in stories that in their vertiginous morality and nefarious excitements have a *fin de siècle* decadence closer to Stevenson's exotic fables than Doyle's essential respectability and develop consciously, as Doyle only suggested, the ambiguous relationship, part fraternal, part erotic, between the two male characters.

Hornung was not the only writer to imagine a criminal version of the hero-detective. Arthur Morrison, best known for his plain-man detective Martin Hewitt (see pp. 73–4), also created in *The Dorrington Deed-Box* Horace Dorrington, a private inquiry agent whose activities were often 'of a more than questionable sort' (1897: 52) and does not even hesitate at murder. But for all his purposeful malice Dorrington never succeeds very well. In the most memorable story, 'The Case of the "Avalanche Bicycle and Tyre Co. Limited"', vividly set among the new craze for bicycling, Dorrington realises that a business fraud is in progress and tries to take financial advantage of the villain, but is himself eventually trapped in an enamelling oven and, having escaped, never presents the bank bill for £1000 he has gathered in the process.

Another author better known for more morally focused stories, R. Austin Freeman, writing as 'Clifford Ashdown', with the help of J. J. Pitcairn, a prison medical officer (Donaldson, 1971: 53–61), produced a number of stories beginning in *Cassell's Magazine* in 1902, published as *The Adventures of Romney Pringle* (1902). Officially a literary agent, but really a fraud about town, Romney intervenes for his own interest in other people's criminal adventures: the fine story 'The Assyrian Rejuvenator' has him scare off a man selling a bogus source of sexual invigoration and steal all the postal orders that arrive at the office. Unlike Dorrington, he gets away with his profits, and Pringle has real criminal skills – he cuts keys to the Rejuvenator office and, in another story, forges a diplomatic message which causes France to break off relations with Britain, and as a result he cleans up on the Stock Exchange. Much more lively than the sombre Thorndyke stories for which Freeman is far better known, Pringle's adventures, like those of Raffles and Dorrington, indicate that not all the audience for crime stories in the wake of Sherlock Holmes were entirely interested in those who fully abided by the law.

Other writers were more directly ironic about Holmes. One, like Hornung, was very close to Doyle. Robert Barr, a Glasgow-born Canadian journalist, moved to London in 1881 and became Doyle's friend and smoking companion (tobacco was close to an opiate for these writers and many of their characters). As well as creating a French detective in *The Triumphs of Eugène Valmont* (1906), a self-regarding and less than successful Parisian super-detective who to some extent parodies Holmes, he wrote two amusing pastiches of the great detective. 'The Adventures of Sherlaw Kombs' is a well-known early response from 1892 in *The Idler* (which Barr co-edited with Jerome K. Jerome); the other, 'The Adventure of the Second Swag', appeared in *The Idler* in 1904 after Doyle had revived Holmes: in this witty story, forgotten until recently, Doyle kills the annoying great detective and then, with the help of his publisher George Newnes buries him, literally, in the Strand (Barr, 1997).

Another path for variations of the great detective was towards fantasy. In M. P. Shiel's stories about *Prince Zaleski* (1895) the prince's remarkable insights were Stevensonian in their fantasy, combining a Prince Florizel-like figure with an unlikely weight of learning, and they seem to have been too strained for lasting success. A livelier figure of the après-Holmes movement was Arsène Lupin. Even more vainglorious than Valmont, but also more criminal, Maurice Leblanc made him a super-Raffles who was capable of acting morally at times, in the fantasised French tradition of Rocambole and Fantomas. Starting in magazine stories in 1906, Arsène is given a Raffles-like sobriquet in the first collected stories, *Arsène Lupin: gentleman-cambrioleur* (1907), but not only does the gentleman-robber arrange remarkable thefts and frauds, he is also the master of extreme disguises and masquerades. He mocks and steals the watch of the English master detective, called in French Herlock Sholmès, but in English translation the duller Holmlock Shears.

Arsène Lupin has been much overlooked in the history of crime fiction, perhaps because the stories are so lightly entertaining, but as a firmly moral master criminal he is both a projection of the idea Poe had in Dupin, a genius beyond both crime and common morality, and also a sign of the increasing twentieth-century interest in the role played by the criminal in the moral dramas surrounding crime. Lupin is also a medial figure in another area of crime fiction history: as a master of disguise both for identifying and committing crime he bridges the two centuries. It is noticeable that in the nineteenth century it is normal for the detectives to go in disguise, often of an elaborate and melodramatic kind, from Vidocq to Holmes, while in the twentieth century it is much more common for the criminal to conceal himself or herself in some way – physical, social and certainly moral. As the detective becomes a stable and credible identity, the multiplicity of criminality is more easily realised, and Leblanc appears to gather both these threads in his hands more than any other contemporary, even Doyle.

Not all the ironic treatments of the Holmes model were playful. A sterner figure was the legal expert Randolph Mason, created by the American lawyer Melville Davisson Post in *The Strange Schemes of Randolph Mason* (1896). In some ways Mason seems unheroic: his 'expression was at the same time sneering and fearless' (1896: 21) and his practices are also surprising, using his knowledge of the law to counteract what seem like proper legal decisions. The second set of stories was initially called *The Man of Last Resort* (1897: the 1923 reprint only carried the euphemising sub-title, *The Clients of Randolph Mason*) and both collections have thoughtful introductions: the first suggests that the law is 'a textbook for the shrewd knave' (1896: 9) but asserts that this is not necessarily a negative view, that a critique of the holes in the law, such as Post has been offering, can in fact be a guide for a better law. The second introduction makes it clear that some critics have been suggesting Post has created a handbook for legitimised crime, but he insists that the stories are meant to improve legal practice, not indicate its loopholes (Norton, 1973: 72).

In the first story in the first volume, 'The Corpus Delicti', Mason is in fact nothing but a criminal's attorney, getting an acquittal for a murderer on the basis of insufficient and over-circumstantial evidence. But as the stories continue, Mason grows more sober, tending to be on the side of equity and against negative legality, as in 'The Grazier', illustrating Mason's ironic maxim: ' "To the law," he said, "all things are possible – even justice" ' (1897: 257). Post's challenge to naive ideas of law, however well defended in his introductions, seems to have been too bold to sustain: by the third volume, *The Corrector of Destinies* (1908), Mason, as Donald A. Yates comments, 'does a turnabout and labours now on the side of justice' (in Herbert, 1999: 349). Post's early cynical tone, not unlike that of the Pringle and Dorrington stories, became moderated here, and the process went further: he remains best known as the author of the far more traditional 'Uncle Abner' stories, published as *Uncle Abner, Master of Mysteries* (1918), where a rural, patriarchal, almost biblical, figure solves crimes by a mixture of deep popular knowledge and close observation.

IV LOW-LEVEL DETECTION

Uncle Abner's intensified form of folk wisdom is a mythicised American version of another kind of response to Sherlock Holmes, the demotic treatment found in the 'Martin Hewitt' stories by Arthur Morrison. These, appearing first in *The Strand* in March 1894 when the Holmes series was well established, deliberately made the detective a plain man. Well known in the period for his Zolaesque revelations of London's poverty-ridden East End, like *Tales of Mean Streets* (1894), Morrison made his detective start as a young law clerk, rather like one of the humble investigators of the 1850s stories, but his success led him to set up as a private detective, working entirely on his own. He employed, as his journalist narrator remarks, 'no system beyond a judicious use of ordinary faculties' ([1984] 1976: 3). The crimes relate to urban business and fraud and Hewitt relies on no more than acute observations to identify that a parrot stole the jewels in 'The Lenton Croft Robberies' or that a hollow walking-stick concealed the missing plans in 'The Case of the Dixon Torpedo'. As Bleiler remarks in his introduction to the reprint, 'Hewitt is obviously based on Sherlock Holmes via the identity of opposites' (1976: xiii): Hewitt is plump, pleasant, low-key and co-operates readily with the police. This makes for capable and competent stories, but not for the high romance or the ideological complexity of the Doyle stories.

Other uncomplicated investigations from what Hugh Greene called 'the rivals of Sherlock Holmes' in his three anthologies (one was the American rivals) also tended to be two-dimensional and not long remembered. Paul Beck, the creation of the Irish lawyer and later judge, M. McDonnell Bodkin, is in the sub-title of the initial 1898 collection called the *Rule-of-Thumb Detective*. He is 'a stout, strongly built man ... suggesting rather the notion of a respectable retired milkman than a detective' (1898: 8) and, much like Hewitt, Beck says 'I ... muddle and puzzle out my cases as best as I can' (1898: 30). His solutions usually turn on a technical device like a jewel case with a false bottom or a pistol fired by the sun through a magnifying glass (an idea that turns up again in an Uncle Abner story).

The inherent limitations of this plain detection appear to have led Bodkin into variations, including a woman detective Dora Myrl (see pp. 78–9) who would marry Paul Beck and produce a son who would himself detect as *Young Beck, a Chip off the Old Block* (1911). But not all writers were to find the plain approach dull. J. S. Fletcher is now a largely forgotten name, but in the early twentieth century he was a large-scale producer of simple detection. A journalist, he produced both short-story collections and mystery novels, sometimes focused on a detective as in *The Adventures of Arthur Dawe (Sleuth Hound)* (1909). The cognomen 'sleuth-hound' comes from the vigorously thriving American weekly dime novella market – 'sleuth' was a Scottish word for trace or track and a 'sleuth-hound' was a tracking dog: the contraction to 'sleuth' alone is also early American. Dawe has a 'business-like-looking office' (1909: 10) and both the style and the narratives are as plain and slightly clumsy as that phrase. In the first story, 'The Mystery at Merrill's Mill', Dawe (like Tabaret) has retired and devotes himself to 'the one hobby of his life – the study of crime and criminals' (1909: 12). Squat and elderly, he nevertheless has eyes 'dark, inscrutable, steady as steel, with a luminous penetrating light that seemed to burn far back in mysterious, unreachable recesses' (1909: 12). In spite of this inner trace of the surveilling hero, Dawe's successes come through very simple means such as observing bloodstains on the floor through a borrowed magnifying glass, though the Gothic element suggested in Dawe's eyes recurs at a banal level: he uses a severed hand to force a confession from the murderer.

Never a very thoughtful writer – Melvyn Barnes speaks of his 'almost total lack of characterisation' (in Reilly, 1980: 581) – Fletcher produced, among a flood of other titles, including poetry and local history, a steady flow of competent, simple murder mysteries, many of them set, with some sense of veracity, in quarters of London. Very popular – President Wilson is said to have highly favoured *The Middle Temple Murder* (1919) – Fletcher represents the strong but largely forgotten undertow of unimaginative business-like mystery writing. It flourished in the booming single-volume novel market that followed the collapse of the three-decker novel market in the 1890s, and was a mainstay of the developing lending libraries, as well as the public libraries – as Colin Watson reports (1971: Chapter 2), extensive lending libraries were found in high-street shops like the chemist Boots or the newsagent Smiths.

A writer with none of Fletcher's banality who also loved London and created a detective in conscious reversal of Sherlock Holmes was G. K. Chesterton. This larger-than-life figure (himself to become the model for John Dickson Carr's Gideon Fell) was closely interested in crime fiction. *The Man who was Thursday* (1908) is a parodic thriller and in 1902 he published a much-noted essay which argued, surely on the basis of reading Doyle, that crime fiction was a modern epic of the city ([1902] 1974). In order to create his own ideal of humble, intelligent, populist Catholicism, he created Father Brown, in many ways the reverse of Holmes, but at least his equal in insight and moral authority. The stories were first collected under the simple, devout title *The Innocence of Father Brown* (1911). In the first, 'The Blue Cross', Chesterton tries to create an epic London story in accordance with his earlier prediction, sending Father Brown across the reimagined city after those who have stolen the religious treasure of the title. It has the typical Chestertonian revealing paradox – Brown identifies the thief Flambard as no priest because he criticises reason – but it is also over-fantastic and improbably based on coincidence. In the following stories Chesterton settles into a morally, rather than topographically, focused world where Brown's penetrating insight disentangles the truth from mysterious events, increasingly involving murder, all highly coloured with the power of Chesterton's imagination. A garden containing a corpse with two heads, a body hidden among the dead at a battle, the sartorial identity of waiters and gentlemen are typically exotic keys to the mystery in stories that, especially for those interested in the religious possibilities of the form, have often been thought the only rivals to Doyle's work in their combination of ideas, wit and fluent writing.

A lower-level contemporary of Father Brown was Baroness Orczy's *The Old Man in the Corner* (1909, in the US *The Man in the Corner*). First appearing in *The Royal Magazine* in 1901, this was a successful series in which Bill Owen – distinctly unprepossessing in appearance (Kayman calls him 'pale, thin and impolite', 2003), and often illustrated as such – sits in a London café and discusses with a young woman journalist crime reports from the newspapers: tying and untying knots in a piece of string, he simply unravelled the problems. With limited impact as mysteries, the stories have, E. F. Bleiler claims, historical importance as 'the first significant modern stories about an armchair detective' (in Reilly, 1980: 1142) – but they add little to Dupin's similar method and may owe their contemporary success just to the unusual presentation of the mysteries.

If there were varied versions of a down-market, but still complex, representation of the hero detective, there was also a much simplified version of his heroics. The hack writer Joyce R. Preston Muddock (in fact a man, who later hyphenated his last two names) wrote thrillers under the name 'Dick Donovan'. He started before Holmes was well known with Waters-style collections like *Caught at Last: Leaves from the Notebook of a Detective* (1889) but, among his many other productions, turned to crime stories. Typical are *The Knutsford Mystery* (1906) and *The Fatal Ring* (1905): they lack a recurring detective but are full of heroic adventure, violence and general mystery and, like many in the form – including sometimes the later Doyle – create a super-villain as a way of simplifying matters for everyone, especially the writer. Symons was able to tolerate Muddock's style as being like 'rather inferior Trollope' (1992: 102) but its inherent turgidity is evident, especially when compared with the all-action tabloid-style intensity of the Nick Carter series which had started in America with *Nick Carter, Detective* (1891). Clurman notes that 'over a thousand Nick Carter stories were published between the late 1800s and the 1920s' (1963: x), written at an amazing rate – like a novella in two days – first by John A. Corryell and then by Frederick Van Rensselaer. Carter often uses disguise, carries an amazing range of weapons and tools with him, yet remains smart in dark jacket and derby hat as he rushes about New York facing all dangers. In *Nick Carter, Detective* he knocks down a villain on the street and then has to deal with a surprise: 'a hooded and hideous head of the cobra was raised menacingly over the senseless man's breast' ([1891] Clurman, 1963: 47). Nick is marksman enough to deal with this curious pet, or concealed weapon, and the story races on in one-sentence paragraphs.

A consciously diluted version of the great detective was Sexton Blake, who lived in Baker Street, making chemical experiments, with a housekeeper and an assistant, Tinker, straight out of Holmes's boy irregulars. Sexton Blake's adventures were all action, combating criminal gangs and evil foreigners with many chases and much gunfire: they flourished from 1894 in the twopenny magazine *Union Jack*, which became in 1933 *Detective Weekly* without any diminution of jingoism. Many authors churned these out, often in a spirit of fun – in 'The Plague of Onion Men' by Gwyn Evans (1932) a French mastermind, Aristide Dupin, who wishes to restore the French monarchy, uses as his footsoldiers the Breton onion-men who regularly visited Britain, commanded by one Hercule Bolo, with a familiar waxed and pointed moustache. Sexton Blake survived into British radio and television in the 1960s and Nick Carter for even longer, and American and English versions of the simplified adolescent-oriented great detective have thrived, especially in films, to the present.

V WOMEN ON THE CASE

Another link with recent crime fiction is the extent to which after Sherlock Holmes, in seeking variation to the dominant model, some writers turned – as had also happened in the 1860s – to the idea of a woman detective. She first appeared in book form in 1894 when Catharine Louisa Pirkis, a prolific writer of romance, produced *The Experiences of Loveday Brooke*, who worked for a detective agency on Fleet Street – the continuation of the Strand itself. Only 'a little over thirty', she has a 'neat primness' but though she is unexceptional in appearance, she is 'the most sensible and practical woman I ever met' (1894: 6–7). In both looks and manner she is like her contemporary Martin Hewitt, but she has a lively side: she uses disguise to investigate and in the first story, 'The Black Bag Left on a Doorstep', shows a wide knowledge of both the London music halls and the culture of cab-drivers. The crimes she encounters range from theft to murder, and the emphasis is on Loveday's capacity to comprehend and, at the end, explain everything.

A similar approach is found in George Sims's *Dorcas Dene, Detective: Her Adventures* (1897). A minor actress, after her artist husband went blind Dorcas drifted into detection through a police inspector neighbour. Combining 'a pretty womanly face' and 'soft brown wavy hair' (1897: 6, 44) with 'plenty of good common sense' and being 'a good observer' (1897: 6), she tends to see through the criminal plan in a moment of insight – the opening story, 'The Helsham Mystery', is an old-fashioned inheritance drama based on baby-substitution. Most of the other cases focus on theft and sometimes murder in a family. Dorcas Dene can use disguise spectacularly – as an old gypsy woman, for example – but mostly she operates on the inside, acting as a parlour-maid in 'The Diamond Lizard' where she does, unusually, solve the matter by detecting a tiny blood spot. Not really any advance on Forrester's Mrs G – and much less interestingly written – Dorcas Dene did well enough for a second series of stories to appear in 1898, which suggests there was an audience hungry for even such limited examples of gender-varied detection.

Dora Myrl, The Lady Detective (1900) is how M. McDonnell Bodkin presents his gender variation of his Holmes variation Paul Beck. She is as respectable as her predecessors, but more sharply characterised, not so much in her 'winsome figure' (1900: 6) but by her status as a Cambridge wrangler, a maths specialist. There is something of the possibility, and mystery, of the New Woman about her: she has trained as a doctor but cannot find her place in the world of work, having been, she says, 'a telegraph girl, a telephone girl, a lady journalist. I liked the last best' (1900: 6). After being involved in a story of a baby-exchange that never occurred (Bodkin clearly had

Gaboriau's *The Widow Lerouge* in mind), she sets up as a detective and has a card printed with 'Dora Myrl, Lady Detective' – a motif presumably borrowed from Pirkis, whose first volume had Loveday Brooke's very similar business card actually pasted on the front jacket. Though Dora's intellectual capacity is stressed, the stories tend to turn on simple tricks: in the anthology piece 'How He Cut His Stick' Dora realises the railway thief has hooked the proceeds onto the electric wires with his walking-stick because she spots the groove this has made. Dora can be brave and active – she at times carries a gun – and there is social meaning in her qualifications and lack of work to match them, but essentially the stories, like Futrelle's, combine the promise of intellectualism with the actuality of rather mechanical, trick-based detection.

Another woman detective of some status is found in *Lady Molly of Scotland Yard* (1910), by the well-known romance writer Baroness Orczy. Lady Molly is noted for 'her shrewdness and ingenuity' (1910: 29) though she also has 'pretty shoulders' and a 'graceful figure' (1910: 44, 102) according to the narrator, a policewoman who later becomes Molly's private secretary. Not unlike a gallant duchess from Orczy's 'Scarlet Pimpernel' stories, Molly, as we learn in 'Sir Jeremiah's Will', is the daughter of an earl who has secretly married the handsome military son of a feuding family. When his grandfather dies he is convicted of murder; Molly joins the police to clear him, and eventually brings this about by uncovering an ingenious impersonation: the idea probably comes from Wilkie Collins's husband-defending wife in *The Law and the Lady* (1875). After her triumph Molly gives up her police work, but the stories that detailed her detective activities are an interesting early example of a woman detective who is not, like the others, restricted to a quasi-male role. More like Mrs G— or Mrs Paschal from the 1860s, Lady Molly operates among women – in 'The Ninescore Mystery' she forces a confession by playing on a woman's fears about her child's health, and the narrator refers rather grandly to 'we of the Female Department' (1910: 1).

Julian Symons dismissed all these women detectives, finding Lady Molly 'more disastrously silly than most of her kind' (1992: 96), and, a little more perceptively, saying that Dora Myrl was 'no less absurd than other stories of the time about women detectives, who retain an impossible gentility of speech and personality while dealing with crime' (1992: 101). It is true that for these writers there is very little space in which to imagine a woman detective, at least until

Wentworth, Sayers and Christie mobilise the image of the spinster in that way. But the creators of the early women detectives were trying, against the tide of the male magazines as much as against social attitudes, to offer different and inherently subversive positions and values for detecting crime. The idea that they all pursued – with the difficulty that enables Symons to dismiss them – was that crime can both threaten and be explained by a woman as much as a man. This idea was in fact to emerge as a main feature of the first new movement forward in crime fiction, in novels by American women which combined mystery and emotion, and presented them from a firmly female viewpoint.

4
The Clue-puzzle Forms

I HAD THEY BUT KNOWN

Novels focused on murder existed in the nineteenth century, but apart from Anna Katherine Green no major writer produced a substantial series of death-based mysteries. As the novel became a dominant form around the turn of the century and, it would seem, as women increasingly became recognised as both authors and readers, two things occurred: death became the threat which the fiction would dissipate and writers found ways of involving readers in the operations of the story. Neither Gaboriau nor Green consistently laid out clues for the reader to follow in any organised way, nor did they assemble a wide range of possible suspects to entice and bemuse the reader's speculations. There developed, though, an increasing desire to amaze the reader: the two best-known crime novels of the turn of the century both end with startlingly unpredictable revelations. In *The Big Bow Mystery* (1892) Israel Zangwill, a radical journalist who was better known as an energetic and influential Zionist, ends a locked-room murder mystery with the amazing, and barely credible, revelation that the detective committed the murder after breaking into the room. This may seem parodic, but it was written for a popular newspaper where such melodrama could seem normal. Priestman has seen a left-wing political thrust to the novel: 'in being hoodwinked into looking the wrong way by the detective cult, the public are overlooking the only real source of social solutions' (1998: 18). With even greater complication than Zangwill, Gaston Leroux in *Le Mystère de la Chambre Jaune* (1907, published as *The Mystery of the Yellow Room* in 1908 in the US, 1909 in London), makes Larsan the police detective in fact a master criminal who engineers the murder in a supremely isolated locked-room situation. Zangwill's villain reveals all in a confession, but Leroux uses Rouletabille, a young journalist – he is only 18 – to achieve a solution which, as Arthur Athanason commented, 'stretches coincidence beyond all credibility' (in Reilly, 1980: 1545), particularly in the fact that the murderer is apparently the detective's father and the victim his mother – a situation which, as Priestman notes (1998: 18), might well invite a Freudian interpretation, if not merely seen as a game.

These novelists created an emotively realised domestic murder – their tone was more Gothic than was found in Green or Gaboriau, and their use of genuine surprises and their awareness of the reader as a potential presence in the fiction suggested a pattern that was to be developed influentially by two American women, writing at much the same time. Carolyn Wells was a librarian whose success with her novels based on Fleming Stone, a somewhat bland but authoritative private detective known as 'the great man', led to a life of writing: by her death in 1942 she had produced over 80 mysteries, as well as scores of children's books. She started with short stories in 1906 but established herself with *The Clue* in 1909, though this was not published in London until 1920, and many of her books only appeared in America. Her world is, like Green's, one of modern American comfortable wealth: her normal focus is not New York but a small town in the north-eastern states. In *The Clue* an orphaned heiress is found dead, apparently by suicide, the day before her marriage. The house was locked at the time, and family members and servants are suspected in turn. A lawyer, much like Robert Audley, attempts interpretation of enigmas such as the apparent suicide note, and the clue of the title is a single tiny cachou. The coroner's inquest moves very slowly and when, quite late in the book, Fleming Stone is called in, he is able to show that an uncle, because of his engineering experience, was able to enter the house through a very narrow tunnel and commit the crime. There is little proof, but fortunately he confesses, and stabs himself.

This highly dramatic narrative is told in the calm, assured, slightly stiff style that Christie will use so successfully, as in the description of Stone: 'He was nearly fifty years old, with greying hair and a kindly, responsive face' (1909: 274). Somewhat mechanical though the novel seems, and quite reticent as Wells is about the melodramatic elements of the story, by removing the Green type of story from the city and its social world, by making a whole family the location of the mysterious tensions, and by moving meticulously through suspicions and possibilities, Wells has imagined into being the essence of the 'golden age' story, which largely ignored social messages to concentrate on the deep-seated deceptions and possibly fatal betrayals of life in extended but also isolated families. Wells had neither the literary style nor the technical polish that brought fame to later clue-puzzlers, but she deserves at least some recognition. She is not even mentioned in Panek's book, subtitled 'Crime Fiction in America' (1990), but her status as someone who focused the preceding tendencies into what became the clue-puzzle is strongly supported by her full and thoughtful book on the form.

She had clearly studied many crime stories when in 1913 she published *The Technique of the Mystery Story*. Usually overlooked, this is a close account of the essential features of modern mystery. Wells appears to be the first of many better-known commentators to reflect on the classical heritage of crime, from the Sphinx and Herodotus through the Arabian Nights to Voltaire's Zadig (and its Arabic source). She notes the 'stirring mental exercise' (1913: 63) of modern detectives and mentions Leroux, Futrelle, Reeve, Barr, Green and Orczy as well as Poe, Gaboriau and Doyle. Recognising a heritage in them, Wells also sees a need for consistent innovation – she dismisses as hackneyed recurrent features like snow and fog, secret panels, initialled handkerchiefs and footprints. She admires orderly sequences of clues as in Green and in Collins's *The Woman in White*, is critical of logical errors and insists that murder is 'the crime *par excellence*' (1913: 219). Her advice to the writer includes creating false trails and not making the police too absurd or the details of the crime too implausible. She feels that motive must be interesting, and recent, but that the identity of the criminal should be invisible to the reader until the very end. She is against a final explanation, preferring action which reveals the criminal, and she recommends little humour and a simple style, with 'accurate English even more than polished expression' (1913: 319).

Wells is strongly aware of the role women have played in developing the mystery and gives (1913: 315) a list of her contemporaries who are now quite forgotten, worth repeating in the hope of stimulating research into them: A. M. Barbour, Stella M. Düring, Augusta Grüner, Natalie Lincoln, Florence Warden, Mary E. Wilkins. She acknowledges Orczy again, and also mentions a contemporary who has not been forgotten, and who had already developed the Wells technique in a less rigid way, Mary Roberts Rinehart. But it may not be only Rinehart she influenced with her study. Although it was not published in England until 1920, Christie started writing *The Mysterious Affair at Styles* in 1916 and she had American links in a godmother – her father, dead for some time, was himself an American. That she had read Wells is suggested not only by the fact that she follows Wells's advice fully, apart from avoiding final explanations, which Christie always liked, and her complex plots needed, but by one particular paragraph which suggests 'a clever dodge is to suspect the characters in order, and though A was exonerated long ago, prove at the last that he was the real criminal after all' (1913: 240): this is the key to the plot of Christie's first novel.

Mary Roberts Rinehart matched Wells's plan for the mystery novel in a distinctly livelier style: she also exploited the emotion of a female context to a greater extent than Wells had done, and more than Green too, though her Amelia Butterworth mysteries and the later Violet Strange stories had brought crime fiction firmly into a world of female knowledge. Rinehart's style of emotional suspense may derive in part from the sensational adult novels of Louisa M. Alcott. Trained as a nurse, married to a doctor, Rinehart had already published widely in magazines when her second novel sold very well and gained her a strong reputation. *The Circular Staircase* (1908), like all her work, was recognised internationally, being quickly published in London. She was a major figure who alone indicates that the 'golden age' was by no means an English or between-wars phenomenon. Rinehart uses a woman narrator who tells the story in the past, with a constantly emotion-aware narrative. The texts insist on 'the complete identification of the reader with the central character' (Joanne Harack Hayne, in Reilly, 1980: 766) and the woman narrator's comments from the present on what happened in the past both humanise and emotionalise the narrative: this led to the name of 'Had I But Known' for the approach, used usually by American men in a demeaning, even sexist, sense, denying the value of the emotions in favour of the (itself not unemotional) 'tough guy' position.

Rinehart brings sensation into the somewhat austere world of the mystery as Wells had outlined it, and romance, both tragic and happy, is a recurrent feature. There is little professional detection in *The Circular Staircase*, though 'Mr Jamieson the detective' does appear, and does receive the final credit. Rachel Innes, the housekeeper, plays the central role, telling a story with a mysterious body (and others to follow), a veiled lady visiting, a servant found dead in a cupboard, a disappearing nephew and a secret room in the house where Rachel bravely ventures, to be attacked by the murderer. He is killed in the final action, and turns out to be a family bad seed, an embezzler. Behind the melodrama there runs a conflict between settled America, symbolised in the comfortable old house, and the new figure of the corrupt, criminal businessman, who destroys lives and even damages the house itself in the process of stuffing it with money: Bachelder comments on 'the gradually emerging central theme: the passion for money' and sees in the staircase itself the symbol of 'an inward-turning spiral of dishonesty and criminal intent' (1994: 17, 18). There are thematic depths to Rinehart's early work, at least, that have been largely ignored, and tend to disappear in her later fiction where, though Hayne finds her plots 'increasingly implausible' (in Reilly, 1980: 766), Rinehart does at least keep up the emotional tension. At the end of *The Door* (1930), the butler is revealed as 'the monster' who committed the crime and the narrator faints away: as Bachelder comments, this is a novel of 'many conflicts' focusing thematically on 'appearances hiding a more complex reality' (1994: 54, 56).

A less sensitive bearer of emotion was Rinehart's only series detective Nurse Hilda Adams, an inquirer sharp enough to be called 'Miss Pinkerton', in novels where the central issues are fidelities and betrayals focused on gender and family but, as Freier notes, she tends to get weaker and the police detective stronger as the novels continue (1995: 133). A lighter-weight female detective appeared in the long-running *Saturday Evening Post* series starring Letitia or 'Tish' Carberry. Cohn comments that Rinehart 'altogether altered the form of the mystery novel by adding flesh and muscle to the skeleton of plot' (1981: 188) and from the viewpoint of the present, when women writers have staked out their own areas of knowledge and authority, Rinehart and Wells did much to redirect the masculinist and unemotive course of crime fiction in their period. It may be that by heightening emotion and making sentiment evident they were largely restricting their audience to women, but their location of a mystery in a emotion-rich family setting was – had they but known – to be the starting point for the huge development of 'golden age' writing.

II HOW GOLDEN WAS THE AGE?

The phrase 'the golden age' is very often used in commentaries on crime fiction, but does not always mean the same thing, and has some implications worth considering. It is usually taken to mean the period between the two world wars, as in Symons (1992: Chapters 7 and 8), though Howard Haycraft, writing in 1942, who appears to have been the first to use the term, dated his 'golden age' from 1918 to 1930, calling the period from 1930 to 1942 the time of 'The Moderns' (1942: Chapters IX and X). Panek regards the 'standard view' of the period as starting from the publication of E. C. Bentley's *Trent's Last Case*, that is, 1913 (1979: 11; the novel appeared in the US in 1914, as *The Woman in Black*), and it might well be wise to pursue this example further and embrace Leroux (in translation), Rinehart and Wells in the period by dating it from 1908. The end of the period is also debatable. Many of the classic writers of the so-called 'golden age' went on writing in their familiar modes well after 1939, though presumably most commentators think that the growth of private-eye fiction and other modes after the 1930s meant that the classic clue-based mystery was after the war no longer dominant enough to be called 'golden'.

But to think in terms of specific periods as if they belong exclusively to a sub-genre is to falsify the complex, overlapping and multiple ways in which sub-genres and their audiences operate. Doyle produced Holmes until 1927; the private-eye story was alive by the early 1920s. It seems better to think of the classic clue-puzzle as a form which came to prominence for particular reasons – not least the influence of those who wrote and read the form, those culturally prestigious people who were able to give their form some of the power that has been described as cultural capital. The term 'golden age' itself has some of that aura: Sally Munt has criticised it as 'replete with romantic associations' (1994: 8) and, through its associations with the Roman imperial period and renaissance pastoral leisure the term has given the sub-genre an aura of static harmony which is quite belied by the tensions revealed in the texts. The classic 'golden age' writers did not, in any case, make much gold from their novels: as Haycraft shows in his chapter 'The Murder Market' (1942: 259–71), successful authors sold quite small editions in the period before paper-backing and film tie-ins and almost all the writers were people with other incomes, either through professional work or through family or marital sources of wealth. The alleged 'golden age' is no more than another competing sub-genre with its own audience and patterns, though one in which some of the best finished and most technically skilful work in crime fiction was achieved.

The characteristics of 'golden age' writing can in isolation be traced to much that has gone before – but the novels of the period, whether by major writers or long-forgotten names, have a coherence and a self-consciousness that is not shared with, for example, the varied product of the emergent detectives of the 1850s and 1860s or the short-story magazine heroes of the 1880s and 1890s. As a result it is possible to shape a list of features that make the clue-puzzle an identifiable sub-genre of crime fiction.

The crime will be murder and this is increasingly recognised in the titles – Christie starts in 1920 with the traditionally euphemistic title *The Mysterious Affair at Styles* (1920) but her second clue-puzzle is *The Murder on the Links* (1923). Particularly in America, death and blood find their way into titles that have previously been almost entirely reticent, even if they were based on murders – and quite often English books with euphemistic titles, like Christie's nursery-rhyme series, are made explicitly bloodstained in their transatlantic forms. This murder will take place in an enclosed setting – the sub-genre does not provide the urban epic of Chesterton's early imagination, and even if they are set in London they will be confined to an area, whether fashionable like Sayers's Mayfair or respectably middle-class as in Patricia Wentworth's mysteries. Particularly urban are the American clue-puzzles by 'S. S. Van Dine', 'Ellery Queen' and Rex Stout. In social terms most examples on both sides of the Atlantic are set among the comfortable upper-middle-class (only rarely aristocratic) country settings, with a few parallels like Innes's academic Oxford or Marsh's theatres and hospitals, and there may be continuity in this feature: Raymond Williams saw the classic murder as a modern evolution of the English country-house tradition, now in capitalist rather than landed gentry form (1973: 298–9).

The social setting is also exclusive. Professional criminals and members of the working classes play very minor roles and servants are used only as passing suspects – Georgette Heyer's title *Why Shoot a Butler?* (1933) is an ironical expression of the social elevation of the puzzles and their concerns. Nor is social conflict outside the murder scene noted: though capitalist malpractice is the motive for murder in Rinehart's *The Circular Staircase*, such issues disappear: the first chapter of *Trent's Last Case* makes a dramatic statement about Sigsbee Manderson's ferocious business practices, but they play no part in the motives for murder, and Christie makes Roger Ackroyd's background as a manufacturer of wagon-wheels irrelevant to his murder.

The victim has some wealth and authority, a person against whom malicious hostility and envy can credibly be raised, and also, it would seem, a person whose wealth and status bring danger, in a complex message of identification and anxiety for the wide audience, few of whom are owners of lavish country houses. Most of the real suspects will be relatives or close associates of the important dead person, and they will almost all have something to hide that makes them become what Wells recommended as a series of suspects. But finally they will be reduced to one, or sometimes two working together; they will be revealed by the detective, possibly forced to confess; but they will not be punished. Sayers is rare in making her detective in *Busman's Honeymoon* (1937) recognise with some pain that in identifying a murderer he too has sent someone to death. The knowledge that explains the puzzle seems a sufficient ending to a classic mystery.

The detective technique, that ensemble of actions, thoughts, attitudes and appearance that constructs the values which the fiction offers against the threats of crime and deception, always emphasises rationality – the classic detectives are clever, insightful and persevering rather than flamboyantly active or coincidentally fortunate like heroes of the detective past and of other sub-genres. Some of this learning may rub off on the style, as with S. S. Van Dine's or Rex Stout's leisured connoisseurs, or the languid amateurs of Dorothy Sayers and Margery Allingham. But, equally, the clue-puzzle may be pared down to emphasise the puzzle, as in Christie's plain, close-to-cliché style or the ploddingly mechanical technique of Freeman Wills Crofts. In the elaborate case the audience is invited to share the lofty perceptions of the hero as a marker of his value; in the plainer form a more banal approach is imbued with quality by the text as a low-level position in which readers can feel confident that harm will avoid them.

Notably absent in most cases are humour and romance. The hero may be witty at times, and minor suspects can pair off finally, but the most widely admired examples of the classic form are those where there is little but the puzzle and its conceivably readable clues to interest the reader. Central to the clue-puzzle is the idea that you the reader can in fact solve this ahead of the detective – not just admire the detective as a brave man, a thoughtful woman, a true leader, a reliable dullard; you can now actually stand in for the detective. Readers could in fact do this: both Edgar Wallace and Jacques Futrelle offered a prize for explaining the solutions to a particularly weird mystery and in both cases, *The Four Just Men* (1906) and 'The Prisoner in Cell 13' (published in *The Thinking Machine*) the prizes were claimed; many people can pick up at least some of the clues in a Christie novel, and the simpler keys to many a mundane clue-puzzle are not hard to identify for an experienced reader. And yet not all readers worry about clues, and many people re-read a clue-puzzle novel knowing who did it: it is not just an enigma with a single solution as its meaning. Rather, the idea that the reader can be a detective is part of the mystique of the sub-genre, implying that an individual can be clever enough – in play at least – to construct defences against a murderer. It is a telling fiction, which is still strong in the modern 'cosy' novels and in many film and television series where a least likely suspect is suddenly sprung on the viewer, and of course in the substantial numbers of 'golden age' crime fiction that are still newly appearing or being kept in print.

III   GOLDEN ROYALTY: AGATHA CHRISTIE

While the patterns of crime fiction are shaped by the dominant concerns of a period, and shaping power also rests in the means of publication, the types of audience, the social and contextual forces, there are also clear instances of a single author catching a moment. Just as Poe combined the Gothic and the rational and Doyle shaped for a century the image of the heroic detective, so Agatha Christie had the intellect and the technical skill to make of the clue-puzzle what Wells conceived it could be: she isolated in her technically brilliant plots, her restrained characterisation and subtle thematic nuances just what a dedicated reader could hope for as a fictional defence against feared crime.

It is not hard to see the main influences on her – she had obviously read Doyle, from whom comes the initial model of detective and narrator, and Green's domestic dramas and Leroux's remarkable complications also seem obvious sources. Neither of these locates the murder in an English country house – though there are traces of this in Doyle. The prime source of Christie's setting, and perhaps the major instance for her to write at all, appears to be E. C. Bentley's *Trent's Last Case* (1913). Bentley, a friend of Chesterton, later said he meant to present a detective, partly in a spirit of parody, as being, unlike Sherlock Holmes, 'recognisable as a human being' (1940: 252). Philip Trent investigates the bizarre murder of the wealthy American financier Sigsbee Manderson, but his character certainly humanises the situation – partly by getting the solution quite wrong and partly by falling in reciprocated love with the widow. Just as

Christie borrowed in reverse the image of a super-detective, and domesticated the melodramatic complication of Leroux, so she used in a calm and unironised way the setting that Bentley had imagined. That was a bold and influential move, both in terms of technique and location. Before Christie the detective novel was still in some sense unfocused. When the successful author of thrillers and romances A. E. W. Mason turned to mystery in 1910 he set *At the Villa Rose* in France with a French detective and a mode quite unlike the clue-puzzle: the murder is a gang-killing, it is solved half-way through and the last half of the novel is lengthy explanation. But by 1924, a form had been constructed: Mason's *The House of the Arrow*, though still set in France with Inspecteur Hanaud, is an effective Christie-like structure, with deceptive mirrors, a pen that is really a poisoned arrow and multiple suspects: all these enigmas lead to a final disclosure. The mystery novel has become fully rational and focused on a puzzle. There can be little doubt that it was the influence of Christie that had made this change in Hanaud's work.

She started writing crime fiction in 1916, in response to an earlier challenge by her older sister to write a mystery. Like some other deeply original books, *The Mysterious Affair at Styles* (1920) found a publisher with some difficulty, being rejected three times (Mann, 1981: 128). The novel at once recognises the impact of the war, as the Watsonesque narrator is a wounded officer and the detective is in the area with other Belgian refugees. But if the context is post-Edwardian dismay, that has nothing directly to do with the plot, which focuses on the reasons why someone from her extended family has poisoned the wealthy Mrs Inglethorp. As with Doyle, the focus of a Christie book is often the personality and value of the detective, but she reduced in various ways the impact of the hero. Hercule Poirot is in name and plump fussy person clearly the reverse of the masculine and English Holmes. Christie's investigators are all passive but clever in persona – first the Belgian super-sleuth with his interest in 'the little grey cells' and his alleged use of psychology, then the perceptive village spinster Miss Marple, the quiet and partly intuitive Superintendent Battle, the self-mocking erratic novelist Ariadne Oliver and, most recessive of all, the ghost who avenges the dead, Harley Quinn – or Harlequin. Much as she seems to have liked Miss Marple, through whom 'the ordinary, gossipy, unsung life of an old lady is shown as a powerful force for good' (Shaw and Vanacker, 1991: 46), Christie seems to have most enjoyed operating without a central detective: in her autobiography she says her favourites were two basically detective-free novels *Crooked House* (1949) and *Ordeal by Innocence* (1958) and one where Miss Marple plays a minor and late role, *The Moving Finger* (1942) (Christie, 1972: 520).

As becomes recurrently clear, Poirot's claim on rational and psychological mastery is a Holmes-like front for a simpler method; but here it is not male clerical-style observation, but the types of knowledge that are classically, and stereotypically, female. The Styles mystery is largely solved because Poirot can understand why a set of paper spills on a mantelpiece have been disarranged; in Christie's masterpiece *The Murder of Roger Ackroyd* (1926) Poirot focuses on why a chair has been moved, and he knows that a scrap of starched cambric must come not from a handkerchief but a maidservant's apron. Before Miss Marple is invented Poirot already represents a heightened version of female domestic knowledge as a weapon against fictional disorder (see Knight, 1980: 109–10). It is on this basis that the reader is invited to read the clues and join the detective in his deciphering of what Todorov (1977) has identified as the hidden narrative – the story both lived and concealed by the murderer. The reader's quasi-detective role was stressed in the varied contemporary accounts of the murder mystery, and the first of the highly elaborate American 'Ellery Queen' novels actually printed a 'Challenge to the Reader' to say that all the clues needed for the solution had now been given.

Some of Christie's puzzles can seem a teasing game with her readers, such as *Ten Little Niggers* (1939) (in the US titled, to avoid the racist impact, *And Then There Were None*, 1940, though it later appeared as *Ten Little Indians*, 1965, itself now dropped). Here the (apparent) first victim is the killer; in reverse, in *Murder on the Orient Express* (1934) all the suspects acted together. But in most of Christie's work the quest for the killer is a more searching inquiry into threats and tensions, and the final revelation has ethical force. The cause of disorder in her novels is consistently a matter of major personal betrayal – typically by a husband and his woman associate in *The Mysterious Affair at Styles,* and this sense that you cannot trust anyone at all is a threatening message coded into the whole 'golden age' form. As Gillian Gill outlines, Christie does not take the simple path of making the murderer a stranger, a foreigner or a servant (1991: 136): the threat is closer, more disturbing than that. Christie gave this sense of intimate danger a powerful formal as well as thematic impact when in *The Murder of Roger Ackroyd*, with considerable impact, and much fuss that she had been technically unfair, she made her murderer not only the trusted village doctor, but also the narrator of the story.

A major reason for Christie's success was that she did not tire of her central method of identifying a betrayer by close observation: in her best novels the procedures by which she invited the reader to identify this figure were both detailed and clever, as in *Cards on the Table* (1936), searchingly analysed by Gill (1991: 135–48). As time passed, she did become less elaborate and made do with one key deception or misconception, like the crucial event from the past that motivates all the mystifying action in *The Mirror Crack'd from Side to Side* (1962: in the USA just *The Mirror Crack'd*), and she did sometimes repeat herself – the detective-free *Endless Night* (1967) reprises the central idea of *The Murder of Roger Ackroyd*, and the trick in the short story 'Three Blind Mice', the source for the endlessly running play *The Mousetrap*, was also used in *Hercule Poirot's Christmas* (1938 – in the US both *Murder at Christmas*, 1939 and *A Holiday for Murder*, 1947).

Commentators recognise clearly Christie's technical power: Symons felt she was the first to make the mystery 'a puzzle story which is solely that' (1992: 113) and Priestman sees her as the originator of 'a pattern of extraordinary resilience' (1998: 19). There are some other factors in her remarkable success, such as her simple style – she is often read by English language learners around the world – and the professionalism of her long-term (though not original) publisher, Collins, and her agent, Edmund Cork. But the key to the long-lasting and genre-shaping power of Christie is her capacity to realise in formulaic, repeatable mode a sense of personal unease and possible danger that emerges even in – especially in – a world secluded from social and international disorder. As Robert Barnard has commented in *A Talent to Deceive*, 'beneath the surface calm of village life there lurks a seething lava of crimes, sins, oddities and other potential disruptions' (1980: 28) and Alison Light, from a viewpoint encompassing both gender and social politics, has seen personal uncertainty as a basic pattern in the novels (1991: 57–9). P. D. James, in many ways Christie's strongest follower, summed up in a television interview (reported by Gill, 1991: 202) the way in which Christie realised 'the very tension between the surface law and order of a traditional English village and certain violent passions below the surface'. Many commentators, especially but not only Americans, feel the 'golden age' mystery is a sunny account of a coherent, if unreal, community, but they seem to overlook the repetitive traumas of betrayal that are central to the form and which provide the basis for the reader's need to be consistently assured that the calm, clever, domestically observant detective can, in fiction at least, protect from such dangerous anxieties.

Not all Christie's work achieved this level. Her simplistic and jingoistic mystery adventures, from *The Secret Adversary* (1922) to *Postern of Fate* (1973), have not lasted: the potential attraction of a married couple with the wife leading the adventures is negated by the obviousness of the plotting and characterisation and the political naivety of the ideas – which may well be the author's own: the sociopolitical neutrality of the clue-puzzles protected them from such a damaging effect. And it may be that even the best of the novels have for most people now taken on a primarily period interest. There are clear signs in the shops that Christie's once massive sales are ebbing, and the recent films and television series lay heavier stress on period nostalgia than on the mystery itself. But although it took quite a while for her to be established as a leader – Sayers, in her ground-breaking introduction only refers in passing and somewhat negatively to Christie as someone who retains the Watson figure ([1928], 1974: 198) – it is clear that her formidable intelligence and her technical clarity enabled her to create, as Doyle had done before, a classic form for a type of crime fiction which had many other writers and very many readers.

IV   AMERICAN GOLD

American commentators on crime fiction enjoy making a distinction between the unrealistic and conservative English clue-puzzle and the bracingly realistic American private-eye story, or 'tough-guy' novel as they uncritically – even sentimentally – prefer to name it. How realistic, or indeed bracing, that sub-genre was will be discussed below, but the real curiosity is that Americans seem largely to forget that their own country saw a major and highly popular transplantation of the clue-puzzle.

Willard Huntington Wright was an American author and editor who, while he was ill for two years in 1923–4, read widely in crime fiction, and then took up the form under the consciously imposing name of 'S. S. Van Dine'. *The Benson Murder Case* sold extremely well in 1926, and by 1939 Van Dine had followed with ten other titles using exactly the same verbal pattern but substituting for 'Benson' another six-letter word, such as Canary, Casino, Dragon. The same meticulousness pervades his detective's self-image. Philo Vance is linked by William Ruehlmann to Sherlock Holmes (1974: 39–40), but a better explanation, as Symons suggests (1992: 125–6), is that he is an American version of Lord Peter Wimsey (Sayers's first novel *Whose Body?* came out in 1923): languid, learned, given to self-gratifying jokes and mock-pomposity, but also very perceptive. Symons values the real quality of Vance's (and Van Dine's) scholarship, but the presence of pompous footnotes and the extremity of Vance's manner does suggest that, like Bentley, Van Dine started off with a spoof mystery that became serious when people, including himself, accepted it as such.

The books move slowly, with great detail about the setting, the detection and the range of suspects – a Van Dine book is twice as long as an average Christie. Crimes are always murder: in his commentary on the form Van Dine insisted that there 'simply must be a corpse in a detective novel, and the deader the corpse the better' ([1928] 1974: 190). The context of death in his novels is wealthy mercantile New York society, and although the detail is close, the effect is basically unreal, more like a masque than a play. Dashiell Hammett, reviewing the first novel, wryly said that because the gun that shot Benson would in reality have knocked him half across the room, he assumed the detective would trace the person who had lifted him back into his chair ([1927], 1974: 382): but the author neither knew nor cared about ballistic facts. Vance's skills include understanding 'the exact psychological nature of the deed' (1926: 336) and Van Dine's version of criminal reality was to chart the deep-seated urges that are so well concealed in respectable people. The plots usually centre on financial advantage and the dark side of the American acquisitive dream. They also, in another form of materialism, involve masses of physical data: Vance can work out and elaborately explain how a criminal bolted a door from the wrong side. The enormous popularity of the books arose no doubt in part from their high polish, bringing the new American value of sophistication to crime fiction – Wright had before his illness been editor of the New York social-mobility magazine *The Smart Set* – as well as the notion that close observation in the context of masculine learning (quite different from the values of Poirot) was a credible fictional defence system.

Van Dine's success in European Americana weakened under the rise of the West Coast private-eye stories, but he was by no means the last American to recreate with success the special limits of the clue-puzzle. 'Ellery Queen' was the name under which two cousins, Frederick Dannay and Manfred B. Lee, wrote the most closely argued and obsessively detailed of all clue-puzzles, using a detective also called Ellery Queen. With a number of resemblances to Philo Vance (Nevins, 1974: 17–18), he is an amateur (in fact a crime fiction author), though as his father Richard is a New York police inspector the ambience is semi-professional. Panek feels that the novels moved 'into the realm of games' and links this with the fact that Queen is the first writer to be self-conscious about the sub-genre which had very recently been codified by Van Dine and the English Monsignor Ronald Knox – Wells's efforts having been forgotten (1990, 133: 134). As the 'Challenge to the Reader' indicates, everything in a Queen clue-puzzle works – however improbably: Panek has a set of criticisms to make of *The Roman Hat Mystery* which he feels amount to genuine flaws in the logic (1990: 132). Not as foppish as Vance, but more elaborately intricate in his inquiries, Ellery Queen presides over a world highly mandarin in tone but also suddenly revealing the violence, malice and mutual hatred that can lurk in the modern metropolis.

The Ellery Queen team produced nine titles with, like Van Dine's, a repetitive pattern, from *The Roman Hat Mystery* (1929) to *The Spanish Cape Mystery* (1935) and into the 1970s they wrote many other mysteries in which, as Francis M. Nevins Jr says, 'Ellery gradually becomes less priggish' (in Reilly, 1980: 1230): these included the highly complicated series of four novels written as Barnaby Ross, using as detective a retired actor named Drury Lane – Nevins calls *The Tragedy of X* (1932) 'a book of staggering complexity, stunning ingenuity and dazzling fairness to the reader' (1974: 27). They edited crime fiction reprints and anthologies, as well as *Ellery Queen's Mystery Magazine* in which many of the major writers, not only of clue-puzzles, placed lucrative short stories. The Queen cousins, like Dorothy Sayers and Julian Symons in Britain, were influential in both the production and the criticism of crime fiction, and the range and impact of their work indicates how deeply rooted was the American version of the clue-puzzle.

A third major figure in that form was Rex Stout, creator of the impassive, even immobile, Montenegrin-American detective Nero

Wolfe. Based more on Mycroft than Sherlock Holmes, but also having links to Gaboriau's Tabaret and, perhaps more closely, as Isaac notes (1995), to the many 'Old' detectives from the American dime novels, Wolfe has an unusually energetic and sometimes even intelligent Watson in Archie Goodwin, who moves around the city gathering information and negotiating with characters on Wolfe's behalf – rather like Lecoq with Tabaret. Stout's novels are still basically clue-puzzles, though there is both romance – mostly for Archie – and a good deal of action, but it only rarely includes Wolfe himself. The first, *Fer de Lance* (1934), has some relationship with the melodramatics of the dime novels, especially in the snake in a packet, and both Wolfe's interest in business and Archie's hyperactive enthusiasm seem unlike the basically dry observant tone of the clue-puzzle proper. The detection involves understanding the possibilities of a golf club as a weapon and also a mysterious snake poison; that combination of the familiar and the exotic is characteristic of Stout, and in the same way Wolfe the eccentric orchid-fancier and beer-drinker can be both feyly idealistic and also bluntly material in his decisions and motives. There are, in the pace and the central figure's authority, as well as the series of dubious characters who through Wolfe's mediation find their way to gaol or to forgiveness, some striking ties with another hybrid figure, Erle Stanley Gardner's Perry Mason (see p. 122), and Stout's work shows both the strength of the clue-puzzle pattern in America and also an American-based extension of its limitations.

The three well-remembered writers, Van Dine, Queen and Stout were by no means the only American contributors to the clue-puzzle. One of the most striking was C. Daly King, a psychologist whose 'Obelists' series deploys academic psychologists as suspicious commentators on the crime (an 'obelist' is one who suspects), complete with references and footnotes, and uses one expert, Dr Pons, as a series detective along with Michael Lord of the police. Very detailed, and wavering between brilliantly ingenious and creakingly contrived, the series has a plethora of maps, charts, lists of clues. The first, *Obelists at Sea* (1932) is often referred to as the best, but *Obelists en Route* (1934), entirely set on a train and possibly inspiring Christie's *Murder on the Orient Express*, which appeared later the same year, is as densely conceived and mechanically adroit as anything Queen produced, though it was never published in America.

A lighter-hearted American clue-puzzler than King is Craig Rice (really Georgiana Randolph); her *8 Faces at 3* (1939) was the first of a series which used a puzzle form with a lawyer detective and a cheerful helping couple called, no doubt ironically, Justus. Rice liked dubious jokes, as in the later title *My Kingdom for a Hearse* (1957) and she Americanised the sub-genre with a light comedy tone not unlike Hammett's in *The Thin Man*. Because of this she has been described by J. Randolph Cox as 'the first writer of humorous hard-boiled fiction' (in Reilly, 1980: 1264), but she is more like an American Margery Allingham with some ingenious plots among the jazz-age ambience.

Further diluted than Craig Rice were the very successful, and still reprinted, adventures of the teenage sleuth Nancy Drew, starting in 1930 with *The Secret of the Old Clock*: the author's name was 'Carolyn Keene' (actually Mildred Wirt Benson at first, employed by the multiple publishers of romance, Edward Stratmeyer's Syndicate). Over 50 mysteries have been produced, selling towards a hundred million copies: Nancy remains 18, virginal, enthusiastic, super-intelligent, multi-skilled and consistently defending wealthy whites, with their faithful servants, mostly black, against the threat of foreigners, tramps and the unwashed in general. The popularity of these preposterous stories must derive, especially in their 1930s context, from the conservative charm of these fables about, as Bobbie Ann Mason puts it, 'a fading aristocracy, threatened by the restless lower classes' ([1975] 1995: 91), and the whole Drew phenomenon has attracted justified attention in recent years, with an essay collection edited by Dyer and Romalov (1995).

King, Rice and Keene do not exhaust the exotic American variants of the clue-based detective story. Before Van Dine wrote, the clue-puzzle was transplanted to the furthest American west by Earl Derr Biggers in the detection of Charlie Chan. The first, *The House without a Key*, is fully set in Hawaii and Sergeant Chan, 'the best detective on the force' (1925: 68) resolves an adventurous Pacific mystery, a sub-genre better known from Australia in the period (Knight, 1977: 164–5) – the actor Errol Flynn wrote a highly competent one called *Showdown* (1946). Charlie is physically unusual: 'very fat indeed' but with 'the light dainty steps of a woman' (1925: 68). That contradiction matches the combination of his over-rich and error-prone English (' "Appearance are a hellish liar," ' he says sagely, 1925: 110) with his subtle insights into what has happened. From the second novel, *The Chinese Parrot* (1926), on Charlie tends to be located mostly in California – where he originally worked as a house boy, a comment that, as with much of the representation of Chan, could be taken either as containing the figure or making it the more disconcerting. Much about Charlie Chan is stereotype, and his great success in early films must in some way operate as a euphemisation of a perceived Asian threat in America, yet the novels ensure that Charlie is the authority throughout. He was based on a real Honolulu detective, and Biggers, a thoughtful journalist, clearly meant him, as Landrum notes (1999: 123), to be an 'inverted image of the Oriental criminal mastermind', an antidote to the Eastern villains who swarmed through thrillers of the time. In spite of what now seem racist features, the Charlie Chan stories can be read as some move towards a multicultural recognition of America and the earliest of what Margaret J. King calls 'the cross-cultural detective' (in Reilly, 1980: 120).

V   ENGLISH VARIATIONS

The thirst for the clue-puzzle was strong in between-wars America, but there was nothing like the flood of writers who turned their hand to the mystery in England. In 1920, when Christie started, two other writers who were highly regarded at the time published their first novels. Freeman Wills Crofts's *The Cask* combined an exotic mystery (a body shipped around northern Europe in a barrel meant for a piece of sculpture, this and much more being organised by a master villain) with his famously plodding detail, concentrating, as in all his books, on the niceties of travel by rail. His famous detective did not emerge until 1925 in *Inspector French's Greatest Case*. For Crofts, it is a very dramatic title: he is the epitome of what Symons calls the humdrum, but his imperturbable mastery of detail and blank personality can still have a hypnotic quality.

Another figure from this year, H. C. Bailey, is now almost completely forgotten, but was at the time regarded as a major name. An established author of adventure novels before he turned to crime fiction in *Call Mr Fortune* (1920), he offered a collection of stories that were in sequence (this formal mix of the short story and the novel was a feature of the period – the Barr and J. S. Fletcher stories, Orczy's the 'Old Man in the Corner' and Futrelle's *The Diamond Master* were others in this hybrid mode). The boyish detective, Reggie Fortune, with a 'round and cheerful countenance and a perpetual appetite' (1920: 8) combined Dr Thorndyke's medical skills with the apparently foolish manner soon to appear in both Wimsey and Vance: Bailey is

likely to be the direct source of this feature, though Panek relates it
to P. G. Wodehouse's foolish hero Psmith (1979: 74). The stories can
be very lively: Fortune personally throws a villain to his death out
of a window, and Bailey writes with real vigour. He later created the
vulgar and self-seeking lawyer-detective Joshua Clunk and until
1950 published stories about both his detectives – even in the same
novel, as in *The Great Game* (1939).

The Fortune-like Lord Peter Wimsey was created by the formidable intellectual Dorothy L. Sayers in 1923, and by 1937 he had
appeared in 12 novels and three short-story collections. Sayers was
heavily involved in the London-based 'Detection Club', a basically
unserious assertion of the significance and structure of the clue-
puzzle form, and she was also, through her reviews and her confident introductions to several widely sold anthologies, a major force
in asserting the identity and the credibility of crime fiction. Others,
including the crime writers W. H. Wright, R. A. Freeman, and
cultural heavyweights who also wrote crime fiction like Monsignor
Ronald Knox and C. Day Lewis (writing as 'Nicholas Blake'), and
the young but very well-known poet W. H. Auden, were to con-
tribute to this self-conscious boosting of the clue-puzzle sub-genre,
indicating its social and cultural appeal, as well as this social
sub-class's power to make their obsessions seem important.

Sayers had in her time and since a powerful following, especially
among well-educated women readers, because of the feminised and
intellectualised masculinity of Lord Peter. Not all admired it:
Symons finds it hard to be positive about Sayers (1992: 122) and
Edmund Wilson was even more dismissive of her amplification than
of what he saw as Christie's aridity ([1945] 1974, 391–2). Her mysteries tend to be based on single tricks, like the haemophilia in *Have
His Carcase* (1932), the arsenic in *Strong Poison* (1930) or the missing
tube of white paint in *The Five Red Herrings* (1931), or centred on
highly improbable events like the murder methods of *Murder Must
Advertise* (1933) or *Busman's Honeymoon* (1937). As Panek shows
(1979: 72–111), Sayers had a varying level of commitment to the mystery as such – only *The Five Red Herrings* (1931) is a densely plotted
pure clue-puzzle. Gill Plain has argued for a development through
the novel series from an initially dysfunctional hero to a man who
finally conquers his military trauma through love (1996: 46–67);
another varying theme is women's roles, at first restricted to
Miss Climpson, Wimsey's spinster assistant, but expanding into the
major character Harriet Vane.

Sayers's novels compensate for their limited mystery plotting by containing a good deal of non-mystery material, rarely found so richly in other authors, such as the bell-ringing and local colour in *The Nine Tailors* (1934) or advertising in *Murder Must Advertise*. These elaborations can arouse strong responses – *The Nine Tailors* has especially divided audiences between distaste and devotion: Edmund Wilson thought it 'one of the dullest books I have ever encountered' ([1945] 1974: 392), while John Cawelti feels it is 'Sayers' best work' ([1976] 1988: 193). Equally charming or irritating to readers has been the recurrent and uncertain relationship, from *Strong Poison* on, between Wimsey and the detective novelist Harriet Vane; he falls in love as he rescues her from a charge of poisoning. A more thoughtful but also more romantic authorial self-portrait than Christie's Ariadne Oliver, Harriet is an early feminist figure and relates to Sayers's strong view, developed by the late 1920s, that puzzles alone are not enough, and that the mystery form should develop towards 'the novel of manners' ([1928] 1974: 108). Later she said more overtly that detective fiction should return to its origins in writers like Wilkie Collins and Sheridan Le Fanu and aspire to the status of 'a comedy of manners' ([1937] 1974: 209). Responses to this view and to Sayers's work in general are at their most extreme in the case of *Gaudy Night* (1935), a novel which spends much time bringing Lord Peter and Harriet nervously together, and so is in many ways outside the developed traditions of crime fiction: Sayers indicates her awareness of that by making it a mystery without a murder. As well as being a high-minded guide to Oxford, the novel explores fully the value of women's higher education and a range of kinds of fidelity; its tone is characteristic of the searching but sometimes playful intelligence Sayers brought to crime fiction.

A figure of some importance in the period, though now an object of interest only for specialists, agreed strongly with Sayers's view of the limited nature of the formal clue-puzzle. Anthony Berkeley Cox was a Detection Club enthusiast and as 'Anthony Berkeley' wrote *The Poisoned Chocolates Case* (1929), one of the most entertaining self-referential texts of the period (the other, much less well-celebrated, is Christie's witty *Partners in Crime*, also from 1929). Cox created Roger Sheringham, an anti-heroic detective (a Trent with brains and a bad temper), in the classic puzzle *The Layton Court Mystery* (1925) but before long he decided it was more important to write 'the story of a murder rather than the story of the detection of a murder' (1930: 7). To do this he exploited the potential of Freeman's 'inverted story', this time to foreground not the detective's cleverness but the rationale of the criminal – Cox, as it were, told a third story, unconsidered by Todorov, the one that lay beneath the criminal's behaviourial narrative and explained it.

He had written his Sheringham stories in thin disguise as 'Anthony Berkeley'; for this new venture he chose 'Francis Iles', the name of an ancestor – presumably not by accident, one who had been a smuggler (Turnbull, 1996: 5). In the first of his two major efforts in this direction, *Malice Aforethought* (1931), he explores the neurotic anxieties and dangerous fantasies of a mild-mannered husband and doctor turned callous murderer: the combination of Dr Bickleigh's actual insignificance and his private murderous hyperconfidence is highly effective. In some way the book is a diluted and demotic *Crime and Punishment*, but there is some residue of the clue-puzzle's final evaluative revelation in the neat trick by which Dr Bickleigh is executed not for his own crimes, but for a casual killing by one of his own victims. The book also, as Priestman puts it, 'carries an in-built safety-net in the comedic style typical of much golden-age writing' (1998: 41). A more thoroughly unsettling innovation is in *Before the Fact* (1932), which Hilfer calls 'a richer, stronger novel than *Malice Aforethought*' (1990: 92). In this the view-point is mostly that of a woman who loves a sociopathic husband. Steadily his folly and malice grow worse and develop into the murder of a friend. By the end it becomes clear that her own death will be the end of this relationship and, more unsettling still, that the title implies a general complicity with murder on her part and indeed that of the reader.

Julian Symons arranged his treatment of the 'golden age' so that the Francis Iles books were its climax, because he clearly felt that Cox in this mode was the most forward-looking writer of the period – though he was reluctant to credit Sayers in this category as well. Cox's work certainly points to the powerful work in the psychothriller of later writers like Margaret Millar, Symons himself and Patricia Highsmith. Like Sayers, he shows that the classic clue-puzzle was being rejected by some as soon as it was recognised as a sub-genre. While Sayers wanted to humanise the clue-puzzle through reducing the mechanics and increasing the colour, Cox went deeper. He was dissatisfied with one of the clue-puzzle's simplicities – the notion that the criminal is simply aberrant, a prejudice that gave great strength, as well as oversimplification, to Christie's work. Cox was able to turn the sub-genre's mastery of

detail, the obsession with formal completion and indeed the involvement of the reader in the process of the novel, into something a good
deal different from the run-of-the mill clue-puzzle. He shaped a fictional form that was used by other writers of the period whose work
has survived strongly, such as Patrick Hamilton, an author known
for his intensity in both politics and drinking (Thomas, 1987), whose
best novel *Hangover Square* (1941) advertises its psychiatric interest with its subtitle 'The Man with Two Minds', or Graham Greene,
whose 1930s thrillers strongly emphasise the consciousness of the
criminal, a process typified in *A Gun for Sale* (1936 – in the US, *This
Gun for Hire*) and culminating in his powerful *Brighton Rock* (1938).

Another writer who basically dissented from the colourless nature
of the classic clue-puzzle was Margery Allingham. With parents
who wrote historical and adventure stories, her work is always to
some degree elaborated: H. R. F. Keating uses the words 'rich and
romantic' to describe her approach (in Reilly, 1980: 29). Only some of
her books are formal mysteries focused on her recurrent detective
Albert Campion, a fey, insightful figure, who first plays a central
role in *Mystery Mile* (1930). He is mysteriously, and playfully, aristocratic or even royal in origin and sometimes, as in *Look to the Lady*
(1931), behaves in a princely way. The lively *Sweet Danger* (1933) is
an exotic mystery adventure, but in *Police at the Funeral* (1931)
Allingham showed she could write a sombre, though at times also
ironic, investigation of family betrayals, and *The Fashion in Shrouds*
(1938) both satirises London society and foregrounds Campion's talented and troubled sister. With a restless mind and verbally precise
intelligence Allingham uses the crime form, in its broadest possibilities, as a way of representing attitudes of the 1930s that range from
snobbery and a taste for sado-masochism to an almost child-like
desire for simplicity and fantasy.

VI   SUPPORTING CAST

If Sayers, Cox and Allingham in various ways sought both
escape from and complication of the pure puzzling and intimate
betrayals that Christie brought into formalised focus, many other
writers were happy to imitate the form without major variations.
Prime among them is the American John Dickson Carr, so prolific
that he also wrote as Carter Dickson. He started with a French
juge d'instruction Henri Bencolin, a sophisticated descendant of

Lecoq and Rouletabille, in richly detailed but not especially probing mysteries like *It Walks by Night* (1930), and, using the same
narrator, wrote some stories in the American tradition like the dense
Poison in Jest (1932), seeming like a masculine derivative of Rinehart.
But he became famous for highly intricate and richly coloured
novels featuring larger-than-life caricatures as detectives: first, and
most, Gideon Fell, a version of G. K. Chesterton with his learning,
bulk, and domination of every scene including criminal investigation, and after that, as Carter Dickson, he created Sir Henry
Merrivale, both bluff and shrewd and allegedly based on the pre-
war Winston Churchill (Panek, 1979: 163–4).

Very productive – with 22 Fell stories and 23 Merrivales to his
credit, as well as a number of one-offs – Carr cherished the locked-
room mystery and in Chapter 17 of *The Hollow Man* (1935: in
America *The Three Coffins*), Fell gave a famous lecture on approaches
to this ark of the clue-puzzle covenant. The novel, with its wonder-
fully intricate solution depending on mirrors, lights and tight time-
schedules is widely thought his finest performance, though many
also admire the more historically oriented and distinctly Gothic
detective-free *The Burning Court* (1937). All of Carr's work tends to
foreground the performing brilliance of the author in a way avoided
by most crime writers, and his literary references are as heavy as his
English nostalgia, both laid on with the passion of a convert. In the
same hyperbolic way, he saw gruesome and grotesque detail as a
central part of the form, as Joshi outlines (1990: 98–101). C. Day
Lewis, writing as 'Nicholas Blake', felt Carr's work has 'the mad
logic and extravagance of a dream' (1942: xxv): the combination of
rigorous explanation, very confident writing, emphatic literariness
and a sado-masochistic sub-text euphemised by those processes
gives the John Dickson Carr and Carter Dickson novels an unusually strong, even indigestible, flavour.

There were many other writers who did well in their time, attract-
ing occasional devotees even now, and exhibiting variations of the
major patterns. The London-based New Zealander Ngaio Marsh
was a lover of theatre who turned to crime fiction one wet day in
1931 (Lewis, 1991: 55): she named her detective Inspector Alleyn
after Christopher Marlowe's lead player. Her solutions can be very
contrived, as in *A Man Lay Dead* (1934), where the murder involves
someone leaving his bath, sliding head first down the banisters
and planting a curved knife into someone's back so precisely that
it penetrates his heart, but other solutions can be over-simple as

in *The Nursing Home Murder* (1935), where it is just a matter of changing gas cylinders in an operating theatre. Marsh's contexts, especially to do with theatre and art, are particularly effective and helped substantially towards her long-lasting success.

In a reverse process, an English migrant in Australia, Arthur Upfield, became the author of a series of stories that, with all the inauthenticity of the imperial spirit, located the clue-puzzle in out-back Australia and focused them on a part-aboriginal detective demeaningly named Napoleon Bonaparte. Typified by *Wings above the Diamantina* (1936 – in the US titled more plainly *Wings Above the Claypan*), the stories celebrate the grim splendour of the country and make some recognition of the alterity of native culture. But Bony's intelligence is at least half European; his dark side is never much more than a touristic totem and the novels seem both condescend-ing and naive in modern multicultural Australia; their world-wide popularity derived from American reprints (before they were avail-able in London) when US troops were in Australia in the early 1940s (Knight, 1997: 158–61).

There was no shortage in Britain of clue-puzzlers with ideas how to vary the form without altering it. Patricia Wentworth's Miss Silver, a quiet, hard-knitting, clear-thinking single woman appeared in 1928 in *Grey Mask*, her ninth novel: as Christie's Miss Marple appeared in 1930 it is conceivable that Miss Silver was her inspira-tion. Although this novel is in many ways a mystery adventure, as its title suggests, Miss Silver is announced as a 'sleuthess' (1928: 69) and is in charge of explanations, though she does not operate fully as a spinster-detective until *Lonesome Road* in 1939. Not always focusing on crime – some of the novels are also romances – and never very complex (Craig and Cadogan note that for her 'corrup-tion and goodness are absolute qualities', 1981: 178), Wentworth is nevertheless a sign of how important a woman's voice was for the audience. So is the work of Gladys Mitchell, the consciously feminist creator of Mrs (later Dame) Adela Lestrange Bradley, a government psychologist. Starting with *Speedy Death* (1929) and best known for *The Saltmarsh Murders* (1932), Mrs Bradley sweeps around in her large car, providing, Craig and Cadogan say, 'genuinely comic detection with serious undertones' (1981: 182). Though she some-times has only a marginal presence, as in the powerful *The Rising of the Moon* (1945) where Mitchell uses her experience as a school-teacher to realise the narrative vividly from a boy's view-point, Dame Adela is a strong force. Capable in the first novel of committing murder in a good cause, she is a feminist predecessor whose vigour matches that of her creator: an early member of the Detection Club, Mitchell's last novel, *The Mudflats of the Dead* was published 50 years later in 1979.

There are many specialists' favourites from the period who often go unmentioned by chroniclers: E. R. Punshon's *Crossword Mystery* (1934) reveals and exploits the link with other word-based puzzles of the time – the London Sunday newspaper *The Observer* had a famously demanding puzzle-setter named (for the Inquisition figure) Torquemada who also reviewed crime fiction. Major Cecil Street wrote many novels as 'John Rhode', possibly the plainest of all. An efficient plotter, thanked by Sayers in *Have His Carcase* for his help with the details, he wrote 72 novels featuring his main detective Dr Priestley, a diluted descendant of 'The Thinking Machine' and Dr Thorndyke, starting with *The Paddington Mystery* (1925), as well as 63 as 'Miles Burton' featuring police detectives. The only Poet Laureate to write crime novels (John Masefield restricted himself to historical fiction) was Cecil Day Lewis who in 1935 wrote, as 'Nicholas Blake', a mystery (allegedly to pay for a new roof). *A Question of Proof* introduced Nigel Strangeways, an attractive and, not surprisingly, very literary amateur detective, physically based upon W. H. Auden. The writing is sprightly and the plots are perfectly competent, but the most unusual feature of Blake's work is his liberal political position, which by the late 1930s had stiffened into the anti-fascism found in *The Smiler with the Knife* (1939). This used a combination of national ideology and vigorous action, usually the domain of right-wing adventure-story writers like 'Sapper' (H. C. McNeile), in order to expose the idea of a fascist coup in England. This is bravely opposed and somewhat improbably defeated, with a somewhat Pauline-in-Peril role being played by Strangeway's wife Georgia, an artist. With some gentlemanly assistance she saves England for democracy. It is hardly a proletarian position: Strangeways is described as 'a young Oxford man, who has taken to investigating crime' (1935, synopsis facing title-page), but even an *haut bourgeois* leftist voice was unusual in crime fiction of the period, though it was also heard in Montagu Slater and Maurice Richardson (see Croft, 1984) and, in the context of spy fiction, Eric Ambler.

Elizabeth Mackintosh, a Scottish physical education teacher, gained fame both as the playwright 'Gordon Daviot' and as a crime writer under the name 'Josephine Tey'. In 1929, she produced

The Man in the Queue (first published under the name Daviot),
a mystery dealing with lower-class criminals and confused crimes in
a London that presaged Graham Greene's uneasy world and used as
detective Inspector Grant, a thoughtful populist version of Wimsey
who gets everything thoroughly wrong – but in a spirit of realism,
not irony. There are some wry jokes – an actress called Ray Marcable
is for Panek a 'bilious pun' (1979: 15) – but the novel has a serious
realistic element: Talburt comments that Tey was 'ahead of her time
in recognising while writing her first novel the limitations of the fiction in which the great detective is the center' (1981: 53). A similar
spirit of new realism pervades the vivid waterside detail of
Josephine Bell's *The Port of London Murders* (1938). Both these
women writers bring to the formal puzzle, like a breath of foul air,
the kind of cross-class, credible realism that had been displayed
throughout the century by the most often ignored, because so
unclassifiable, of English crime writers, Edgar Wallace.

Born in 1875 and trained as a journalist in England and South
Africa, between 1906 when *The Four Just Men* appeared and 1932,
with *When the Gangs Came to London*, Wallace published 89 crime
titles, most of them dealing with domestic and international villainy
disturbing the peace of England and especially London. As David
Glover outlines (2003), his output was very varied. Some went close
to clue-puzzles like the short stories in *The Mind of Mr J. G. Reeder*
(1925) and many were crime adventures including police like the
best-selling *The Ringer* (1927), which started as a very successful stage play (Lane, 1938: 319–22), and told with relish of the dangerous return of a master criminal and multiple disguiser from
Australia to London. There is something of the nineteenth century
about Wallace: his vigorous, simplistic stories are often close in feeling to Vidocq and, as Glover has argued, to theatrical melodrama
(1995: xi–xii). His novels may not have appealed to the quotation-
hungry audience of Sayers or Allingham, usually being 'hybrids of
detection and adventure' (Glover, 1989: 73) but he had a substantial
readership in America and a massive one, still largely uncharted, in
translation through Europe that lasted until well after the Second
World War. The social and cultural power of those who wrote and
relished the clue-puzzle and its variants should not conceal the fact
that popular fiction, of an active and naive sort, continued to flour-
ish even in the England of Monsignor Ronald Knox: for every one
person who read a Christie, let alone a Sayers, there were ten who
read Wallace or Sexton Blake, and the actual broad-based audience

in England was not as different as that in America – with its own up-scale investigators – as many people on both sides of the Atlantic would seem to like to think.

VII THEMES AND EXPLANATIONS

Along with their ways of making the clue-puzzle appear significant by locating it in Oxford or substantial country houses, the Detection Club and their colleagues were great ones for speculating on the significance of the form. Sayers, following Wells, and curiously paralleling Régis Messac's book of 1929, in her well-known anthology introduction (1928) gave the clue-puzzle an antiquity to quell any sense of modern inauthenticity – Sophocles, Herodotus, the Bible, Voltaire were all bandied about as validations, if not sources. But other commentators explained the meaning of the clue-puzzle in modern terms. Chesterton's wish to give it a secularised religious role (1902) and C. Day Lewis's argument that the mystery compensated for 'the decline of religion and the end of the Victorian era' (1942: xx) were applauded in W. H. Auden's influential essay 'The Guilty Vicarage' ([1948], 1988). He asserted that the form mirrors the Christian world in bringing murder like a serpent into Eden, and in displacing guilt onto the single identifiable murderer as a scapegoat via 'the miraculous intervention of a genius from outside who removes guilt by giving knowledge of guilt' ([1948] 1988: 24). Combining the consolations of Christianity with the fashionable intellectualism of anthropology, the argument holds up as long as it is not applied to any actual stories, which show the initial situation as being fraught with tension, unlike Eden, and creating unacceptable infidelity, not expiable guilt, in the identified murderer. While Auden's approach meshed with the simplicity of the sense of evil found in Chesterton and Christie, satisfied that sin is in the world and can be cast out, it does not explain the obsessive nature of the recurrent quest for the signs of certain guilt.

A contemporary reading that interprets guilt in a quite different and certainly obsession-related way is Freudian. Marie Bonaparte read Poe in Freudian terms (1933), and it does not seem surprising that the story of murder in the night with mysterious stains, clues and signs of upheaval could be read as representing a child's fantasised view of parental sexual activity. Geraldine Pederson-Krag (1949) advanced this idea, elaborating in 'primal scene' terms an

earlier suggestion by Leopold Bellak that the violence gratifies the id
and the detective's actions represent the censoring order of the
superego (1945: 403–4). Charles Rycroft developed the specifically
sexual Freudian reading in his book *Imagination and Reality* (1968).
Few literary commentators have wanted to let crime fiction be controlled by such a strongly simplifying explanation, in spite of its
evident force and the neat relationship between the knowing but
innocent detective and the observing eye of the child in primal scene
theory. It has been easier to accept in a general way the link between
the clue-puzzle and a version of psychology more rigorous than
Poirot pretends to offer. Zizek's account of the detective as analyst
(1990 and 1992) has seemed the most acceptable, though there
may be a way of combining both a fully Freudian view and other
approaches, including broader psychiatric ones, offered by the
analysis of Richard Raskin, to be discussed below.

An essentially more conservative explanatory approach, in that it
consciously ignores content, is a formalist or structural one. Jacques
Barzun is the best-known advocate of appraising crime fiction in
terms of its technical aesthetic qualities, insisting that it is essentially
a folklore-like tale, albeit one with 'superior sophistication' (1961:
16). Thereby he removes it from a political present and dispenses
with any disturbing or exciting content it might have. Barzun is not
troubled by disagreeing with most readers: his formalist faith leads
him into the curious position of insisting that a 'pure detection'
Sherlock Holmes story like 'The Six Napoleons' is much better than
the famous adventure-like story 'The Speckled Band' – a judgement
which suggests the limits of an approach based on evaluating technique above content. The more rigorously structuralist approach of
Todorov (1977), reading the sub-genre in terms of its double narrative, one by the narrator and the other hidden by the murder and
deciphered by the detective, is itself in principle content-free, but is
such a potent tool for disentangling the stories that it has value for
analysis of content and indeed ideology. The influence of Northrop
Frye's primarily descriptive genre-based approach leads Grella also
to read the form as a form of folk-tale, the sort of harmless thing that
people just do ([1976] 1988), while Panek follows Frye in seeing the
whole activity as being ludic, without conflict, and insisting the
audience must just admire these strange and engaging practices
(1979: 18–19). John Cawelti also links his structural analysis to Frye,
seeing crime fiction as primarily 'a ritual drama' (1976: 90), but he is
consistently aware of the context and the audience and what they
make culturally, if not politically, of the patterns they enjoy.

If these authors tend to treat crime fiction as a basically cultural phenomenon, value-free and without sociopolitical implications, some other explanations for the rise and the power of the clue-puzzle seek to relate it more firmly to context. Post-war angst is often seen as being dissipated by the sub-genre. Some analysts think that the fiction works by ignoring the conflicts of the time – Priestman sees it as 'A Version of Pastoral' (1990, the title of Chapter 9); others feel the sub-genre displaces these pressures into manageable form – Max Perkins, Van Dine's editor, saw here 'the anxieties and afflictions of a tragic decade' (Tuska, 1971: 20). One of the most thorough investigations of the displacing mechanisms at work in the clue-puzzle form of crime fiction is an essay by Richard Raskin, which sees four levels on which it engages the reader's attention (1992). One is simply 'Ludic', the author's game-playing with the reader, who enjoys the sport; the second is 'Wish-fulfillment Functions', involving the reader's identification with murderer, detective and victim – sado-masochism appears here as a significant element. Then Raskin describes the more elusive 'Tension-Reduction Functions' in which anxiety is successfully displaced through the punishment of the villain and, more unnervingly, the death of the wishfully vulnerable victim, a theme Zizek has explored further in his discussion of the detective as something of an analyst, but one who relocates rather than identifies guilt (1990 and 1992). Finally, and very broadly, Raskin refers to 'Orienting Functions' which deal with social myths, or what might be more realistically called ideologies: the issues of class, race, gender, the underlying – and so pervasively persuasive – politics of crime fiction, patterns which have been discussed by sociopolitically oriented commentators such as Knight (1980), Porter (1981) and Mandel (1984).

Raskin's analysis relies heavily on the male-gendered premises of Freudian theory, and feminist crime fiction writers provide different forms of identification and tension-reduction, as will be discussed in Chapter 8, but to read Raskin's categories against major crime fiction texts is to find much to discuss. He suggests with considerable strength that this form did not succeed just because it posed good puzzles, but because the good puzzles were also able to encode a deep and disturbing range of ideological issues at a level that was both personal and social.

In both areas the US-based innovators of the private-eye form were different from the clue-puzzlers, whether they came from England or America.

5

The American Version

I ORIGINS AND ATTITUDES

In the nineteenth century, as Part I has shown, American writers both adapted European patterns to their own circumstances, as with Charles Brockden Brown and Anna Katherine Green, and also developed patterns based on features of their own culture, like the wealth of private-detective fiction from Jem Brampton to Nick Carter. Poe is in both camps, seeming somehow based in both Paris and New York at the same time. Largely unnoticed as it has been, there was a richness and a variety about the kinds of American crime fiction in the nineteenth century that survived into the twentieth century: writers like Wells and Rinehart were substantially innovative and America-based, while the New York clue-puzzlers were effective adaptors of a European model. But the position is more complex with those writers who shaped what has become an enduring image of American fiction, and indeed the American consciousness. The creators of private-eye fiction combine tradition and innovation much as Poe did before them – and with his world-wide impact.

The general impression is that one magazine and two writers basically invented a new form of crime fiction that started in *Black Mask* (a curiously old-fashioned name: the tough crooks never wore masks, not even the cowboys who sometimes appeared), and was developed especially by Captain Joseph Shaw who edited the magazine from 1926. The usual story is that Dashiell Hammett in the 1920s first created the adventures of a solitary, honest private detective among the corruptions and betrayals of the modern American city, and Raymond Chandler in the 1930s brought wit and a literary polish to the newly identified sub-genre. This narrative is almost entirely based on Chandler's own arguments in the famous and highly persuasive essay 'The Simple Art of Murder' (1944). He separated what he insists is modern American realism from what he

110

stigmatised as the unrealistic, irrelevant and in any case feeble mysteries of, in a memorable phrase, the 'Cheesecake Manor' school, meaning Christie, Sayers and their followers. To the American version he allots a reality about crime and a type of language that are contemporary and urgently real, and for them he claims a vigorous morality based on the detective who is 'neither tarnished nor afraid' ([1944] 1974: 237), in spite of his threatening environment.

It is rare for critics to accept so fully the self-analysis of a writer, but there has been little dissent from this view in America, nor indeed in England where Chandler had high status while still writing – *Trouble is My Business* (1950) *The Long Goodbye* (1953) and *Pearls Are a Nuisance* (1953) all appeared first in London. But in spite of its general acceptance, Chandler's critique of the English clue-puzzle as mechanistic and trivial overlooks the actual tensions and complexities of the sub-genre and is clearly for him – as for many later American commentators – a way of positioning the American model as being more truth-telling and indeed more masculine. The tough detective was seen as a modern but also traditional American hero, like the earlier pathfinder or cowboy, an idea offered by Leslie Fiedler (1960: 476) and influentially elaborated by George Grella ([1974] 1988: 106–10). Few have dissented from this view, at least before feminists made their critique of the private eyes: William Ruehlmann is unusual in making the title of his book *Saint with a Gun* (1974) ironic, relating the image of the private eye to the self-validating violence of the vigilante culture in America.

This highly valued, even nationally focal, hero became internationally known especially through film: the vigorous action, limited dialogue and stress on personal relationships converted to the screen very well, and a major impact was made by the work of outstanding directors such as John Huston with *The Maltese Falcon* (1941) and Howard Hawks with *The Big Sleep* (1946), translating the dangerous personal encounters and city settings of the novels into the style that became known as *film noir*. Film as a genre favoured the action and attitudinising of the private-eye form, while the characters of the clue-puzzle, whether reticent or self-mocking, fitted awkwardly into the hyperbolic style of Hollywood film, and there were also technical problems: the partly concealed clues of the Christie style of crime fiction were much harder to film effectively – the camera overstresses the clues. So film, the dominant technique of American culture, powerfully transmitted the private-eye detective as an icon of the national self-concept.

But in spite of this canonisation of the modern American urban crusader, a study of the texts reveals a range of ways in which they do not in fact descriptively match Chandler's persuasive eulogy, and also ways in which they may seem less evaluatively admirable than in his presentation. Crime writing with violent action went back a long way in America, certainly to the 1860s with Jem Brampton and the beginning of the dime novels: the idea of a lone moral hero cleansing the filth of the modern city is basic to the popular detection of the late nineteenth century. This is also true of language. The tough talk of the private-eye world has been accepted in Chandler's terms as a distinctively new American form of realism by Jameson (1970) and felt by Narremore to represent a post-war 'suspicion of noble language' (1983: 53), but the earlier dime detectives spoke with a brisk and brusque style that was quite un-British, and so did the ethical criminal 'Boston Blackie' created by Jack Boyle who appeared in *Redbook* magazine from 1919 on.

Another area of possible dissent from Chandler's arguments lies in the crimes that the tough-guy writers dealt with. He insists that it is modern, corrupt, gangster-ridden America that the hero will fictionally cleanse, and that this is a crucial difference from the private and artificial concerns of the English form. In fact, as will be discussed below, while the early stories of Hammett and Chandler do deal specifically with gangsters, and while Hammett always retains some sense of social crime, in the private-eye novels the real crimes solved, the deepest threats faced by the private eyes, come from personal betrayals, mostly by women. Gangster corruption is in the private-eye tradition almost always a smoke-screen for treacheries every bit as personal as those represented in uncamouflaged form in the Christie tradition.

That persistent personalisation of the private-eye form is not so surprising when the heavily individualist nature of the sub-genre is considered: the private eye operates alone, judges others by himself, shares no one's values and mores. Nor even facts: he rarely detects very much, using his movements, observations, consciousness (and his frequent unconsciousness) as his primary method of unravelling a mystery. He is I rather than eye, and his story is in the first person – again, with the exception of much of Hammett's work.

It is through this sense of isolation that the private-eye story is in fact most innovative, bespeaking a sense that social values, communal mores, have no real value. This is a distinct difference not only from the English clue-puzzle and its socially 'centered' detectives

(Malmgren, 2001: 147–8) – even including odd figures like Poirot (Danielsson, 2002: 47) – but also from the earlier American detectives. Whether 'Old' and inclined to be passively wise or energetic like Brampton, Pinkerton and especially Nick Carter, they were much more positive, fully committed to the can-do, know-how atmosphere of American social and business activity. The world-weary feeling of the Hammett–Chandler detective seems related to a growing dismay with modern mercantile society – a theme already found in Rinehart and Van Dine, but also general in the post-war period, with its recurrent sense of lost dreams and the dangers of over-sophistication. Where Jem Brampton or Nick Carter functioned without problems as the implicit agents of a respectable, law-abiding and business-like community, devoted to rooting out the thieves, fraudsters and cobra-carrying menaces who threatened the social order, personal safety and prosperity of the American citizen, the between-wars private eye has a much more personal quest and a much more individualised set of values.

The setting is a crucial part of this modern and innovative sense of anomie, in the shapeless, valueless, traditionless cities of the far west, places that could be described, like Mike Davis's Los Angeles, as a 'deracinated urban hell' (1990: 38). A compulsive image of the private eye is alone on watch on the street, on the move to another scene of danger in his car, even, as counterpoint to the usual rapid movement, alone and inactive in his office. Innate rectitude, determination and bravery are coupled with isolation, and this mechanism is inscribed in the plots in an extraordinarily compulsive feature. Over and over again the detective is told, or realises, that the case on which he has been employed is now over – usually about a quarter or a third of the way through the book. But he always decides to continue with his inquiries, to satisfy himself and some personal sense of justice. Though the private eye is a professional – a paid worker like most people – he is not, in the crucial part of the story, an employee: his time, his courage, above all his values, are controlled by himself. He is as far from the real working police and positive social agents as he is from gangsters and their negative social operations.

II HAMMETT'S INITIATIVE

If Chandler is to the private-eye story the Sayers who defends the sub-genre and its literary qualities, in a different way Hammett is curiously like Sayers in that he challenged the limits of the form and – more like Cox in the deep-seatedness of his rejection – was never satisfied with the simple structure that others happily used. Hammett never wrote two books in the same mode, though a number of his early short stories do repeat a pattern that is the basis for the private-eye story and were the acknowledged core of *Black Mask*. What makes it all the clearer that Hammett is the originator of this potent form is that in one story he appears to show the reader consciously what he is doing.

'The Tenth Clew' is a very early 'Continental Op' story, appearing in *Black Mask* in March 1924 (reprinted in 1975, ed. Marcus). It opens much like *Trent's Last Case*: an important man's body has been found, with some mysterious objects on it. After looking into the case, the Op sums up nine particular clues of the traditional kind, including a typewriter, a false list, a threatening letter. The dead man's shoe is, as in *The Hound of the Baskervilles*, missing but then reappears. It seems as if Hammett is deliberately parodying the techniques of classic detection, from Sherlock Holmes via Trent to Hercule Poirot. But the Op decides to abandon all that – the 'tenth clew' is that the other nine are all artificial, fabricated by the criminal as nonsense. So the Op does not sit around puzzling over clues, or clews, but plunges off into detective activity of the Pinkerton kind that America had seen in fiction before and Hammett had personally experienced. The Op watches, questions, acts, is knocked out, flung into San Francisco Bay, manages to survive, and in his turn knocks out the criminal he can now, as a result of his vicissitudes, identify. The pace of the story and the intense self-commitment of the detective shape the private-eye story on the deliberate ruins of the clue-puzzle.

The characters and context of the early Hammett stories involve professional criminals – as in the very violent, almost documentary account of a major attack on a city's banks in 'The Big Knockover' and its sequel '$106,000 Blood Money' (reprinted in 1966, ed. Hellman) where the surviving criminals, to the Op's great advantage, fall out for the money. Or the villains can just turn to violent crime as in 'The Gutting of Couffignal', where a similar raid is organised by Russian emigrés – Hammett's sources quite often have internationally exotic elements, like the mysterious Maltese Falcon itself. Here the Op becomes personally involved enough at least to admire the female criminal, but he does not allow her to get away – though, like Sherlock Holmes, he can at times dispense justice beyond the mechanism of the law, it will be based on social, not personal judgements: here, as she expects his admiration to let her escape, he plants a shot in her shapely calf.

Chandler paid warm and very persuasive tribute to Hammett's style: it is vigorous and always clear, but also quirky, with occasional unusual phrases or a piece of fastidious description to slow and re-focus the rapid action and invest the Op with a depth of knowing – in 'The Tenth Clew' O'Gar the detective 'dresses like the village constable in a movie' (1975: 25). A less immediately obvious emphatic feature is the shortness of the chapters, or, in the stories, demarcated segments. On a pages-per-chapter count, Hammett is the shortest of all the private-eye writers, with many of his stories and novels having on average only five pages, sometimes even less, as a brisk segment of action and reaction to make a chapter. In the much more expansive *The Maltese Falcon*, largely because of two unusually long final chapters, the average is close to ten pages per chapter – but Christie is always above that and can go as high as fifteen pages per chapter: Sayer's norm is a good deal more.

In plot and in style, the private eyes seem less likely than clue-puzzlers to dwell on matters, whether they are relevant to the story or not, but this does not mean that they do not include material outside the crime itself. Hammett had been a private detective and had life-long left-wing views and in his first novel, *Red Harvest* (1929, serialised in *Black Mask* in 1927–8), a deliberately tough view of detecting on the street combines with a radical critique of modern American society. Personville, pronounced Poisonville, is a site of industrial oppression and public corruption, both of which include the police. The detective, here still a Continental Op, to tidy things up sets crook against crook and sees some very rough justice done. His motives seem largely social and his target is the corruption that Chandler was later to identify as the sub-genre's main opposition. But the text is more personalised than is sometimes thought. The Op lets himself, as if subject to his own corruption, slide into the world of drinking and violence, even feels himself becoming 'blood-simple' ([1929] 1963: 137). He wakes after a night's dissipation to find himself clutching an ice-pick buried in Dinah Brand's breast, and facing a murder charge. He is able to extricate himself from his own involvement and the charge of murder, yet his final position is isolated, and less than triumphant as a corruption-fighter: he doubts that the town will be 'a sweet-smelling and thornless bed of roses' ([1929] 1963: 190). This is neither the realistic account that

Chandler offered nor the heroic crusade that popular reaction has bestowed on the private eye. Romantic only in its appreciation of nihilism, and realistic only in its sense of the inability to change modern urban culture, *Red Harvest*, like *The Woman in White* or *The Murder of Roger Ackroyd*, is one of those genre-shaping books that were never quite matched again, and whose effect was inherently diluted to make it repeatable and acceptable.

Hammett himself did not so much reduce the impact of his first crime-exploring novel as move away from it; in *The Glass Key* (1931), which he thought his best, he produced a story of restrained subtlety focused on a semi-criminal but ultimately heroic figure who finally withdraws from crime into tentative romance. Symons praised it simply as a novel, not just a crime story, saying Hammett here used 'violent events to comment by indirection on life, art, society' (1992: 158). Hammett did not use in these novels a first-person narration to validate the hero's lonely identity, but he has the power to convey interpretations through a Hemingwayesque loading of third-person narration with suggestions about how a character feels and works. By leaving a greater ambiguity about the actual feelings, Hammett can in fact – as with Ned Beaumont in *The Glass Key* – suggest greater depths and vulnerabilities than seem available to Philip Marlowe and his never-ending flow of controlling responses.

Mediated by a third-person voice as it is in Hammett, the individualist escape is the major journey made by the private-eye heroes, but Hammett takes it towards existential nihilism. In *The Maltese Falcon* (1930) Sam Spade's friendship with Archer and affair with his wife appear to have no personal emotive meaning, and that brutal isolation, and a sense of automaton-like rectitude, is the point of the famous ending: Sam Spade asserts a form of communal duty that is also a threat to his own personal happiness when he finally decides to turn in for murder the woman he probably loves. In *The Thin Man* (1934) Nick Charles has a marriage and a busy social circle, but he has withdrawn into alcoholism in a way that suggests the hard-drinking Hammett here ironises himself: Narremore has suggested that here he is 'satirising his form' (1983: 69), but there may be a darker interpretation. In this his last novel the missing man, buried in the cellar, is as famously thin as Hammett was himself, and it is tempting to read the story as Hammett's dark prediction of his own incipient silence. He remains a major, if always enigmatic and elusive influence and figure, rather than, like Chandler, a producer of a clear and imitatable model of the new sub-genre.

III CHANDLER'S VARIATION

Neither Hammett's flexibility nor verbal restraint is matched by Raymond Chandler. Although he has the reputation of an art novelist, with fine style, incisive insights into modern life via a well-judged mixture of contempt and positive feeling, Chandler's novels are in many ways the work of a formulaic series producer. He uses consistently the same central character, speaking in the same voice, in the same setting and with a remarkably similar range of characters and plot elements. Where Hammett was always experimental – and perhaps ran out of energy for that reason – Chandler worked a narrow vein in crime fiction, effectively formularising his sub-genre much as Christie had done. The five novels from *The Big Sleep* (1939) to *The Little Sister* (1949) are very similar in technique. *The Long Goodbye* (1953) is longer, more intensely evaluative and, some feel, sentimental – and has a higher page per chapter account accordingly – but is no more than an elaborated Marlowe novel. *Playback* (1958), originally written as a film script without Marlowe (*Raymond Chandler's Unknown Thriller*, 1985), is in novel form a late version of the formula, having more sexual licence, a (no doubt related) reduced aggression towards women and a maturer kind of disconnection from the world.

Chandler's life seems less coherent than the pattern of the novels. Born in Chicago, he was educated in England at Dulwich College, a high-class private school in a leafy part of depressed south London – the British fascination with class divides remained with Chandler to the end. Clever at school, he worked for the government in London afterwards, and wrote youthfully fluent and earnest prose and poetry for the London magazines (Chandler, 1973, ed. Bruccoli). He returned to America in 1912 and worked in the Californian oil business, a far remove from the world of Georgian poetry.

Chandler turned out, it seems, a poor employee, given to drinking and some extramarital activity, as if he was beginning to live the life of a Hammett character. Writing about them was certainly his interest when he lost his job and he published in *Black Mask* and other magazines from 1933 on. He started uncertainly: typical is the over-elaborate and over-sentimental novella 'Pearls are a Nuisance' – the hero Walter Gage talks 'the way Jane Austen writes' ([1953] 1964: 45), the pearls were never faked out of the old jeweller's unrequited love for the old lady, and Henry the giant chauffeur and obvious criminal likes Walter too much to avenge his retrieval of the pearls. In later stories, like 'Finger Man', where the hero is Marlowe, or the substantial John Dalmas sequence of novellas such as 'Red Wind' and 'Trouble is My Business', the initial themes of male homosociality, the narrator's elevated perceptions and the presence of feeling are brought into control with a plot containing far more action than before and a tighter, even ironic, hold on moments of sentiment. What Chandler learnt from Hammett was to control the over-rich feelings and stylistic mannerisms of a young literary person through the self-consciously tough and obsessively active self-concept of an American idea of heroic manhood that went back into the nineteenth century but worked very well as a response to, and also withdrawal from, the mean streets of modern America.

Chandler turned to the novel from the story ten years after Hammett, and he managed the generic transition – structural to the development of crime fiction itself – by turning stories into novels by linking them, usually through making two characters into one. Chandler wryly called this 'cannibalisation' and, as Durham shows (1963: 124–9), it was the basis of three of his first four novels – not *The High Window* (1943), similar though it seems to the others. There is an advantage to Chandler in the fact that the novels are either based on two stories or fall easily into two halves. They are not plot and sub-plot, nor yet Todorov's distinction between the detective's narrative and the murderer's narrative. Rather, the Chandleresque double story makes the whole feel of the narrator's experience the more mysterious, errant; it gives a dream-like, even modernist, feel to the strange narrative locations where Marlowe must attend.

The 'cannibalisation' process suggests that plotting was not as important to Chandler as characterisation and style, but his plots work well in their deliberately meandering way. Obviously he was not as focused on plot as the clue-puzzle writers, but scepticism is recommended about the story so loved by unreflective journalists: that when Hawks asked him during the filming of *The Big Sleep*, he did not know who kills Owen Taylor. It is perfectly clear in the novel, when carefully read, and if Chandler chose not to tell Faulkner and Hawks, perhaps it was because he felt they might read the novel and find out in return for their huge Hollywood incomes.

The outcomes of the private-eye stories deserve attention in general. In Hammett everyone, including the detective, is more or less criminal. In Chandler, as in Christie, there will be a final identification of a bad person who has soured the world and threatened the detective, not only with failure but usually with death or at least disgrace. For Christie there will be a constant, reader-teasing variation in the nature, age, status, gender of the villain, but Chandler is more consistent in his demonisation. In 'The Simple Art of Murder' he traced crime to corruption and gangsterism, but his practice does not pursue this scheme. The early novellas, notably the bravura 'Finger Man' (which mysteriously has never been filmed) do tend, like Hammett's Op stories, to deal with realistic gangsters and the ways that their feudal activities, and their feuding, impact on ordinary lives.

But when it comes to the novels, a short story originally with a gangster theme, like 'Killer in the Rain' is in *The Big Sleep* used as a preliminary offer of corruption, but a story with a much more personal focus, 'The Curtain', is structurally dominant. The mad girl killer of 'The Curtain' is made the same as the girl who is pestered by gangsters in 'Killer in the Rain' and so Chandler constructs a pattern where the opening part of the novel deals with criminals, gangsters, the threatening dark streets as so much developed in 'The Simple Art of Murder', but as the novel continues these issues fall away and we find that the lost gangster, Rusty Regan, has been killed for entirely personal reasons – which bear threateningly on Marlowe himself in the final scene (for fuller discussion of this pattern see Knight, 1980: 153–8 and Roth, 1995: 26). The gangsters are either easily mastered people, like Joe Brody; or those whose villainy is directed personally at Marlowe, not society, like Lash Canino; or they are admirable men who understand and even value Marlowe, like the nobly named Eddie Mars. There may well be corrupt cops as in *Farewell My Lovely* (1940) but they too are presented as a personal threat to Marlowe and in *The Lady in the Lake* (1944) the murderously bad cop betrays not the community he serves but a woman he has loved. With both police and gangsters, the emphasis on personal values and personal dangers tilts the plot away from the kinds of criminal reality that Chandler argued for in 'The Simple Art of Murder', though it is striking to see how the film of *The Big Sleep*, made in the strong Hollywood tradition of gangster realism, constructs a new retributive climax where Eddie Mars dies from his own men's guns.

If the threat of gangsters and corruptions is in Chandler's novels a charade, real villainy is simple and consistent: it was a woman who did it. As a rule, the detective will be finally threatened with death, humiliation, identity-erasure by a woman whose physical attractions are only matched by the depths of her infidelity and depravity. Rabinowicz has argued that these woman-focused endings are deliberately incomplete, and that the reader really understands that the gangsters are still out there, unpunished (1987: 200–5). But this view seems to match neither the final self-satisfaction of the woman-freed detective nor the attractive names given to the genial gangsters like Eddie Mars in *The Big Sleep* and Laird Brunette in *Farewell My Lovely*.

Here it is only women who are in disguise, as Chandler presents a dramatic series of murderous masquerades. The pretty, amoral Carmen Sternwood, the torch singer turned millionairess Velma Grayle, the demonic, multiform Muriel Chess, the less than deadly but still secretive secretary Merle Davis coupled with the brutal and dragon-like Mrs Murdock, the vicious screen star Dolores Gonzales, the coolly deadly beauty Eileen Wade, but not, finally, the troubled Betty Mayfield in *Playback* – the treacherous women of Chandler's novels reveal a deeply gendered set of evaluations at the core of his novels, never so clear as when in *The Big Sleep* Marlowe rejects in horror the naked Carmen, and she hisses at him, a serpent in woman's clothing who later tries to put him to death – a dragon in all but appearance (Knight, 1995).

This dark revelation of masculine anxiety is very striking when compared to the cheerful heterosexuality of the film of *The Big Sleep*. But the sexist violence of Chandler's resolutions is thoroughly, if not completely, euphemised by the bouncy wit and topographic vitality of the fiction. In Marlowe's constant driving and sense of Los Angeles' topographic grandeur Chesterton would have found his urban saga. Chapters often begin with an address: the first megalopolis is realised and explored, relished both for immediate ill and a persistent underlying sense of excitable good in these novels of self against, and in, the city.

Style is another benign force. We know how witty and sensitive Philip Marlowe is because he tells us, all the time, in his images and implications as much as in his direct dialogue with characters. Moving from the stories into the novels, Chandler steadily perfected similes that only Chaucer has matched for point and punch, as in 'old men with faces like lost battles' (*The High Window* [1943] 1951: 60). He developed real mastery, markedly better than Hammett's, in varying the pace and intensity of the story, interweaving action, description and introspection skilfully and using two forms of dialogue – Marlowe to ordinary people and Marlowe, far more eloquent, to himself and the reader. Though Chandler theorised the private-eye story as Sayers did the clue-puzzle, his impact was that of a west-coast Christie, giving it a confident shape, a distinctive style, and providing many less gifted writers with a model to aim for: they could miss by a distance, but still write acceptable versions of the form. His rewards were in some ways considerable – he revelled in English admiration – but were never financially enormous; yet his ambitions were so literary that to have so powerfully moulded a sub-genre would probably satisfy this querulous but deeply gifted man. His work has certainly lasted, and better than that of Hammett, who retains the pathfinder's honour but is much more rarely in print now. And this may well be in part due to the sheer vitality of Chandler's writing: many women readers are well aware of the sexist thrust of his books but still revel in and read against the grain his elegant, supple, multivocal style, or styles – almost as if that flexible, reactive voice has itself, ironically, escaped from the confines of the blunt masculinity of the usual private-eye novel, and has achieved a double-gendered persona that Chandler's heroes, and conceivably Chandler himself, could never admit as possible.

Between them Chandler and Hammett tower in complexity, contradiction and conundrum over the other writers in the sub-genre, more even than Christie dominates the clue-puzzle: her mastery is primarily of technique alone. And this may in part explain why, although the last 40 years have seen literally thousands of Marlowe and Spade imitations in novel, film and comic, in the 1930s and 1940s there were not in fact many to pick up the form of private-eye fiction. There had been a substantial school of writers for *Black Mask*, as there were scores of English clue-puzzle writers, but even the best of them, like Carroll John Daly and Raoul Whitfield, did not make the transition of Hammett and Chandler into successful novels and so into giving the hero the expansive powers to judge, condemn and even execute the modern world for its corruptions, particularly those that impinge on the free spirit of the sensitive individual. With the sort of alchemy that occurs in rapidly changing societies (and had been present at the birth of the sensation novel 60 years before), out of a crassly masculinist mode of writing, as banal in value as it was limited in vocabulary, came a form that exhibited at once the personal aspirations and the painful limitations of contemporary American manhood.

IV   OTHER AMERICAN CRIME WRITERS

The private-eye model was not the only possibility, or the only success, that came from the west coast. One of the early *Black Mask* writers was Erle Stanley Gardner, a Californian lawyer turned writer. In his early novels Perry Mason was like his earlier namesake Randolph, a ferocious defender of people's rights against the apparent power of the law. As Gardner went on, Mason's practices became less sharp, though he always has elements of cunning and stealthy preparation in his battle against the law. Though the structure of the stories is quite unlike that of the tough detective's inquisitive ramblings – actual detecting is allotted to Mason's assistant Paul Drake and is usually off-stage – and though the climaxes are in court not in a gunfight in some seedy location, Gardner's characters are much the same as the over-sharp businessmen, the money-hungry women and the identity-changing minor players who throng the world of the private-eye novel. But for all their alienated Californian context, the precision of the stories and their great use of physical evidence makes Gardner's novels basically a hybrid of the clue-puzzle style and the private-eye world, and accordingly they place great emphasis on plot and little on characterisation and colour.

Another major difference is that the central figures in Hammett and Chandler are full of self-doubt and possible guilt, but though Mason may be suspected of weakness and sometimes crime by the police and even his loyal but untouchable secretary Della Street, he is always in charge: he has disciplinary power as a Foucauldian panoptician of the west coast. The closed-off, formulaic certainty of the Mason stories made them especially successful on television, more so than Gardner's more open other work, a partly comic series with Bertha Cool and Donald Lam (written as A. A. Fair), and a shorter set of novels foregrounding in Doug Selby the kind of troubled district attorney that Mason routinely humiliated. From the beginning, with *The Case of the Velvet Claws* (1933) through 81 more instances, the Mason titles are repetitive and slightly playful in form, epitomising a technically skilful, undemanding, unthreatening and immensely successful series.

A different type of certainty was even more successful than Gardner's. Mickey Spillane's first novel, *I the Jury* (1947), opens with Mike Hammer waking from drunken sleep to see his army buddy lying murdered. This situation would bring trouble for Marlowe or the Op, but the police never suspect Hammer – partly on evidence but basically because the text never places his authority, moral and physical, in any doubt. Hammer is a blunt instrument, an imperme-able hero fired with missionary violence in support of an unques-tionable right. Moving very quickly, Hammer and the story pursue a personal vengeance the police are not trusted to deliver. There is little trace of Hammer being actually employed as a detective: all his frenetic detecting through corrupt New York is on personal grounds in the service of his own dedicated vigilante ethics. He is at a sort of raging ease with women: his secretary, Velda, is an inviolate beauty (though occasionally we can relish her torture by soon-to-be-annihilated villains), glamorous vamps offer themselves to Hammer, occasionally with brief success, but he regularly has an ideal woman like the beautiful Charlotte of the first novel, whom he mis-takenly adores like an adolescent and cannot bring himself to defile.

This mix of sadism and fantasy – Fiedler called it 'brutal semi-pornography' (1960: 477) – races to a violent conclusion. The Hammer novels are famous, or notorious, for their ferocity: petty criminals are savagely beaten, treacherous and less than masculine men are cruelly killed and, most memorable of all, the lovely and deified Charlotte, who is behind all the evil, is with sadistic care shot in the stomach as she finally strips in an attempt to distract Hammer from his vengeance. Yet Spillane is in some ways a skilled crime fic-tion writer. Even his severest critic, Anthony Boucher, agreed that he was 'one of the last of the great story-tellers in the pulp tradition' (quoted in Collins and Traylor, 1984: 27). The structure is lucid, with-out confusing sub-plots, and with more detection and clues than are found in Hammett or Chandler. Written with pace and impact (though not with Hammett's disturbing staccato effect – the page-per-chapter count is quite high), the Hammer novels create an unproblematised American masculinity, bringing the blunt voice of the comic strips for which the young Spillane wrote dialogue to the previously rather complex private-eye story.

Spillane, unlike either Hammett or Chandler, consistently con-denses the corruption theme with personal betrayal – Charlotte masterminds a heroin ring, Juno in *Vengeance is Mine* (1950) runs a pornographic blackmail business. This gives the novels both potent self-righteousness and sociopolitical force, but it is not directed in any way towards liberalism or democracy, in spite of the populist worker-friendly nature of Hammer's personality. The weight of punishment falls on characters seen as aberrant to the American way of masculine life – women, especially seductive ones, are always a threat, and there are more exotic dangers. In *Vengeance is Mine* Anton is both homosexual and a former Nazi collaborator and Juno, the beauty who has throughout aroused Mike's devotion and sexual excitement, turns out to be a man in drag, to be stripped, humiliated and executed. In Spillane's later novels the enemies become communists: Mike mostly exterminates them in McCarthyite fantasy, though in *One Lonely Night* (1951) a society beauty who has erred leftwards is stripped so he can, with belt and buckle, beat her pink body. Grella has felt the need to separate this position from the individual frontier hero from whom he feels the private eye rises, and he stigmatises Hammer as 'the perversion of the American detective novel' ([1974] 1988: 116). Some have been less negative: James Traylor and Max Collins see Hammer as a product of post-war dismay and the novels as 'a savagely lyrical description of the wounded American soul' (in Herbert, 1999: 422). Cawelti more sharply locates Spillane's fury as being an 'agonised but final outcry of the evangelical subculture of moral America' (1976: 190).

If Spillane channelled the energies of post-war gender anxiety and the Cold War into the private-eye form, Ross Macdonald, writing (it may be surprising to note) at the same time, continued the Chandler model of doubt-ridden and anti-social inquiry. He gained high popularity at the more sophisticated end of the market in the 1960s and 1970s, when he was most prolific, but seems now to have been largely forgotten. Macdonald – born Kenneth Millar – taught English Literature at university and had a strong interest in psychology. Starting with *The Moving Target* (1949, published under the name John MacDonald and successfully filmed as *Harper*), Lew Archer works in Santa Teresa, a fictional town based on Santa Barbara, like Chandler's Bay City–La Jolla connection, and his cases take him back through puzzling present events into their origins in family trauma, usually secrets of parenthood. Macdonald stories can seem like versions of the nineteenth-century inheritance puzzles updated in broadly Freudian terms, and Archer's role is close to that of a psychoanalyst. He is rarely physically active, though sometimes he is assaulted. Family traumas abound, usually from the past, so often that there is little sign of family as an ideal: Woody Haut has argued that Archer is 'a kind of Laingian detective, relentlessly attacking the totalitarianism of family life' (1999: 16).

Most commentators see Archer as the good liberal of private-eye fiction – Landrum admired his 'sensitivity to people who are caught in the conflicts of social change' (in Reilly, 1980: 989). A less supportive eye might see some neurotic traces in the recurrent portraits of the women going physically to seed who thrust themselves at Archer, and some signs of textual trauma in the angry boys and the cool professional men who are consistently victims and villains in these well-shaped but sometimes slow-moving narratives: Macdonald can present conversations over several pages. At his best he combines a closely worked 'tragedy of manners' style with images of wider power, as in *The Underground Man* (1971) where a dysfunctional family's troubles are co-extensive with ecological threats to the Californian environment, or in *The Wycherley Woman* (1961) where a false-identity plot set in the shoddy motels and trackless suburbs of southern California represents a widespread 1960s sense of personal and social anomie. Eric Mottram goes so far as to suggest that *The Underground Man* 'signals the end of a genre, the death of the detective's moral security in self-righteous investigation' (1983: 112), and Macdonald can be seen as the last, and the most serious-minded, of the Californian private-eye tradition, though as Part III will discuss, there have been many ways of renovating the sub-genre and its tough, but also sensitive, American hero.

V THE CRIME NOVELISTS

To think of the 1930s as dominated by private eyes is a selective cultural memory. Not only does it overlook the still booming New York clue-puzzle, it forgets a major contribution to crime fiction made largely in America, which is best called the crime novel. This sub-genre – Hilfer calls it an 'anti-genre' (1990: 1) – does not structurally emphasise the processes by which the criminal is identified and punished, as most crime fiction has done from the *Newgate Calendar* onwards, but rather it focuses on the criminals and their feelings before, during and especially after the crime. Rejecting shared social mores for an interest in aberrance itself, the form can be seen as relating to rapid social change and evaluative uncertainty – Mandel describes the crime novel as 'a phenomenon of social decomposition' (1984: 94). This pattern is also found early, in similarly disrupted times – the 'Tales of Terror' and the Newgate novels are an exploration of crime and its emotional context, but, probably because they were often criticised for appearing to be also an exploitation of crime, or perhaps in Mandel's terms because Victorian society became more settled, the crime novels tended to fade away, and sensational fiction glimpses the criminal mind at some distance as in *Lady Audley's Secret* or Maria Belloc Lowndes's *The Lodger* (1913).

Australia alone, with its strong convict heritage and a sturdy anti-authoritarian spirit, remained receptive through the nineteenth and twentieth centuries to what Knight calls 'the criminal saga' (1997: 49–56). In England, as soon as A. B. Cox sought to make the crime novel more interesting the path into the criminal's mind was an obvious and successful one – it is implied in *Before the Fact* (1932, written under the name 'Francis Iles') and direct in *Trial and Error* (1937, written as 'Anthony Berkeley'). But none of these were as intensely committed to realising the world and the responses of the criminal as what came out of the realistic crime writing of the 1920s and 1930s in America. W. R. Burnett wrote, as George Grella puts it, 'powerful, accurate, cynical explorations of criminals in their own environment' (in Reilly, 1980: 233). Priestman sees a resemblance between *Little Caesar* (1929) and the nineteenth-century Newgate novels (1998: 39), and Burnett produced 18 books that can be considered crime novels, the best-known others being *High Sierra* (1940) and *The Asphalt Jungle* (1950). They show people developing and delivering plans for stolen wealth by way of murder; there is conflict among the criminals, over money and sex; there will be betrayals and violence, but also courage and a deep-seated sense of commonality among the antisocial criminal comrades. Ultimately things will go wrong, and all that the criminals have is a sense of having lived boldly in hard times.

The pattern, it is clear, is tragic; Burnett's stories and their kind have been the mainstay of Hollywood at its best as modern tragedy. Simply by admitting that a criminal can be admirable in some ways, crime fiction can access some of the most powerful and moving structures of emotional narrative. *Little Caesar* in both plot and form – it uses a great deal of dialogue – has clear similarities with drama and the reader is emotionally engaged on behalf of the criminal; as Hilfer comments, 'maneuvered into various forms of complicity' (1990: 2–3). This kind of sympathetic realism was of course a major mode in the period and it can only be called crime fiction if there is formally a crime at the core of the stories – John Steinbeck's sagas of human suffering under contemporary capitalism like *The Grapes of Wrath* (1939) or Horace McCoy's accounts of people crunched in the industrial mechanics of the American dream like *No Pockets in a Shroud* (1937) or *I Should have Stayed Home* (1938) are outside crime fiction, but central to the crime novel is the work of James M. Cain.

The Postman Always Rings Twice (1934) is in the antique form, frequently found in the early nineteenth-century journals, of a convicted man's reminiscences. But it also has potent modernity: the
sexual frankness of the book and the original film generated many
responses, negative and positive, but the novel is new in other ways.
Cain presents two people who, obsessed by sex and money, or a
mixture of the two, are led into crimes which they not so much
regret as feel is natural, part of their fate. Powerfully caught in the
1946 film, there is an existential, automatic quality about this world
which, combined with the Hammett-like clarity and brevity of style
and the passion of the stories make Cain's work all the more powerful, especially in the film versions – they include *Double Indemnity*
(1944), which Chandler co-scripted with the director Billy Wilder
from a Cain story that appeared as a serial in 1936 in *Liberty* magazine. As Madden comments, Cain's stories are entirely focused on
individuals and 'deal in broken American dreams' of the Californian
urban wilderness, in 'a vacant glare of a sunlight that gilds the
cheapest artifacts of transient American technology' (1970: 110, 108).
Albert Camus regarded Cain as an existential novelist and, as
Madden notes, his masterpiece *L'Étranger* is in a major way derived
from Cain (1970: 171–5).

Other Americans moved away from the private-eye tradition and
towards the crime novel, notably women writers. One who continued to work in the spirit of Rinehart, but also made her heroines
become involved in the meshes of criminality, was Mignon Eberhart.
Her novels combined real puzzles with richly emotive and often
Gothic settings and action. Starting from *The Patient in Room 18*
(1929) with a series based on a nurse and a detective, she strengthened the Gothic element by making her heroines subject to many
pressures – including being the main suspect as in the well-crafted
and richly written *The Dark Garden* (1933, published as *Death in the
Fog* in London, 1934). Good at dialogue and at managing shifts in
the roles of characters – the weak grow strong, the strong often
crumble – Eberhart, born in 1899 but writing into her and the century's eighties, shows that with dedication and enough skill, a sub-
genre can find an audience long after the experts have declared it
out of date by borrowing strengths from contemporary successes –
both the private-eye and the crime novel lend elements to her often
powerful stories.

Dorothy B. Hughes did recognise the private-eye form and used a
male detective figure, but placed emphasis on how characters –
often wealthy – could become involved in a crime and only escape

its consequences with difficulty and at great cost to themselves, as in *The So Blue Marble* (1940). An experienced journalist, Hughes wrote with great attention to detail, which comes to be laden with symbolic meaning through her characters' nervous and often psychotic reactions. Chandler thought she was the only one of these writers who was genuinely scaring ([1962] 1973: 55), but she could go further into the crime novel proper, as in her powerful *In a Lonely Place* (1947), in which a returned war hero, the first-person narrator, is also a psychotic killer.

Hughes was not the only woman to treat flexibly the male private-eye tradition: Leigh Brackett's first novel *No Good from a Corpse* (1944) involves a corrupt detective and a woman killer who comes to love the amateur investigator, but finally dies in an accident that he causes, like Miss Wonderley's version of *The Maltese Falcon*. With bigger and better parts for women than any of the male writers, including Macdonald, Brackett shows what can be done with the form but seemed not to want to repeat the performance: her later work was often in film, including co-writing *The Big Sleep* with William Faulkner, but like Hughes she moved towards the crime novel, notably in a serious analysis of teenage crime, and the dangers of a vigilante response to it, *The Tiger Among Us* (1957).

A writer with perhaps less innate talent than Brackett but more acceptance of the detective form was Dolores Hitchens. Some of her novels are basically parodic – *Sleep with Strangers* (1955) directly mocks *The Maltese Falcon* with a dangerous beauty called Miss Wanderley (who is not a criminal). Others, written as D. B. Olsen (her married name), construct a positive form, using an elderly spinster as a central figure as in *The Cat Saw Murder* (1939). This looks back to Rinehart in structure and, like Craig Rice's work, has a breezy tone that also separates Hitchens from the earnest, at best ironic, mood of the male private-eye stories that in various ways she resists.

These women, discussed by Haut in a separate chapter on 'Femme Fatality' (1994: Chapter 4), moved away from the private-eye story towards the crime novel, but there were also masculine developments of a parallel kind. It could take the form of urban Gothic, as in the work of Cornell Woolrich, who also wrote as 'William Irish'. Like Cain, he gained high opinions in France for his existential elements, but his novels are generally less serious in effect than the intensity of Cain. His first novel, *The Bride Wore Black* (1940), tells how a woman widowed on her wedding day hunts down and kills the men responsible. It is a grisly game more than a real spine-chiller, and at the end she turns out to be mistaken, as if Woolrich is the E. C. Bentley of the crime novel. Responses have differed to what Glover calls Woolrich's 'histrionic universe' (2003). Some have admired the power of his work – Hilfer speaks of him as creating 'one of the most consistently ontologically pathological worlds of any crime novelist' (1990: 35) and his novels certainly realise a sustained level of male neurosis: he likes especially mother–son relationships gone wrong, and aberrant marriages. This impact and a trickily dark imagination give Woolrich's stories a memorable curiosity, but his frightening openings can be weakened by trite endings: in *Phantom Lady* (1942, published under his pseudonym William Irish) a master criminal who bribes every conceivable witness is the highly unlikely explanation of a genuinely unsettling story. Chandler felt there was a tendentious element in Woolrich, saying 'you have to read him fast and not analyze him too much; he's too feverish' (1962: 55).

The crime novel could become much less playful and stress the masochistic, self-lacerating potential of the American criminal. The classic author in this mode was Jim Thompson, also a film writer, and one of the cult figures of American crime writing. *Nothing More than Murder* (1949) is an imitation of Cain's criminal sagas with enhanced violence and a darker ethic that substitutes nihilism for tragedy. Collins comments that 'in Cain there is a sense of fate behind events – in Jim Thompson there is no sense in things' (1989: 41). *The Killer Inside Me* (1952) is a seriously sadistic book: its brutal scenes recur with the regularity and incremental obsessiveness of pornography. The book still has interest because it is structurally a private-eye story reversed, with a clever, resourceful, self-obsessed criminal acting like an ethically deranged Marlowe: as Horsley comments, it takes 'to a logical conclusion' and puts 'into practice the secret wishes harboured by others' (2001: 122).

Yet Thompson can also write with unmeretricious power, as in *The Getaway* (1959): here, Hilfer comments, he 'presses tough-guy conventions to a surrealistic extreme' and it seems that the characters are symbolically located already in hell (Hilfer, 1990: 137, 138). Compared to other crime novelists, Thompson provides, as Collins comments, 'stronger, darker, medicine, the violence and sex starkly, unapologetically depicted, the protagonists' mental state constantly verging on mad, often entering into psychosis' (1989: 38). In Thompson's work Chandler's idea of hard realism is fulfilled, but

without any of the values that Chandler realised: Thompson takes to
an irrationally logical conclusion the entirely personalised terms
towards which almost all of the American thrillers had tended and
as a result he produces, at his rare best, powerfully modern versions
of the old 'tale of terror'.

Less celebrated than Thompson, but more even and focused in
his work, is David Goodis: as the author of what Glover (2003) calls
the 'noir classic' *Dark Passage* (1946), famously filmed with Bette
Davis in the lead, and then a story of paranoia (also filmed) *Nightfall*
(1947), he gained 'huge commercial success' (Francis M. Nevins, in
Pederson, 1996: 425). Nevins likens his work to Hemingway and
Woolrich but here and in *Cassidy's Girl* (1951) the pace and intelligence of the writing seem more like a variant version of the private-
eye initiators, and Haut argues with some reason that Goodis
'updates and revises Hammett' (1994: 21). Haut is one of the few
commentators to offer a full analysis of Goodis's work (1994: 21–34):
it combines a real drive with a refusal to follow the heroism, either
meretricious or liberal, of the Hammer and Macdonald school, but
also is less extreme and emotively manipulative than Cain and
Thompson. Unfashionably setting a number of stories in
Philadelphia, and avoiding the hyperbole into which American
'tough' writing can easily fall – Horsley calls him 'reliably pessimistic' (2001: 166) – Goodis is a major author who, like Hammett
and Chester Himes, was admired more in France than in his home-
land – François Truffaut's film *Shoot the Piano Player* was based on
Goodis's *Down There* (1956).

VI THE 'TOUGH GUY' ABROAD

The private-eye form has long been imitated in American culture
and around the world, but one of its earliest international locations
has been, it seems, almost completely forgotten. Some British writers turned their hand to the private-eye story in the spirit, like the
New York clue-puzzlers, of transatlantic imitation. James Hadley
Chase and Peter Cheyney cranked out vaguely set and linguistically
bizarre quasi-American thrillers in the late 1930s. The great surprise
was Chase: actually named René Raymond, he was in the book trade
when he decided to try the 'tough guy' approach. *No Orchids for Miss
Blandish* (1939), in spite of its society-sounding title, was a grimly

realistic and sadistic story set in the American south and with some elements of Faulkner in it, especially the plot of *Sanctuary* (1930): a probable further source was the recent *Thieves Like Us* by Edward Anderson (1937). It had pace and vigour – George Orwell, while disapproving of the book's value-free Americanism, as he saw it, still called it 'a brilliant piece of writing' ([1944] 1984: 30). The violence, sex and above all the sadism made it both a banned and a best-selling book. As Horsley notes (2001: 157–8), Chase continued to produce into the 1980s novels that were increasingly focused on sex rather than violence, though in 1961 he produced a heavily cut version of his famous novel for the English market. He did occasionally show greater subtlety, as in *Trusted Like the Fox* (1948, first published as by 'Raymond Marshall') which deals with a war-maddened British veteran who is a worse criminal than a pro-Nazi traitor, an interesting theme from Chase, who had served with distinction in the Royal Air Force throughout the war.

Less well known than Chase was Carter Brown – actually Alan G. Yates, a mild-mannered businessman who, after war service in the British navy, settled in Sydney and turned out a huge flow of tough-guy novellas for publishing houses first in Australia and then around the world. His joke-like titles (*Strip without Tease* (1953) and *Homicide Hoyden* (1954) are typical), his euphemised violence, and a focus on rich food rather than sex all seemed to target an early adolescent audience. Carter Brown showed how the private-eye form had a world-wide audience, but retained an American form – his stories were set in a vague imaginary USA.

One English writer went further, at least in geographic terms. Peter Cheyney was once very well known indeed, but now is almost completely overlooked, and out of print. During the war his sales matched Christie's, and he established himself before Chase as a pasticheur of Hammettesque thrillers – he started before Chandler had published a novel. *This Man is Dangerous* (1936) introduced Lemmy Caution to a British audience – first located in London but soon reverting to the USA. It was published in New York in 1938, with some success – according to his biographer Michael Harrison his sales there reached 300,000 a year, which, intriguingly, was only a third of his sales in France (1954: 274). A fantasy of a tough, self-satisfied, loud-mouthed American, Caution actually works – another unlikely feature – for the FBI. Cheyney was criticised in England for being so un-British with Caution, so he created in *The Urgent Hangman* (1938) Slim Callaghan, a suave, handsome, resourceful, Mayfair-based private detective who is Irish – the nationality was perhaps a tease for Cheyney's patriotic critics.

Through Caution's crass violence and Callaghan's dubious polish, both overlaid with a sexism focused on seductive clothes and, especially, shoes, Cheyney sold very well. The stories are fairly thin, based on chasing about in fast cars, interrogating people, giving and taking punches, outwitting the treacherous 'dames' and unreliable foreigners who fill this two-dimensional world. Rather richer in plot and details, including sadistic ones, are the 'Dark' series of spy stories that Cheyney produced during the war – Chandler thought *Dark Duet* (1942) was 'damn good' ([1962] 1973: 59). By then Cheyney had mercifully abandoned Caution, but his death in 1951 (he was only 55) curtailed a remarkable career that, had it continued, might well have relocated the private-eye form in Britain in the way that Leo Malet's Nestor Burma series, started in France during the war, had an influence that has lasted to the present in French culture and crime writing.

But nobody after Cheyney wrote like him in England. Not only has that limited the range of the post-war British crime writing, but the absence in itself seems to have helped create the simplistic divide between England as the home of the clue-puzzle and America as represented only by the private-eye story. Clearly the two sub-genres did take special root in the different countries, yet much misunderstanding has been caused by reading the two forms as being only national in nature. They were, rather, two ways of handling the situation where the detective was firmly established and death was accepted as the core of the mystery that was to be faced. In their ways of treating both the clue-puzzle and the private-eye story, as well as its reflex the crime novel, writers had by the time of the Second World War already shown a large range of varieties in treatment that constructed varieties of attitudes and ideology. There were to be, in the decades to come, major variations in those forms themselves, as well as the generating of what amounted to new sub-genres. While neither the clue-puzzle nor the private-eye story were as limited to the between-wars period as has often been thought (both, as has been argued here, had an earlier life), that was still the period when they were most fully developed. Both these major sub-genres survived in varied ways after the Second World War, but great changes were also to come: with detection and death firmly in place, the decades of diversity in crime fiction lay ahead.

Part III
Diversity

6
Continuities with Change

I AFTER THE 'GOLDEN AGE' IN BRITAIN

The major patterns of British crime fiction continued after the Second World War, as for decades Christie, Marsh, Wentworth and Mitchell produced on average a book a year, and pre-war newcomers like Cecil Hare and 'Michael Innes' (J. I. M. Stewart) maintained their recondite mysteries, with legal and literary treatments respectively. There was also change. Sayers wrote no more crime fiction, apart from her unfinished mystery *Thrones, Dominations* (1998, completed by Jill Paton Walsh). Allingham was mostly sombre, as in the moody London thriller *The Tiger in the Smoke* (1952). Tey varied the classic form in the crime novel *Brat Farrar* (1949) and a historical mystery *The Daughter of Time* (1951). Carr produced only four Gideon Fell puzzles after 1950, focusing more on historical mysteries, though from 1944, in *The Case of the Gilded Fly*, his entertaining puzzle style was recreated by 'Edmund Crispin' (Bruce Montgomery). Michael Gilbert, another newcomer, also had a light touch – Symons calls him 'an entertainer' (1992: 233) – but most in this period struck a darker tone, like his namesake 'Anthony Gilbert' (in fact Lucy Malleson), who, having started with classic clue-puzzles as early as 1925, developed 'a rather shocking addition of realism' with her exploration of 'woman's powerlessness' (Coward and Semple, 1989: 47), as in *And Death Came Too* (1956). Celia Fremlin produced stories where crime arises from social breakdown, like her first, *The Hours Before Dawn* (1958), a powerful study of a mentally tormented woman which, though it lacks a murder, won an Edgar award; Josephine Bell continued to chart the deprivations and emotional strains of post-war London as in *To Let Furnished* (1952, in the US *Stranger on a Cliff*). Christie maintained her tricky plotting, but her later novels darken somewhat, recognising changes in class mobility, as in *Hickory Dickory Dock* (1955) and the country's new dependence on America, as in *The Mirror Crack'd from Side to Side* (1962, in the US *The Mirror Crack'd*).

The clue-puzzle was by no means dead but it seemed mostly more serious in weakened post-war Britain. There would be many more creators of the death–detection–explanation model, but almost all of them now recognised a need for some form of realism, either character-based or contextual or frequently both. Priestman sees these 'new "realistic" influences' as coming in part from America and in part television (1998: 25), but the form they take is domestic. It can be the much increased use of a police detective, normal in the long series of what are often called 'cosies' (or in the US 'cozies'). These were usually set, with some credible detail and cross-class sociology, in a provincial region of England, where a senior detective investigated an unexotic crime with its roots in local and usually familial hostilities and obsessions. Alan Hunter's long-running series with an Inspector named Gently, mostly set in East Anglia, is typical of this low-toned development of the classic mystery, and another example is Dorothy Simpson, with her Inspector Thanet plodding around the lanes and unheroically mean streets of a small Kent town.

These were still clue-puzzles in basis. Though much of the new realism is related to police activities, the thrust is not yet procedural: this is a glum English version of what Dove calls 'the great policeman' (1982: 159). That has been the underlying pattern of authors as different as the witty and ingenious Robert Barnard (though his policemen are intermittent), Colin Dexter's elaborate, Oxford-set Morse series – equally touristic and, as Plain notes (2001: 185–6), sexist – and the tougher, more private-eye-like Resnick series set in Nottingham, by John Harvey. The most internationally successful version of this reconfigured heroic detective, P. D. James's Adam Dalgliesh, makes clear both his relation to and his difference from the tradition of the golden age. Selling massively in modern America as the archetype of the Christie tradition, and presumably inspiring the sometimes improbable English-set clue-puzzles of American writers like Martha Grimes and Elizabeth George, James made Dalgliesh a learned loner, moved at times to admire women but happier with his poetry and the high Anglican religion that recur as symbols of unchanging value. The settings are varied from the golden age: Priestman notes how Dalgliesh often detects in a hospital, a school, a seminary, places that were formerly classic country houses (1998: 26). As in the thoughtfully developed *Devices and Desires* (1989) James also considers the psychological sources of crime and the aberrant desires of both suspects and victims: the two-dimensional parsimony of character on which Christie's plots depended is replaced with a less simply resolved sense of human complexity.

This also occurs in another major English police detective, Ruth Rendell's Wexford. As ready with a quotation as Lord Peter and at times as intuitive as Poirot, Wexford is updated by his daughters' disruptively modern activities and by investigating crimes that derive from contemporary forces like gender, race, consumer obsession and social exclusion, often seen in some psychological depth, as in *No More Dying Then* (1971) where, as Barnard remarks (1983: 147), Wexford's assistant Sergeant Burden is explored with special impact. Rendell has moved outside the traditional puzzle more than James (though the latter's *Innocent Blood* (1980) is a telling and detective-free character study) and Rendell's major achievement is in forms of the psychothriller, to be discussed below, but the continuing, if changing, popularity of the clue-puzzle has kept her faithful to this provincial, demotic and sometimes troubled version of the great policeman.

Not all British continuations of the clue-puzzle form were so serious in theme or tone. After the grim post-war decades much in English life became more light-hearted – or trivialised – including some elements of crime fiction. Colin Watson, author of the entertaining study *Snobbery with Violence* (1971), also wrote the amusing 'Flaxborough Chronicles', set in an East Anglia town burdened by pompous local politicians and incompetent police. In each case the murder is resolved through the insight of Inspector Purbright, in the context of much stupidity and vulgarity by the characters and, ironically, some snobbery by the author. Joyce Porter created a more extreme anti-detective in Inspector Dover, a fat, greedy, foolish and often drunk police inspector who is able to solve the murders basically through the stupidity of criminals. A higher level of wit enlivened a series of theatrical murder mysteries by Simon Brett, led by his often neurotic, but always intelligent and witty detective Charles Paris. Through variations both serious and ironic, the English mystery tradition has survived in renovated form, as is clear from James's international standing.

II THE PRIVATE EYE MODERNISED

The American private-eye story was less affected by post-war pressures. Chandler published into the 1950s and Ross Macdonald and Mickey Spillane continued their differing versions of the private-eye story into the 1970s. Robert B. Parker, from *The Godwulf Manuscript* (1973) to the present, has offered a familiar private eye who through physical endurance and inquiring legwork resolves crimes that derive from domestic strain and small-scale urban corruption. Learned in the form, having a PhD on its origins and values, Parker avows continuity. His detective Spenser, with the Renaissance poet's spelling, is a play on the name of Marlowe, though he is located in Boston; Parker also completed Chandler's unfinished *Poodle Springs* (1989) and *Perchance to Dream* (1991) is effectively a sequel to *The Big Sleep*. Developments do exist: Spenser can be seen as a 'post-Vietnam figure' (Cobley, 2000: 59), his regular girlfriend is the intelligent professional Susan Silverman, and from *Promised Land* (1976) on he has the informal assistance, often crucial, of the black gangster Hawk, though as Willett suggests (1992: 33) this may seem less a reference to modernity than to the original pathfinder's friendship with Chingachgook in James Fenimore Cooper, as if deriving from Parker's PhD. Spenser encountered contemporary diversity especially in *Looking for Rachel Wallace* (1980), where his client, and then object of his quest, is an abrasive feminist, but although with his interest in cooking and his recognition, at some distance, of gender equality, Spenser has some attributes of a new man, his aggression and regular restoration of the normative family make the novels firmly, if sometimes subtly, traditional and patriarchal.

Parker was both typical and influential in the continued private-eye form. In *Sons of Sam Spade* (1980) – a curiously familial title for these alleged isolates – David Geherin describes some developments. One group was basically ironic: Roger L. Simon's Moses Wine is in both name and activity antiheroic, but *The Big Fix* (1973) is rich in plot – Geherin calls his work 'a marvel of inventiveness and calculated surprise' (1980: 107) and, in tune with the early 1970s, the stories are quite radical – Wine sees himself as 'the People's Detective'. Andrew L. Bergman, a film expert, named his detective 'Jack Levine' after a Hollywood street, and in *The Big Kiss-Off of 1944* (1974) set him back in the world of 1940s *film noir* rather than the novel tradition. Stuart Kaminsky's *Bullet for a Star* (1977) starts a series with Toby Peters, an impoverished private eye who nevertheless encounters famous film stars in the classic Hollywood period. In a more literary version of referentiality Joe Gores paid literary homage in *Hammett: A Novel* (1975).

Other writers made a more serious, Parker-like, transplantation of the tradition into the American present, in a wide range of regions. The ultra-productive Donald Westlake, writing as 'Tucker Coe', created Mitch Tobin as a New York ex-policeman private eye in a short series from *Kinds of Love, Kinds of Death* (1966): these were essentially a darker version of the Ross Macdonald tradition, empowered by Westlake's subtly confident style. Lawrence Block, identified by Art Scutt as a 'journeyman genre writer' (in Reilly, 1980: 148) set Matt Scudder, an alcoholic ex-policeman described as 'a much-diminished Spenser' (Bertens and D'haen, 2001: 50), in New York starting with *In the Midst of Death* (1976), and won an Edgar with the violence-focused *A Dance at the Slaughterhouse* (1991), but the stories are more notable for Scudder's self-satisfaction and personal pleasures than any moral or criminographical insights. Greater realism appeared in other work: Loren D. Estleman, from *Motor City Blues* (1980) on, was to locate the distinctly Chandleresque Amos Walker in what Donald A. Adeste (in Pederson, 1996: 344) calls 'the menacing city' of Detroit. James Crumley's Montana-based mysteries in a post-Vietnam mood started with the partly ironic Milo Mildragovitch in *The Wrong Case* (1975), but in *The Last Good Kiss* (1978) he created the more traditionally American C. W. Sughrue: Willett calls him 'one of the educated rednecks of hard-boiled fiction' (1992: 29). Crumley couples liberal anger and male fantasy about drink, women and guns with a style that combines fluency and impact. Stephen Doberman's less tense and mostly non-violent Charlie Bradshaw operates in the Saratoga area from *Saratoga Longshot* (1976): here, as in Crumley, there is a strong democratic liberal thrust to both the context and the detective's attitudes. Robert Crais has had the courage to recreate private-eye stories based in Los Angeles, starting with *The Monkey's Raincoat* (1987): combining the hip and witty Elvis Cole (self-styled 'World's Greatest Detective') and the traumatised but still weapon-focused Vietnam veteran Joe Pike. Updated in some ways but underplaying the tensions of race and gender in modern America, Crais essentially recycles the classic private-eye form, as in *L.A. Requiem* (1991).

Both new and traditional, often politically liberal but also exhibiting the masculine individualism of the past, these private-eye stories are effectively as 'cozy' as the modern English provincial police heroes. Other descendants of the private-eye tradition are more diverse in both technique and attitude. John D. MacDonald, starting with traditional mystery detection in *The Brass Cupcake* (1950) and then producing a long series of adventure and mystery stories, created his major detective figure Travis McGee in *The Deep Blue Goodbye* (1964). He produced 21 McGee stories, all set in Florida: their sensationalist, colour-focused titles, like *The Dreadful Lemon Sky* (1975), undersell the radicalism that coexists with an uninflected masculinism and effectively reworks the tradition. McGee, a former soldier and footballer, lives on his boat in Fort Lauderdale, Florida, and works in marine salvage. Enjoying fishing, drinking, sun and the quasi-pioneer life, he is recurrently engaged, usually on an amateur basis, in murders that derive from a combination of career criminals and corrupt officials in what Haut calls 'the putrefied middle classes' (1999: 18); the crimes not only involve the destruction of ordinary men and women, especially women, but also often bring real threats to the Florida environment.

Because of the evident sexism of the books – women are gazed upon, trivialised and consumed, by McGee as well as the criminals – the novels have fallen in reputation, but in their ecological interests they were innovative. MacDonald's inheritor is Carl Hiaasen, who started his series of what is often called Florida *noir* – highly coloured though the fiction can be – with William D. Montalbano in *Powder Burns* (1981) and from *Tourist Season* (1986) on has written alone with greater vigour, comedy and ecological concern. He combines mainstream American mayhem with immigrant illegality and foregrounds the damage being done to the local environment. To this exotic mix Hiaasen adds a vigorous and often highly comic style and plotting. The novels gain varied vitality by not using a series detective, though there is a recurrent figure, both droll and value-bearing, in the eccentric former governor who has taken to the Everglades as Skink, and who frustrates the villainous exploiters of the region.

A parallel to Hiaasen's exotic regional fables is in the work of James Lee Burke, starting with *The Neon Rain* (1987). Previously a straight novelist, he created one of the best-known recent detectives. Dave Robicheaux has left the police, is as subject to violence as Marlowe, as earnest as Archer, as erratically tough and liberal as C. W. Sughrue, and as visionary – at least – as McGee. He defends his world of the Louisiana delta, social and physical, against local criminals and corrupt officials, often well known to him, as well as invasive gangsters from big cities beyond the region. But he and the plots are also directly concerned with tensions arising from exploitations based on differences of class, gender and colour in the area.

The texts go further: Robicheaux is not just, as Haut puts it, 'liberalism's answer to private investigation' (1999: 91), he also has Faulkneresque capacities for mysticism. In the powerful *In the Electric Mist with Confederate Dead* (1993) he not only detects the long-past murder of a local black, but he is also consistently influenced by dreams about, and identifications with, the confederate soldiers whose bones lie in the same swamp as the black victim's body. Excitable, romantic, sometimes verging on magic realism, Burke's fables of crime and context project a modern version of the vigour, intensity and moral allegory that animated the early stage of the American private-eye tradition.

It was a tradition that travelled further than the many regions of America. Canadians adapted the form in John Nairn Harris's *The Weird World of Wes Beattie* (1963), with a lawyer acting as a private investigator, and Hugh Garner's *A Nice Place to Visit* (1970) deploys 'a washed-up magazine hack with a drinking problem', as he has been described by Howard Engel (1987: 1), while L. A. Morse won an Edgar for his wryly tough *The Old Dick* (1981). Engel himself became the best-known of the Canadian private-eye writers – Symons found his detective Benny Cooperman 'consistently interesting' (1992: 324). The series started with *The Suicide Murders* (1980; in the US, puzzlingly, *The Suicide Notice*) and operating with 'dedication, persistence and believability' (Geherin, in Pederson, 1996: 342) rather than violence and melodrama, Cooperman pursues cases from his small Ontario town into nearby Toronto and even to the distant northern mining terrain in the prize-winning *Murder Sees the Light* (1984). The Canadian detectives are less extreme in behaviour and attitudes than their US counterparts, and clearly make some contribution to a sense of national identity.

In Australia, when separation from Britain was an economic reality and national identity became a focal concern, some crime writers turned away from their largely British attachment to clue-puzzles and Buchanesque thrillers. Peter Corris, starting with *The Dying Trade* (1980), created the trans-Pacific figure of a Sydney-based private eye in Cliff Hardy, a rugged individualist in the national self-image, who traced the hidden causes of crime among dysfunctional families and criminal connections in contemporary Sydney. Corris has been followed more by feminists than male writers, though Shane Maloney's Melbourne-based political adviser-turned-detective Murray Whelan, starting in *The Brush-Off* (1996), has had a good following. Even more rare have been male private eyes in

Britain. In the 1970s there was, in outward-looking 'swinging London', a brief series by 'P. B. Yuill' (actually the well-known novelist Gordon Williams and the better-known footballer, Terry Venables) about Hazell, a moderately tough but mostly smart East-Ender on the town, who was well received on television. Mark Timlin's often violent and distinctly down-market adventures of Nick Sharman, as in *Ashes by Now* (1993), have had some success, but though the private eye has been used by both women and black writers in Britain, as will be discussed later, the figure, though very well known and admired in authentic transatlantic form, seems to have no mainstream appeal when transplanted. The film *Gumshoe* was, like the television series *The Singing Detective*, fully ironic, and the successful television series *Shoestring* was, as its title wryly suggests, based on a detective and a set of crimes (as well as a budget) much reduced from the heroics of the individual white male that still attract American audiences.

III   OTHER CONTINUITIES

In America the tradition of the crime novel was continued by Jim Thompson into the 1960s, and this form of tough, criminal-based fiction has been followed by Charles Willeford, discussed by Haut (1994: 176–88). His first novel, *Cockfighter* (1972), as Haut comments, 'refuses to give the reader an easy way out' (1999: 32); *Miami Blues* (1984) is more liberal in both exposing and explaining the actions and attitudes of a violent, selfish criminal, but at least Willeford's titles kept up the tough spirit, as in *Kiss Your Ass Goodbye* (1987). Donald Westlake has produced (in addition to his private-eye series as 'Tucker Coe') under the name 'Richard Stark' powerful accounts of a criminal from the inside, the gangster novel with a single protagonist, as in *The Hunter* (1962, filmed as, and in the UK titled, *Point Blank*), which 'portrays the Mafia as the quintessential corporation' (Haut, 1999: 33). Much less seriously, under his own name, Westlake has written a farcical series of criminal capers starting with *The Hot Rock* (1970). Elmore Leonard can operate close to this territory, as in a number of his inherently light-hearted gangster novels, like *Cat Chaser* (1982), where he just shows criminals in nefarious action as basically go-ahead Americans, often failing through incompetence or confusion; but, as Cobley argues (2000: 80–5) his most complex narratives, which Haut calls 'anarchic' (1999: 132), like *City Primeval* (1980) and *Freaky Deaky* (1988), can be seen as being in their disruptive form and ironic endings close to the post-modern crime fictions to be discussed in Chapter 10: they give a more serious edge to the ironic gangster novel. The same is true of George V. Higgins, whose dialogue-heavy *The Friends of Eddie Coyle* (1972) challenged both ideas of legality and the form of the crime novel, though his later series using the detective lawyer Jerry Kennedy, starting with *Kennedy for the Defense* (1980), has returned to the tradition of an explaining central figure, aware of criminal threats and legal complexity but, compared to Higgins's earlier central figures, seeming a moralising lightweight.

Amateur detection was not entirely forgotten in America. Though the high days of Vance, Queen and Wolfe were long over, there were still some surviving parallels like John Putnam Thatcher, first appearing in *Banking on Death* (1961), by 'Emma Lathen'. Heffernan (1997) discusses the realistic compromise of a lawyer detective, as in John Grisham's series where the hero, sometimes heroine, confronts corruption both outside and inside the profession. This moralised individualism was highly successful in his first best-seller *The Firm* (1991) and its similar successors. Such a sense of consoling conclusion is not present in the, at first sight, conventional criminal puzzles of Scott Turow, which like later Leonard and early Higgins ultimately interrogate the validity of both lawyers and the law, as in *Presumed Innocent* (1987) and especially *The Burden of Proof* (1990).

The crime novel, whether professional or not, was not a tradition used in mainstream British fiction, though in the 1970s G. F. Newman, also a television writer, produced hard-hitting accounts of criminal activity as in *You Nice Bastard* (1972) and, in the wake of successful English gangster films like *Get Carter* and *The Long Good Friday*, the sub-genre is at least alive in Britain, with a recent success in Jake Arnott's *The Long Firm* (1999). The form has been relatively strong in Australia, with its tradition of empathy for escaped convicts and bushrangers like Ned Kelly (see Knight, 1997: 54–5). Garry Disher has successfully localised the unsentimental crime novel tone of Richard Stark in his 'Wyatt' series, and has been matched for austere violence by John Carroll and, with a difference, by Robert G. Barrett in his basically farcical novels of criminal violence rejoicing in titles like *You Wouldn't be Dead for Quids* (1985).

Though short on private eyes and crime novels, Britain has recently developed some diverse variants of the traditional clue-puzzle. One combines a tourist interest with a mystery and locates the detective and the story in an interesting foreign country. The well-known reviewer and critic H. R. F. Keating created Inspector Ghote of the Bombay Police – according to Ray B. Browne, with the American market in mind (Winks, 1998: II, 1035) – starting in *The Perfect Murder* (1964) a series of ingenious mysteries that avoid racial condescension in their presentation of the exotic but also impressive nature of post-imperial India – Ghote is discussed as a 'post-colonial detective' by Meera Tamaya (1999: Chapter 2). In making detection travel, he may have been influenced by the successful series by Nicholas Freeling, who set his Simenon-like Van der Valk mysteries in modern Amsterdam, and, after killing his hero off, wrote French-based mysteries using Van der Valk's widow Arlette and then a somewhat colourless detective Castang. Lionel Davidson produced a set of well-written and strongly plotted mysteries set in different countries, from Czechoslovakia in *The Night of Wenceslas* (1960) to Israel in *A Long Way to Shiloh* (1966; in the US *The Menorah Men*). Responding more closely to English tourist interests, several series have been based in Italy, mixing local detectives with even more local colour, by Magdalen Nabb, Michael Dibdin and Donna Leon.

A form of internal tourism much loved in England is to revisit the past, and there are now a remarkable number of mysteries which employ the author's special knowledge of a historical period. The initiator was the 'Brother Cadfael' series by 'Ellis Peters', the experienced novelist Edith Pargeter, starting with *A Morbid Taste for Bones* (1977). Set in Shrewsbury and the Welsh border in the early twelfth century these used antique detail, physical and political, to enrich limited but effective plots, focusing on the charismatic central figure of an ex-soldier turned monk with a special love of botany and medicinal herbs. Not all Peters's followers have combined so many motifs beloved of the colour supplements, and many of them offer little more than creaking dialogue, stiff settings and thin plots – indeed Julian Symons thought Peters's work itself was 'cardboard' (1992: 304). Ranging more widely, in the classical tradition of Margaret Doody's one-off *Aristotle Detective* (1978), Lindsey Davis has been successful with mysteries set around AD70 in Vespasian's Rome, though, as in her first, *The Silver Pigs* (1989), her detective Marcus Didius Falco's relationship with a senator's daughter is more extensive and convincing than the boyish hero's escapes and investigations.

Before Peters and Davis ventured into the distant past Peter Lovesey had shown originality in creating nineteenth-century detecting with two policemen in *Wobble to Death* (1970), based on a bicycle race (perhaps inspired by Romney Pringle's cycle-linked activities, see p. 71 above). There was rich detail – the purist Symons thought there was 'too much setting, too little plot' (1992: 20) – and there has been an even greater richness of imitators, such as M. V. Trow's series on the cases of Inspector Lestrade, better-known as Sherlock Holmes's incompetent professional assistant. No period or place is safe; there is now a flood of authors, with increasing numbers of Americans among them: Peter Tremayne with a seventh-century Anglo-Saxon nun Sister Fidelma; 'Bruce Alexander' using Sir John Fielding in the mid-eighteenth century (recalling the short-story collection *Dr Sam Johnson, Detector*, 1946 by 'Lillian de la Torre' – actually Lillian McCue) 'Caleb Carr' in late nineteenth-century New York; Patricia Finney writing about Elizabethan England; Edward Marston on the time of William the Conqueror; Sharon Newman in twelfth-century France; and even Lynda Robinson using Lord Meren, investigator for King Pharaoh. What had been for Agatha Christie an entertainment in setting *Death Comes as the End* (1945) in ancient Egypt has become a minor criminographical industry, as Thomas L. Amos has shown in his scholarly survey of the phenomenon (2001): this new sub-genre indicates both the flexibility of crime fiction, here appropriating the historical novel, and the recurring need among many readers for a fully escapist, even light-weight, treatment of crime.

In case diluted and less than serious detection should seem only an English formation, mention should be made of the recent florescence of American series novels featuring detectives whose determined amateurism gives a basis for exploring unthreatening and sometimes even uninteresting fields like floristry, catering, veterinary science. Reaching their sub-generic zenith (and their detecting nadir) in the work of Rita Mae Browne, where a beloved cat, Sneaky Pie Browne, is the prime agent of restoring order, these American 'cozies', which have their own annual conference in the national capital, have claimed a significant part of the market: Danielsson, in her chapter on 'Special Interests and the Initiated Reader' (2002: Chapter 2), has shown how niche publishing and a 'fanzine' culture have helped develop this modern equivalent of the most anodyne of golden-age puzzles.

IV   THE PSYCHOTHRILLER

Julian Symons's praise of A. B. Cox as a climax to his account of the
'golden age' suggests a direct transition to psychologically concerned British writers of the post-war period, including Symons
himself. But the real development in the potential of the psychothriller took place in America. Both in the crime novel and
to some extent in the women writers who reduced the authority of
the private eye (Hughes, Brackett and Hitchens), crime and its
effects were being represented without the containing and consoling
presence of a detective, even one as recessive as Lew Archer.
Remarkably, it was Ross Macdonald's wife who both stimulated this
element in his own work and also was the first, and still in many
ways the best, writer to realise the psychic trauma that can surround
crime.

Margaret Millar, born in Canada, wrote a range of crime fiction
but her most important work was in the psychothrillers she produced in the 1940s and 1950s. Her first three novels were an implicitly gendered transition from the male genre, humorous mysteries
using a detective called Paul Prye. Then in *Wall of Eyes* (1943) and
The Iron Gates (1945; published as *Taste of Fears* in London in 1950)
she explored the mind of both criminal and victim. These novels
involve a crucial change of emphasis in plot structure: as Reilly comments, Millar chooses 'to direct attention upon the neurotic or psychotic personality, leaving the detective figure in the shadows as an
instrument of plot' (1981: 240). Seen largely through a woman's
eyes, they deepen Cox's work structurally and thematically. While
he, writing as Francis Iles, had separated the strands of victim-
centred and criminal-centred psychothrillers in different novels
with differently gendered subjects, and maintained an ironic tone
throughout, Millar condensed the potential of the psychothriller
sub-genre and made her closely explored female killers the victims
of their own psychoses in novels that combine empathy with
harrowing realism.

Wall of Eyes is in some ways conventional, dealing with a past
murder concealed as an accident, but it opens up the double life of
the murderer and has a consistent interest in social class, as Mary
Jean Demarr notes (in Winks, 1998: II, 685). More subtlety derives
from the mystery's being unfolded through the multiple viewpoints
of characters who are in various ways close to derangement.
Inspector Sands does work things out, but there is a clear move into

the domain of the psychothriller. This is confirmed in *The Iron Gates*, where Lucille Morrow is at first represented as an unstable woman, the victim of her fears and unable to be calmed by a reasonably attentive family. But Millar does not simply let her be a victim of social and gender pressures: Lucille's trauma in fact relates to her long-past crime in exterminating her husband's former wife, and this emerges not from Inspector Sands's marginal investigations but from her own tormented mind. Her punishment is also autonomous. In a tragic climax combining pity and terror with the best, Lucille, both murderer and victim, painfully climbs a barbed-wire fence on the roof of a mental hospital in order to plunge to self-execution.

Millar produced another mystery-based psychothriller in *Beast in View* (1955). This classic schizophrenic study (which Hilfer identifies as a crime novel, 1990: 24) has something of the clue-puzzle about it. There are definite hints at the outcome and a stunning – even Poirotesque – final revelation when Helen Clarvoe sees in her own mirror her own schizophrenic beast. The trickery of *Beast in View* is something of a withdrawal from the undiluted psychothriller power of the earlier novels, and this movement continues in *A Stranger in My Grave* (1960) where Millar uses her first quasi-private eye to resolve the heroine's traumatic dreams – in fact about her father's grave. This sounds as if Millar's husband had in turn influenced her, and she turned to male-focused detective stories like *How Like an Angel* (1962). While these are still very skilful, versions of the private-eye story that recognise the deforming power of both gender and race, they are the work of a more conventional crime novelist than is found in the disturbing novels of Millar's early period.

A likely reader of Millar was Patricia Highsmith, growing up and living in north-east America until 1963. Her novels have a calmer – or colder – approach than Millar to the psychic internalisation of crime, though there is a collection of outrageously Gothic short stories, *Tales of Natural and Unnatural Catastrophes* (1987), and the switch from bourgeois order to grotesque violence is always a possibility in her novels. Where Millar combined inner horror and occasionally brutal action with the domestic banality of a woman's life, Highsmith operates across gender, being one of the few women writers in all fiction who have convincingly created the mundane world and discordant aspirations of a man. After her first novel *Strangers on a Train* (1950), famously filmed by Hitchcock, and other novels about the criminality of ordinary people, she began the unmatched Ripley series which was to occupy her intermittently for over 20 years. This combines the nervous masculine vanity of the hero with an elegantly simple narrative and coolly observed settings to generate, as if inevitably, a sequence of murders and other crimes equally striking in their casualness and their vicious profitability. Without certainty of gender, status or profession, Tom Ripley, like Highsmith herself an American in Europe, is led in *The Talented Mr Ripley* (1955), through a series of selfish and barely even cunning manoeuvres, to murder the man he has for a better standard of living come to impersonate. Then, having married a wealthy French woman and masterminded an art-forging business he is in *Ripley Under Ground* (1970), *Ripley's Game* (1974) and *The Boy Who Followed Ripley* (1980) led into evasions, mendacities and more killings to defend his new-found respectable status.

With her fluent but unassertive style and mastery of suggestion through restrained description, Highsmith, as is noted by Symons, 'fixes character and plot most successfully' (1992: 205). But her power is also thematic, highlighting as Hilfer notes 'the indeterminacy of guilt, the instability of identity' (1990: 124). He treats Highsmith as an exponent of the crime novel at its most interrogative, as she 'deliberately and shamelessly evades the conventional morality of crime and punishment' (1990: 136). Where Millar saw criminality as normal only for a psychologically traumatised person, Highsmith presents it as an everyday activity for a reasonably ambitious and self-concerned individual. Hannah Arendt's powerful and disturbing perception of 'the banality of evil' in the context of Eichmann's war crimes is already written into Highsmith's account of her respectable criminal hero. Much as the continuing American crime novelists like 'Richard Stark' represented the Mafia as being like – and in many ways genuinely being – successful American businessman (an insight found especially compelling in positively titled films like *The Godfather* and *Goodfellas*), Highsmith shows Ripley to be the model of an acquisitive and industrious bourgeois man, self-made and unrestrained by any moral or humane concerns.

Highsmith could do other things. *Edith's Diary* (1977), her first female-focused book, is, as Bell explores (1990), both an account of a woman's collapse into madness and a coded satire on American political life of the early 1960s. The grotesque *Tales of Natural and Unnatural Catastrophes* are baroque satires of America where Highsmith seems to revel in abandoning the linguistic and imagistic constraint that was appropriate for simple, and deadly, Tom Ripley.

But his saga is the summit of her remarkable achievement in showing how profoundly readable, and plainly profound, crime fiction can be. Her books are, as Klein comments, 'too much like and yet unlike her audience to be attractive and appealing' (1985: 196): Bell puts the same idea differently, seeing her as 'one of the most faithful progeny of the naturalist novel' (in Pederson, 1996: 516). Because of the ruthless clarity of mind which author Highsmith shares with criminal Ripley, her psychothrillers are irresistibly, and disturbingly, compelling.

The author who comes closest to matching Highsmith's revelations of civilised horror is Ruth Rendell. In her Wexford series she was muffled by a dominating police presence and by the need to produce a neatly concealed, and sometimes merely tricky, conclusion, but from her second book, *To Fear a Painted Devil* (1965), she has also offered novels which, without recurring characters or a dominating detecting and evaluating viewpoint, show how a crime develops and what the impact is on ordinary people – including ordinary and often Ripleyesque villains. Symons calls them 'studies in abnormal psychology' (1992: 227), but Rendell is at some pains to show that it is normal human functions which in certain circumstances lead to major crime. In what many consider her best psychothriller, *A Judgement in Stone* (1977), it is primarily because Eunice Parchman is illiterate that the influence of an unbalanced acquaintance leads her to gun down the family for whom she works as an overlooked, indeed banalised, servant. In *The Lake of Darkness* (1980) it is because Martin Urban is too greedy to share a win on the football pools with the friend who gave him the numbers that he spirals as a victim into personal chaos.

Both of these novels, though, depend on some tricky plot moves – the chain of events that lead to Parchman's crime, the complicated revenge plot of Urban's cheated friend. Acceptable in the artificial form of the clue-puzzle, these implausibilities are exposed by the greater realism and consequentiality of the psychothriller. Rendell also at times uses the facile mechanism of a deranged person, like Finn in *The Lake of Darkness* or Anthony Jones in *Demon in my View* (1976), without giving the character the central and powerful explanations that Millar could manage. This tendency to short-cut was avoided when Rendell adopted a more fully explanatory technique in the novels she published as 'Barbara Vine', starting with *A Dark-Adapted Eye* (1986). These move more slowly and in frequently compelling detail, often based on substantial research, like the material on the London Underground in *King Solomon's Carpet* (1991). Although they consistently contain a mystery and a final explanation – whose was the child in *A Dark-Adapted Eye*, just what happened in the past in *A Fatal Inversion* (1987)? – they rely successfully on Rendell's power to elaborate the multiple motives and fully credible bizarrenesses of human behaviour. The absorbing revelation of a normal family, with its many partial dysfunctions and how they led to murder, made it clear in *A Dark-Adapted Eye* that this was a major new voice, fulfilling the potential for explaining and experiencing criminality in psychological terms which was evident in the Wexford novels and was, within limits, often successful in the Rendell psychothrillers. At times old habits recur: the brilliant depiction of people, mostly young, adrift in the anomie of Thatcher's London in *King Solomon's Carpet*, is weakened by the conventionally puzzle-like frame that relates the attack on the underground back to the villain's sister's death. But at her best, Rendell as 'Barbara Vine' locates criminal and dangerous behaviour in the full context of the tensions of British social life and their constraining and distorting effect on vulnerable individuals.

It would seem clear that an influence on Rendell, her equivalent of Millar for Highsmith, was Julian Symons, a poet and historian as well as an influential reviewer and analyst of crime fiction. Straight after the war he published capable mysteries resolved by Inspector Bland, starting with *The Immaterial Murder Case* (1945), a classic puzzle told, *Moonstone*-style, in different voices, and Symons was to go further in condensing crime fiction and the novel proper. *The Thirty-First of February* (1950), in which a detective hunts an innocent man to death, marks an imaginative move towards the psychological and novel-like treatment of crime fiction Symons so much admired in A. B. Cox. Later novels like *The Colour of Murder* (1957) and *The End of Solomon Grundy* (1964) outline with developing intensity how crime can grow from the minds and the motives of ordinary criminals in very ordinary English contexts. Without using the coolly amoral dynamic of Highsmith, the intense psychopathology of Millar, or the socially explanatory details that Rendell usually employs, these were potently suggestive outlines of how normal a thing crime can be, a conscious rejection of the simplistic Christie-esque notion that murderers were essentially evil.

An inheritor of the British psychothriller tradition is Minette Walters. Starting to great acclaim with *The Ice House* (1992), she can explore present and past mysteries in considerable psychological depth, as in *The Sculptress* (1993), about the growing bond between a jailed mass-murderer and a woman writer. But Walters varies her approach, as in the fairly traditional *The Scold's Bridle* (1994), updated as it is in gender terms and violence, and *The Breaker* (1998), a murder story which reads – almost deliberately – like a modernised version of Sayers's *Have His Carcase* (1932). Another recent British writer with considerable powers in the psychothriller, but an intermittent commitment to it, is Frances Hegarty. As 'Frances Fyfield' she has written legal mysteries with a man and woman team of amateur investigators, which, like the first, *A Question of Guilt* (1988), can be searching in terms of both gender and social politics, far more so than Grisham; she has also used Sarah Fortune, an intelligent, generous and vulnerable woman as the focus for novels that go to the edge of reason and violence, like *Shadows on the Mirror* (1989). Under her real name, Frances Hegarty, she has produced novels like *The Playroom* (1991), 'more darkly psychological' (Dean James, in Pederson, 1996: 390), not following the crime and explanation model but exposing the horror and frailty behind respectable lives, using multiple voices and stream of consciousness to continue the substantial tradition of the psychothriller in modern British crime writing. The tradition has extended elsewhere: June Drummond, a South African writer setting many of her novels in Europe, located the psychologically dramatic *Farewell Party* (1971) in Durban. In Australia Pat Flower turned from police-based mysteries to make a major contribution to the psychothriller with *Hell for Heather* (1962), her first to be published in London, and continued in the sub-genre: *Hunt the Body* (1968) is particularly effective. Knight calls Flower 'the most unfairly overlooked of this century's Australian crime authors' (1997: 91). Another Australian contributor to this form was Patricia Carlon from her first novel, the English-set *Circle of Fear* (1961), to the powerful *The Whispering Wall* (1969), which does not pale in comparison to Millar's work.

Two things are striking about the psychothriller tradition: one is that almost all of the authors are women. This is perhaps understandable since a sense of hidden threat is common to them all and though this anxiety is by no means always gendered, the power of a male-oriented social order is usually the cause of disturbance. The other unusual feature is that the sub-genre is not so evident in modern America. One of the curiosities of the psychothriller is that, having had so powerful an early voice in Millar, and being so much an element in the crime novel itself, there have not been more American producers – Highsmith herself lived and worked in Europe. Expertise and interest in psychology are hardly in short supply in the land of routinised analysis and massive study of the discipline, and Ross Macdonald and James Lee Burke have shown how powerful an element it can be within the structure of a detective inquiry. The best-known practitioner of psychological mysteries, Jonathan Kellerman, literally moves detection to the analyst's office in his first novel, *When the Bough Breaks* (1985). Alex Delaware, a skilled child psychoanalyst, consistently works on cases referred by the police which lead him, in a high-powered version of Lew Archer's inquiries, to find out what has caused the crime – not always murder – with which the story starts. For all Kellerman's expertise and the effective, though hardly memorable, writing, the novels seem to achieve little more than Ross Macdonald did, and are somewhat muffled by their sentimentalisation of both the victim-criminals and the angst-ridden inquirer.

Psychoanalysis has become so normal in American culture, it may be that as explanation or motive it has become domesticated in both the crime novel and the private-eye tradition, and has not been felt exotic enough to need a breakaway to a separate sub-genre – even in Millar the form fades away to provide explanatory mechanics within a detective novel. And as the major American sub-genre, the private-eye novel is from the start so powerfully dependent on the damaged individual, from Carmen Sternwood to Robicheaux's grotesque enemies, the exposure of the criminal mind does not require freedom from inappropriate sub-generic patterns, as was necessary for Sayers, Cox, Rendell, Walters, Fyfield and Flower, who were working out of the more individualistically restrained clue-puzzle. Equally, the crime novel, always strong in America, easily absorbs the psychological material, and Hilfer has treated the psychothriller as simply a part of this sub-genre. But there seem to be two different positions: the crime novel stresses the *how* of the criminal's activities and the psychothriller emphasises *why* – though obviously these can easily become condensed and the two distinguishable sub-genres can readily be hybridised.

In these ways, the psychothriller technique does not vanish in America. Always implicit in the crime novel and deepening the more serious private-eye novels, the psychological element will also, as Chapter 10 will discuss, play a formative role in the recent treatments of violent aberration within a police detective frame, and the psychothriller's techniques of comprehension and exculpation can recur in the various forms of police procedural that have abounded in modern America.

7
Police Procedures

I ORIGINS

Though nineteenth-century police had their high moments in detection, as with M. Lecoq and Ebenezer Gryce, a condescending attitude to them long dominated the genre, from Collins to Sayers and Poe to Chandler. Even when relative realists like Crofts recognised the fantasy of amateurism by making their hero a policeman and involving him in meticulously realistic inquiries, he was still the single dominating force, what Dove calls the 'great policeman' (1982: 159), like the well-born Scotland Yard idols in Marsh and Innes; and in America, the professionalism of Hammett's Op never became reduced to mere procedures.

Therefore it was a radical change in both the technique and the ideology of crime fiction when writers began to depict the work of police detectives as having a greater relationship to reality: monocles and shoulder-holsters were no longer the only central motifs in the citizens' imaginative defences against crime. 'Henry Wade', an English baronet, H. L. Aubrey-Fletcher, is sometimes cited as an early procedural writer but novels like *The Duke of York's Steps* (1929) are very much like Crofts and although he democratised detection in novels like *Constable, Guard Thyself!* (1934) and short-story collections like *Policeman's Lot* (1933), his work hardly created a procedural sub-genre. Very similar were the straightforward police detection stories of Sir Basil Thomson, himself a Scotland Yard dignitary: after *P.C. Richardson's First Case* (1933), the hero gained remarkably rapid promotion to appear as *Inspector Richardson C.I.D.* in 1934. Nor did a new sub-genre emerge from Helen Reilly's *McKee of Center Street* (1934), the first in a series about a New York detective. It certainly has procedural overtones – the end-papers of the first edition display a morgue-tag hanging off a bare foot, and equipment and technique are foregrounded – but it is still a single mystery heroically solved by McKee himself.

The procedural form proper was to emerge after the Second World War when in fiction and the immediate-effect media of radio and television the new sub-genre really begins. The experienced crime writer Lawrence Treat created in *V as in Victim* (1945) a team led by Mitch Taylor, a procedural detective, in a story described by Panek as offering 'traditional police wisdom combined with cynicism, exhaustion and the attitudes and values of the lower middle classes' (2003). Knight has argued that the new acceptance of collective procedures against crime derives in part from the wartime sense that a disciplined, co-operative, well-equipped body of men is the most valid form of defence against disorder (1980: 168). Mandel has suggested that organised policing is a response to organised crime (1984: 54), but this dialectical view does not seem to match the dates: Hammett was well aware of such hostile forces without becoming procedural. More relevant is Messent's comment that the evident improbability of private eyes dealing with murder and urban decay left a space for a more credible form of policing (1997: 2), and also Panek's argument that the full development of the procedural sub-genre responded to anxiety created by the widely publicised mass murderers of the 1960s, like Manson and the Boston Strangler (2003). Treat wrote another nine procedural novels by 1960, but the early success of the form in the 1950s in both America and England largely relates to the growing impact of realistic narratives, especially the documentary capacities of black and white television. This is clear in the international success of the series *Dragnet*, starring Jack Webb as the workaday cop Joe Friday, first on radio in 1949 and then on television in 1952, which exploited the credible, but also exciting, appeal of vigorous urban action, police co-operation, new technology and a toughly businesslike approach to crime.

II   CONSCIOUSLY POLICE PROCEDURAL

Though television was to become a major form of procedural crime fiction, the sub-genre was primarily developed in literary mode. A more directly stimulating harbinger than Treat was Hillary Waugh, the much-admired all-round writer who in 1952 produced *Last Seen Wearing*..., in which the rape–murder of a young girl is tracked down with the detail, the dialogue, the uncertainty and the final exhausted success that become characteristic of the procedural form: Symons found the book 'remarkably realistic' (1992: 237). Its tone was to be widely continued, including in Waugh's own work and especially in America, but the earliest conscious developments were to occur elsewhere.

In the antiheroic atmosphere of utility Britain Maurice Procter, himself a former policeman, began a long series of self-conscious procedurals. Procter first published novels about ordinary life on the police beat, the first bearing the weightily Wade-like title *No Proud Chivalry* (1946). His fourth was *The Chief Inspector's Statement* (1951), usually cited as being his first procedural, yet in spite of the plain title (in the US enlivened to *The Pennycross Murders*), it included romance and was focused on a single figure, but in *Hell is a City* (1954; in the US *Somewhere in This City*) Detective Inspector Martineau leads a detective team in a dull provincial town, though there remain weaknesses: the writing is fairly colourless and the plot resolution strained – Martineau went to school with the eventually revealed villain.

It seems likely that Procter's procedural initiative had been noted by the enormously productive and multi-generic John Creasey. He had since 1942 used Inspector Roger West, a daring active police hero, though some domestic detail and his use of police helpers and facilities did have a mildly procedural tone. But in 1955 in *Gideon's Day*, Creasey, as 'J. J. Marric', created Commander George Gideon, the formal leader of a large Scotland Yard team that dealt in crisply mechanical ways with a range of crimes across the whole of London. Here the multiple focus of characters and crimes, a basis of the procedural sub-genre, was given canonical form. Gideon is still a 'great policeman' – Symons found the novels 'marred by hero-worship' as well as a 'lack of humour' (1992: 243), but Gideon's heroism includes his own exhausting dedication and a major impact on his own family, and the recurrent realities of crime, its impact on ordinary lives, the reliance on plain police work to combat it, are all put in place by a writer who knew from long experience how to pace a story and interweave plot strands effectively.

The Gideon series continued until 1976, three years after the prolific Creasey's death, and it was very successful on British television, but the major impact in disseminating the nature and value of the new sub-genre was made by 'Ed McBain'. A former GI, born Salvatore Lombino, he had already written crime stories, and had a major success under his novel-writing pseudonym 'Evan Hunter' with *The Blackboard Jungle* (1954), where skilful urban realism offered education as a resolution to problems, including crime, arising from conflicts of class and race in urban America. Always energetic – he has to date published 50 in his procedural series – he varied his productivity with a fresh pseudonym and a powerfully imagined new format. The first novel was not, as reported in Pederson's bibliography (1996: 716), *Cut Me In* (1954), published under another pseudonym, 'Hunt Collins' (that is an unexciting New York literary agent as detective story), but *Cop Hater* (1956) in which as 'Ed McBain' he presented the police squad of the 87th Precinct in a city he called Isola, which is evidently New York: McBain turned the map of New York 90 degrees clockwise, and retitled all its features to create a symbolic metropolis for the modern anomie captured in its isolationist name.

McBain stresses the elements present but not rhetorically emphasised in his predecessors in the police procedural. A substantial police team represents the multiracial character of city life. Steve Carella, the effective leader, is of Italian origin, while the actual chief is of Irish stock. Meyer Meyer, Arthur Brown, Bert Kling are, as their names suggest, transparent versions of the Jewish, African-American and German elements of the modern US city. Hispanic detectives will appear later, though women are not in the squad and make rare and stereotyped appearances. Realistically, the police tend to work in pairs and have many cases on at the same time. Procedures are stressed, with forensic reports and record-searching, but in fact the documentary inserts and illustrations of finger-prints, warrants, criminal dossiers and so on that were so striking a feature of the books very rarely play a part in the solution of a crime. The human impact of the police and their credible reliance on equally human informers is the main thrust of the plots and their resolution.

The crimes investigated also combine outward social credibility with an inner humanist emphasis. Far from the 'golden age' death of an authority or the parallel private-eye concern with mayhem among the rich, it is the ordinary people of Isola who suffer from knives, bullets, blackmail and extortion, and it is the impact on them all which McBain dramatises – even melodramatises – in his recurrent rhapsodies about the glamour and threat of the big city. If this sounds like, and was indeed felt to be, a genuine democratisation of crime fiction, there are areas in which the novels now appear to be more a formal reorganisation of traditional attitudes than a breakthrough into an ideology as liberal and socially critical as the techniques implied. Carella is in many ways an American Gideon, a leader in action and values, if not quite hero-worshipped. But he is the tallest, the best-looking, and that masculinism has what now seems its ludicrous reflex in the fact that his girlfriend and future wife is a beautiful blonde who is literally dumb, and deaf as well, and is reduced in her name, Teddy, to a sexist toy.

The plots are based on personal crises rather than any social critique. In *Cop Hater* it appears that the police have a murderous enemy, and there is some speculation about organised hostility to them, including media malice, but it turns out that – as in Christie's brilliantly artificial *The A. B. C. Murders* (1936; in the US *The Alphabet Murders*) – the early killings are a smokescreen, to conceal the deadly hatred of a *femme fatale* for her police husband, the last to die. A technique-based parallel to this diminution of the apparent social message is that the solution is often found not through solid police work and courage but through a tricky single device again reminiscent of Christie's short-cuts to solution, as in *Lady, Lady, I Did It* (1961) when the immigrant's mysterious dying statement 'Carpenter' turns out to be in his accent the immediately identifying words 'car painter'. A different form of reductive and personally emotive treatment is in the regular use of descriptive detail which approaches sado-masochism. The period allowed McBain to be more explicit about sex and the body than before, but it was the female body he described in heavily gazing detail – the lush charms of the murderess on a hot night in *Cop Hater*, for example – and he approached a pornography of violence in his fondness for close-ups of a woman's body bruised and torn, as in the assault and rape on Policewoman Eileen Burke in *Lightning* (1984).

In its oscillation between collective and private, its combination of urban realism and emotive personalised plotting and rhetoric, the 87th Precinct series can be read as testimony not only to a sense of the need for co-operative and skilled, soldier-like police work, but also as texts that newly and to some degree covertly celebrate individualism. Their full context is not only the post-war awareness and the alarming growth of the cities, but the associated attitudes relating to what Daniel Bell called 'the end of ideology' and to the growth of identity through consumerist commodification characteristic of booming America in the 1950s (Knight, 1980: 182, 189).

III AFTER McBAIN

Both that deep relation to its context and his vividly memorable technique gave McBain's development of the police procedural great impact. Police teams of varying credibility and effectiveness developed across America like the Californian one in *Case Pending* (1960) by 'Del Shannon' (the multi-pseudonymous Elizabeth Linington), led by Inspector Mendoza, who in being a long-arrived Hispanic with personal wealth seems less than probable. Hillary Waugh himself seems to have been stimulated by McBain to return to the pattern of *Last Seen Wearing* ... and he created some of the best-written and most tightly plotted of all police procedurals, starting with a Procteresque small-town police detective team led by the plainly named Fred Fellows in *Sleep Long, My Love* (1959) – the Chandler-like title suggests the yet-unestablished nature of the procedural form – and then in 1969 a New York version under the equally plainly named Frank Sessions in the now fully procedural title *'30' Manhattan East* (1968).

'Robert L. Pike', a forceful pseudonym for Robert L. Fish, created a police team led by Lieutenants Clancy and Reardon in *Mute Witness* (1963, successfully filmed as *Bullitt*) and continued with *Police Blotter* (1965): not without excitements and firmly pro-police, Pike's novels are both less rhetorical and more fully procedural in their techniques of crime-detecting than McBain's. The best-seller author Lawrence Sanders's successfully filmed *The Anderson Tapes* (1970) gave through documents a skilfully procedural account of a crime and then he took one of its minor police characters to, as Grella commented, 'cross the police procedural with the crime novel' (in Reilly, 1980: 1296) in *The First Deadly Sin* (1973). 'K. C. Constantine', whose real name remains unrevealed, produced a strong series based on Chief Mario Balzic of unfashionable western Pennsylvania, starting with *The Rocksburg Railroad Murders* (1972) and continuing into the take-over as chief by Ruggiero Carlucci in *Good Sons* (1996): the dialogue-heavy series has been much admired, with John L. Breen saying it is 'among the best crime fiction being written today' (in Winks, 1998: II, 1135). Joe Gores, private detective turned writer, made the imaginative move of taking proceduralism out of the police in his toughly realistic and wittily written *Dead Skip* (1972), about car repossessors acting to catch a murderer: Donald C. Wall regards the three books about Dan Kearney and his associates as 'perhaps the best procedural series written' (in Pederson, 1996: 428) and like Gores's *Hammett: A Novel* (1975) it combines innovation with assured skill. The procedural has remained a vigorous form, lending its force to many developments in crime fiction, dealing with issues of gender, race and ethnicity, and also surviving in a strong version of its original form in the highly successful series created by Michael Connelly, starting with *The Black Echo* (1992).

The impact of the police procedural as a series form and a quasi-realistic treatment of crime was also strongly seen in television. McBain's novels became a successful television series in the 1960s, and from the 'melting-pot' impact of *Kojack* in the 1970s to the more hectic realism of *NYPD Blues* and *LAPD* in the 1990s, the vulgate form of the police procedural in America was on television. In Britain that development also occurred, from the early and newly realistic (in both class and regional terms) *Z Cars*, starting in 1960 and continuing through the 1970s corruption-aware excitements of *The Sweeney* to the long-running, highly banal but massively popular *The Bill* – enshrining in its title the Cockney slang term for police on the beat, 'The Old Bill'.

But there were other, and ultimately more ground-breaking uses for the procedural form, especially in America. Its inherent realism in abandoning the improbably isolated American private eye (as well as the creaking clue-puzzle) made it a natural form for writers who wanted to challenge the socially normative structures of gender, race and sometimes class that were part of earlier sub-genres. Many of the texts to be discussed later which seek to interrogate social values, especially in terms of race, would use a procedurally developed police story as the basis for their critical investigations.

McBain's initiative was followed in Canada – David Skene-Melvin points out (in Herbert, 1999: 53) that as a national police force was established very early, Canadian crime writers tended to be more positive towards police than elsewhere. Hugh Garner created Inspector Walter Dunant of the Toronto police in *The Sin Sniper* (1970) and Laurence Gough set a pair of police detectives, male and female, in Vancouver in *Accidental Deaths* (1991). Eric Wright uses Charlie Salter, a traditional police detective operating fairly procedurally, in a lengthy series starting with *The Night the Gods Smiled* (1983).

There were other international imitations of the McBain pattern. A close reworking, except in politics, was in the avowedly Marxist series using Martin Beck as a modern detective everyman, written in Swedish by Maj Sjöwall and Per Wahlöö in ten novels from 1965 to 1975, widely available in English. Another international procedural was produced by the South African writer James McClure in a series starting with *The Steam Pig* (1971), containing a good deal of procedural activity and a pair of policemen, Afrikaans Lieutenant Kramer and Bantu Sergeant Zondi. The realism of the series extends to consistent observation of the context – Donald C. Wall comments that the plots 'all impinge on or are complicated by apartheid' (in Pederson, 1996: 722) and Tomara feels that the two policemen are 'a microcosm of the best of South Africa' (1999: 54). Not unlike Upfield's Boney, Zondi has skills highly useful for policing, but McClure treats him and his people's concerns with more seriousness than Upfield's two-dimensional version of indigenousness.

Australian culture has long had such distaste for police that in spite of its equally strong tradition of demotic realism, no true procedurals developed there. Jon Cleary's rare official detective Scobie Malone is a hero policeman, if of an ironic sort – he has to apologise constantly to his Irish-Australian father for being a policeman at all – and the only approach to proceduralism comes in the crime-novel-like tough cops of John Carroll and Philip McLaren's aboriginal police, who are much like the African-American police and the Maori detectives from New Zealand, to be discussed below.

There were clearly procedural influences on the Europe-focused authors discussed by Winston and Mellerski (1992), though Freeling's Van der Valk is heroic enough to be antiprocedural, and the same is true of the Italy-based recent detectives created from England. Jan Willem van de Wettering, writing in Dutch, laid a good deal of stress on ordinary police work as his pair of detectives, Grijpstra and De Grier, approach their solutions. The suggestion has been made by Ian Rankin (1998: 9) that Georges Simenon's Inspecteur Maigret was the first procedural detective, which would contradict the account of the sub-genre's origins given here, but it seems clear that Maigret's heroism, intuitive methods and emphasis on the suspect's psychology, however much his assistants may act procedurally, locate him in the tradition of the great policeman with unusual psychological subtlety basically deriving – as with Gaboriau – from the different, non-evidential, emphases of the French detecting system.

In Britain the idea of plodding realism had considerable attraction. John Wainwright was a major producer of competent, through rarely thrilling, police stories set in a gloomy Northern city and most of the English regional police cosies referred to above have some element of procedures in them: Colin Watson's Flaxborough incompetents are notably unable to handle techniques of any kind. There have been several Scottish versions. William McIlvanney's Laidlaw, for all his gloomy plodding, is really a Scottish great policeman, of an ironical and radical kind, but Bill Knox's *Deadline for a Dream* (1957; in the US *In at the Kill*) was set, if rather colourlessly, in Glasgow and that city has more recently seen novels by Peter Turnbull about P Division, starting with *Deep and Crisp and Even* (1981): Ian Bell has called them 'over-formulaic and rather lifeless' (1998: 190) and a livelier Scottish police series has been that focused by Ian Rankin on the Edinburgh detective, drinker and music-lover, John Rebus. Though his impact partly comes from being a troubled version of the great policeman, he and his helpers engage, as in *The Falls* (2001), in far more procedures than did the 1930s version of that figure. In a similar way police techniques enable the character-rich activities of Reginald Hill's Dalziel and Pascoe, in the Yorkshire-set series, which started with *A Clubbable Woman* (1970) and which can, as in *Under World* (1988), dealing with the 1984 miners' strike, and in the recurrent debate about Pascoe's feminist wife, handle political issues with substantial impact. In their deeply ironical way the flamboyantly written series by 'Bill James' (actually Jim Tucker, like Reginald Hill formerly a lecturer in English), starting with *You'd Better Believe It* (1985), deals often procedurally with the impostures and fantasies of modern Britain: Bell comments that he 'makes no attempt to conceal his cynicism' (1998: 187), and in his new series, as 'David Craig', as in *Bay City* (2000), he shows a police team handling, with mixed success, the wealth and corruption that have variously invigorated modern Cardiff.

Whether as a self-sufficient sub-genre or as a set of positioning techniques for analysis of crimes both social and personal, the police procedural approach is part of the language of modern crime fiction. It implies an audience and a set of writers who can, at last, trust the police – or some of them – to be credible operatives against crime. The humble operations of Waters and Mrs G— have finally merged with the flamboyance of M. Lecoq and the persevering success of Ebenezer Gryce, and so have brought to an end the long period of automatic contempt for officials as low-status bunglers. What Dickens foresaw as a narrative and thematic role in Inspector Bucket has finally become a world-wide and generically renovating reality.

8

Diversifying the Viewpoint: Gender

I   TOWARDS FEMINIST DETECTION

Before the 1920s the few women detectives remained lady-like while solving crimes, and even when writers like Wentworth, Christie and Mitchell began to use a consciously independent woman detective, and others like Sayers, Eberhart and the Nancy Drew authors involved a woman against crime, they still operated within the expectations of a masculine order. Historians like Jessica Mann (1981) and Mary Cadogan and Patricia Craig (1981) describe an increasing number of women sleuths who operated through the decades after the Second World War, but they went no further in terms of gender critique than the forceful but still contained presence of Mitchell's Bradley. The first woman detective who substantially interrogated the situation was herself no revolutionary, with the colourless surname Gray in addition to P. D. James's doubt-ridden title *An Unsuitable Job for a Woman* (1972).

Things have changed. No major publisher or bookshop is now without feminist crime fiction. Walton and Jones have shown how the numbers of authors have risen from about 40 in 1980 to nearly 400 by 1995 (1999: 30). The authors are far more than any survey can handle in any but a highly selective and trend-indicating way, but, compensating for the limits of the present analysis, there has also developed a substantial secondary literature on the new sub-genre of feminist crime fiction, with major studies by Maureen Reddy (1988), Sally Munt (1994), Kathleen G. Klein (1995), Gill Plain (2001), a searching essay-collection edited by Glenwood Irons (1995), and a thoroughly researched overview by Priscilla Walton and Manina Jones (1999).

Commentators identify an inherent difficulty for writers speaking as women, and usually as feminists, in a form which is deeply

162

implicated with masculinism. The violence of language and action of the private eyes, the insistent individualism they share with the clue-puzzle detectives, the extensive male chauvinist traditions of description, attitude and behaviour, as well as the complacent acceptance of a patriarchal social order, all seem contrary to the tenets of late twentieth-century feminism. Palmer speaks of 'a discrepancy of values' (1997: 89) and Maassen sees feminist crime fiction as at best 'the carrier of a compromised feminist message' (1998: 154). Some are more negative: Babener sees 'female sleuths' as 'deputy henchman for patriarchy' (1995: 146) and Geason calls the feminist private eye 'Marlowe in drag' (1993: 116).

Others, like the critic Gorrara (1998) and the major author Paretsky (1990: xii–iii), find real possibilities and values in revers- ing the masculinist trend of the form, and the great effort that has gone into reclaiming the sub-genre from masculinism in itself indi- cates that many writers, whether liberal or separatist feminists, have seen it as much more than a doomed task. However, it is striking that it was the hyper-masculine private eye form that the early fem- inist rewriters chose: Humm commented firmly that the 'feminist detective is not individualist and cannot be a *private* eye' (1990: 249), yet the image of a single urban dissenter was a compelling one, and provided the vehicle for the crucial first moves.

The police procedural might seem a more accommodating form by being inherently more collective but it would have been – and still is – hardly credible to imagine a largely female detective squad-room. Some early gestures were made in a procedural direction – both Dorothy Uhnak, who had herself been in the New York transit police, and Lilian O'Donnell wrote accounts of a woman police officer, but the feminism is distinctly limited. Uhnak's Christie Opara, first appearing in *The Bait* (1968), is brave and effective, but she is also emotively and professionally incapable of resisting the male embrace, metaphorical and literal, and Reddy dis- misses O'Donnell's Norah Mulcahaney, starting in *The Phone Calls* (1972), as no more than a 'patriarchal woman' (1988: 11), though Klein does see an 'independent spirit' in Mulcahaney (in Pederson, 1996: 798). Some stronger moves towards feminist police were made in television in the American female buddy series *Cagney and Lacey* and later in the 'great policewoman' form of *Prime Suspect* – itself based on a real senior woman at Scotland Yard. Yet this has not been a major mode in feminist crime fiction, though it is noticeable that, as will be discussed below, increasing numbers, especially of non-white and lesbian detectives, have recently been identified as police officers, though they usually remain loners on the force.

The clue-puzzle was even less a candidate for feminist reworking: its artificiality and innately, docilely, privatised form has left little room for a politics of gender or any other kind that went further than was achieved by Mitchell and Christie; though, as will also be discussed below, some headway has been made in feminising this sub-genre by writers like 'Amanda Cross', Val Miner, Joan Smith and, most notably, Barbara Wilson.

Starting, and largely succeeding, with the challenge of feminising the private-eye form, and with some success in other sub-genres in the wake of that achievement, feminist crime writers have changed the face of the genre enormously: what was unimagined in Symons's first edition and grudgingly noticed in his third has become a major element of crime fiction. But it may be more than a new power shift: Rowland (2001: 17–18) argues that the whole crime fiction genre, representing the Other of traditional social order, is in itself inherently feminine, and that woman writers have authenticity in controlling its forms and themes. To put it another way, the modern feminist crime writers may be fighting the same battles as the formidable mistresses of Gothic and sensational fiction, with at least some of the same successes.

Sceptical though feminists might be about Reddy's claim that *Gaudy Night* (1935) is 'the first feminist detective novel' (1988: 12), it has been proposed as the point of departure in both characters and theme for P. D. James's venture into the field in *An Unsuitable Job for a Woman* (Campbell, [1983] 1995: 17–20). Responses to this novel – like those to *Gaudy Night* itself – have been varied, both in itself and in relation to the other Gray-focused novel, *The Skull Beneath the Skin* (1982). Munt feels Gray can only operate under the final validation of James's series detective Dalgliesh (1994: 23), but Nixon (1995) sees the first novel as an expression of 1970s feminism, in which Gray finds her tentative way as a professional woman and finally identifies with and exculpates the woman who avenges her son against his treacherous father. However, both the suicide of the killer and the detective's general air of uncertainty make this at best a tentative foray into feminism, and James herself seems to have been less than committed. When, encouraged by readers, she returned to Gray ten years later, her agency focuses on finding lost pets, and both the novel and the detective operate in traditional terms. Nixon (1995) argues that this is a decline into 1980s Thatcherism, with Gray essentially emotive and domesticated, but though that is a wide-spread view Campbell felt that Gray here shows 'new-found strength', is less troubled than in the earlier novel, and that she acts as an authority in the story and as the eyes of the police ([1983] 1995: 25–6). James did return to a woman detective in *A Taste for Death* (1986) with Kate Miskin, who acts as a junior to Dalgliesh and recurs in later novels, but in English style she is seen more in terms of class than gender – she has battled up from a deprived background – and making her the threatened final victim of the killer relegates her, for all her courage and skill, to a role with no more agency than the potential victim.

The uncertainty and ultimate limitations of James's approach to detection by a woman resembles another early move towards the sub-genre: the confident, well-finished but in gender terms essentially limited investigations of Kate Fansler, the creation of 'Amanda Cross' – actually the distinguished American literary critic and feminist theorist Carolyn Heilbrun. From *In the Last Analysis* (1964) on, Fansler is a wealthy, stylish and learned Professor of English Literature in New York and detects as an amateur in the clue-puzzle tradition – Reddy remarks that 'the academy may be an updated version of the country house' (1988: 15). While she can be taken as a role model for a professional woman, Fansler is never in any way deprived or seriously the victim of male oppression – nor, for all her poise and brains, does she have much functional independence: her male lover plays a major role in most of the solutions in the early novels. Yet Cross's plots have a feminist tendency: as Roberts has pointed out, 'all but one of her victims are women, all but one of her murderers ... are male' (1995: 96) and her substantial contributions to feminist criticism, as Heilbrun, made her position a more critical one than James's, academically at least. In *Death in a Tenured Position* (1981) Cross deals for the first time with a woman who is clearly patriarchally oppressed: appointed as a token woman full professor at Harvard, her death seems connected to the offensive treatment she receives. However, Cross conceives the problem of sexism, as Cranny-Francis says, as 'not a social but a personal one' (1990: 74) and the fact that the death turns out to be a suicide makes the novel something of a feminist damp squib, especially when compared with Val Miner's *Murder in the English Department* (1982), where the professor turned amateur detective works out that a sexist professor has been murdered by a graduate student he was harassing, and decisively covers up for her crime.

Cross's work did provide a discursive space for intelligent professional women in the genre, and by using a woman detective does move on from Sayers (though not far from Mitchell), and she certainly gained a wide readership that other writers exploited – Reddy's second chapter, 'Free-Lancing Amateurs' (1988), deals with a number of women like the American Virginia Rich and Lucille Kallen who follow Cross by using professional woman as amateur detectives: elsewhere British writers like Anne Morice and Jessica Mann and Canadians like Alisa Gordon and Medora Sale did the same, and more recently Americans such as Carolyn Wheat, Sharon McCrumb and Nancy Pickard have continued this mildly feminist tradition. But the wealthy, elegant and amateur Fansler is an object of fantasy, not identification, for most readers, and through moving for the most part easily in a man's world, she is structurally equivalent to the 'honorary man' role of the female police in the work of Uhnak and O'Donnell. More fully feminist work by Cross was to come in her later novels like *No Word from Winifred* (1986) where, as in her own scholarly practice, emphasis lies on the construction and recognition of female identities and biographies; but as there is also here much less emphasis on crime and detection, Cross remains no more than a precursor in feminist crime fiction.

II FEMINIST DETECTION IN AMERICA

The first major move in feminist crime fiction was made by Marcia Muller with *Edwin of the Iron Shoes* (1977). The change from earlier efforts is striking, and Reddy connects this to the context: 'By the time Muller's first book came out liberal feminist ideas had seeped into public consciousness' (2003). This novel started what Walton and Jones call 'an immensely influential series' (1999: 20) with her professional detective Sharon McCone, first working as investigator for a legal office and then setting up on her own. From the start McCone displays what have become major features of the woman private eye. She is mature and experienced as well as inquisitive and skilful; she is wary of but not fully opposed to the police; she has sexual identity and also an extended connection with family and, especially, friends, both women and men; she has substantial empathy with victims of crime; she pursues her inquiries with courage, often being alarmed or physically hurt in the process; the crimes she confronts can be violent and distressing, and unlike the male private-eye tradition they derive mostly from a real combination of urban corruption and personal betrayals. She embodies an optimistic sense that crime can be contained and a better life enjoyed for women, even in the big bad city, even among the secrets and dangers of modern human interaction.

Muller, with an authority and impact like Doyle and Hammett in creating an authoritative new model of the detective, transplanted the familiar enough real life of a professional working woman into the world of threats, inquiries and resolutions that is crime fiction. McCone faces various forms of sexism and belittlement – her being part-Shoshone leads a police detective to call her 'papoose' – but she is no separatist: she has an affair with the same man. Though she becomes increasingly frustrated, worrying about her anger in *Where Echoes Live* (1991) as Adrian Muller notes (in Pederson, 1996: 776), she is friendly and cooperative and it may be that this personality helped both Muller and her followers to deflect convincingly the masculinism so strongly rooted in the private-eye form.

Whatever anxieties some critics might retain about the appropriateness of the sub-genre, Muller's intervention worked: she became a regular producer and was to have many followers. Her novels and those they stimulated came to draw an enormously positive reception among the rapidly increasing number of woman readers and book buyers for this new figure who could convincingly represent their interests and anxieties. It was not immediate: her second McCone novel, *Ask the Cards a Question* did not appear until 1982. But after that a new wave, or rather flood, of writers gave crime fiction accounts of the pressures and possibilities of life as a woman in the modern world, a process which, in the face of socioeconomic conservatism under Reagan and Thatcher and some clear elements of anti-feminist backlash, conveyed on the new sub-genre some status as fictional resistance, as well as recognising the legitimate interests of slightly more than half the population.

If Sharon McCone's busy amiability had eased the transition from male to female private eyes, a more aggressive figure was to become a dominant feminist detective in the work of Sara Paretsky. Where McCone enjoyed the pleasures of San Francisco, Warshawski works in the grim bustle of Chicago; unlike Sharon she is known by the initials V. I. and only answers to the androgynous Vic: this sets a standard – Walton and Jones note the frequent use of 'male-identified names' in the new tradition (1999: 115). She always works alone, she lives alone, she is very active, with a penchant for furious driving and night-time break-ins; she is often quite badly hurt, spending a period in hospital in almost every novel. Genuinely tough, she keeps herself fit by running and, if reluctantly, will carry and use a gun.

But she also has skills: like McCone, but most unlike their male predecessors, V. I. will trace enigmas through files and, like Paretsky herself, understands business matters very well – the first novel *Indemnity Only* (1982) has a complex insurance basis. Warshawski was formerly a defence lawyer, but equally important experience came through the women's movement of the 1960s and 1970s, with an emphasis on abortion rights. This all sounds formidable, and there is a driving tone to both her personality and the vigorous prose and rapid action of the novels, but unlike the Continental Op or Marlowe, V. I. is more than a loner. Though not as sociable as McCone, she has casual friends from work or from the past, an occasional lover and useful regular contact in the journalist Murray Ryerson, a close though sometimes acerbic woman friend in Lotty Herschel, a doctor and refugee from Nazism, and after the first books an elderly neighbour in Mr Contreras who worries about her safety, even tries ineffectively to help her at times, and looks after her labrador. Quasi-family as are Lotty, Contreras and Peppy the dog, V. I. is both haunted and consoled by her own real family – a familiar experience for most women readers. The child of a Polish cop and an Italian-Jewish woman, V. I. bears rich but bittersweet memories of her upbringing, her parents' immigrant values and hopes, and her own self-constructed distance from them: as Walton comments, 'Paretsky's focus on race may go unnoticed' (1999: 273) and she gives some emphasis to an issue that Muller left underdeveloped in both McCone's Amerindian inheritance and the San Francisco context.

Family also participate in the plots: in the second novel, *Deadlock* (1984), V. I. investigates the death of her cousin 'Boom-Boom', a famous ice-hockey player, and feels strongly the distance between herself and his clannish and religiose relations. But the solution in this well-constructed novel derives from his involvement in the shipping business, and Paretsky shows her consistent capacity to combine personal loss and threat with broad social corruption – unlike the male private eyes Warshawski focuses a powerful interrelation of the personal and the political, a convincing fictional realisation of the key insight of second-wave feminism. As Walton and Jones comment, ' "Who done it" often turns out to be a societal entity' (1999: 209).

Burn Marks (1990) starts with family: V. I.'s erratic aunt Elena, vagrant, drunk, occasional prostitute, a spectre of a woman alone and out of control, brings her into an inquiry that involves the murder of a young black mother and harm to the detective, but eventually leads back to a land-development scandal high up in Chicago politics. Convergently, V. I. finds that an old feminist colleague is, in order to be elected for the radical cause of Hispanic residents, making common cause with the same crooked politician-businessmen. V. I. cannot accept such compromised means, whatever their promised ends, and continues with her inquiries – to find that her own personal interests are directly involved as Michael Furey, her well-named police lover, is part of the corruption and violence, and finally tries to kill her. Plots and themes interweave compellingly and V. I.'s courage, physical endurance and most of all her determined sense of values are ferociously tested, but finally found sufficient.

The exaggerated intensity of the stories can seem extreme – Plain calls *Bitter Medicine* (1987) a 'feminist fairy tale' (2001: 154), and to some modern women students V. I. seems too embattled, unifocal and perhaps old (she turns 40 in *Tunnel Vision*, 1994) to be a figure for identification. Munt objects to V. I.'s obsession with clothes, shoes and appearance, calling her 'a glamorous spectacle' (1994: 47) – though this could now be read as post-feminist. It is the loner aggression of V. I. that has stimulated much of the feeling that the sub-genre cannot be subverted to feminist purposes, though this intensity is itself criticised in the texts, as Vanacker notes (1997: 67–8), especially by the authoritative figure of Lotty who in *Blood Shot* (1988; in the UK, curiously, *Toxic Shock*) finds V. I.'s sense of duty has become obsessive and damaging to others, including Lotty herself.

The importance of Paretsky's achievement is suggested by two contextual facts. Though she finished the first novel by 1980, it took two years to be published – this was a new and troubling voice. And it remained too troubling for Hollywood: the 1991 film *V. I. Warshawski*, deplored by Paretsky and most women readers, not only condensed and thoroughly garbled the plots of the first two novels, added a long and mindless boat-chase and cast Kathleen Turner in man-mad mode as V. I., but as further sexist containment invented Boom-Boom's daughter to show that V. I. could still be an all-American surrogate mother. As Gorrara has argued (1998), the liberal feminism that V. I. embodies was an important message in the continuing world of gender conflict, and it intensified Muller's crucial initiative into a major renovation of crime fiction and the confident establishment of the new sub-genre of feminist detection.

Often linked to Paretsky, but in a number of ways different, is the work of Sue Grafton. A television writer, she adopted the sub-genre with confidence in its continuity, as is boldly displayed in her first title, *A is for Alibi* (1982): so far she has reached *Q is for Quarry* (2003). Her androgynously named professional detective is Kinsey Millhone, whose cases mostly derive from her connection with an insurance company. Like V. I. she is fit – also a runner – and she lives alone with a quasi-family. There is an enfeebled paternal neighbour, but just as Kinsey's skills and aspirations are less elevated than V. I.'s, her older woman friend runs a bar. There is no quasi-child as Kinsey has no room; small herself, she lives in a tiny flat, and a sense of miniaturised power is recurrent: at the end of *A is for Alibi* she hides from a murderous ex-lover in a beachside garbage bin – and then shoots him as he raises the lid.

Industrious, determined, and intermittently sexually active – also, more unusually, twice-divorced – Kinsey is a recognisable version of the new tough woman, but there are stronger than usual links to the male versions of the sub-genre in the setting (Macdonald's Santa Teresa), the tendency for personal betrayals to drive the plots, the substantial number of female villains and especially in the language. Christianson has noted how in Kinsey's appropriation of Chandler style she 'talks dirty, she talks tough and she talks smart', though he also comments that her wise-cracking style is in the US a working-class feature (1995: 127, 132). The style and the relatively reduced level of feminism and political critique have caused a varied response. Maassen feels that overall Grafton is closer to 'the tradition of Chandler and Hammett than to the doctrines of women's liberation' (1998: 160) but Klein finds this 'compromise' both credible and realistic, that Kinsey is represented as liking women, and the texts offer 'a constructive portrayal of women', especially low-level workers (1995: 113, 107–8). While it is clear that Grafton's purpose is less forcefully feminist than that of Paretsky and the lesbian-focused crime writers to be discussed below, through her steady production, her continuing quality – Geherin feels *K is for Killer* (1999) is 'one of the strongest entries in the series' (in Pederson, 1996: 439) – and, importantly, through her lively and accessible style, Grafton has been able to project the idea of an independent, courageous, irrepressible and witty crime-fighting woman into the mainstream of modern literary culture.

The combined impact of Paretsky and Grafton created many followers in this rapidly established sub-genre. Some, like Susan Dunlap's Berkeley-based Jill Smith, beginning in *Karma* (1984), operate from inside the police, but in terms of her assiduous and sometimes dangerous inquiries, as well as her unstable but hopefully partnered heterosexual personal life, Smith's role and meaning are similar to the woman private-eye predecessors. After four novels based on a sophisticated male actor, Linda Barnes introduced Carlotta Carlyle in *A Trouble of Fools* (1987): formerly in the Boston police but both private eye and cab-driver, tall, fearless, friendly to women and suspicious of men, but still just maintaining heterosexuality. Her intense adventures have attracted a large following and, as in *Coyote* (1990), Barnes consistently tells a fast-paced story strong in social and gender awareness through the eyes of a heroine who is both tough when necessary and recurrently tender.

Stephanie Plum, created by Janet Evanovich in the series beginning with *One for the Money* (1994), is a definitely free spirit from working-class, non-WASP Newark. Aware of her rights but succeeding mostly through luck, improvisation and the appeal of a lurid wardrobe, Stephanie oscillates between half-criminal colleagues and her hermetic family. Bertens and D'haen suggest the novels are 'to a large extent a send-up of currently fashionable women's detective writing' (2001: 124), but beneath a light stylistic touch and often comic action Evanovich communicates a good deal about the world of post-feminist young women and rustbelt America, where extra-legality is one of the few ways of sustaining a viable and entertaining way of life. Sparkle Hayter, a Canadian-born television journalist, produced in *What's a Girl Gotta Do?* (1994) that rarity, a genuinely comic and recurrently witty crime novel which is also aware of gender pressures. The tone is post-feminist – Reddy, drawing on the title of a potent anthology (Duffy and Henderson, 2002), offers the term 'tart noir' for this type of novel (2003) – and detecting does come second to Robin Hudson's jokes and personal fiascos, but there is a still a real surprise ending and also a firm, if also comic, insistence on gender issues.

Fully Canadian versions of the new figure appeared in Lauren Wright Douglas's Caitlin Reece, an ex-lawyer working in Victoria, British Columbia, in *The Always Anonymous Beast* (1983) and in Tanya Huff's Victory (Vicki) Nelson, formerly in the police and tracking down crime in Toronto with a descendant of King Henry VIII in the less than always serious *Blood Price* (1991). More in earnest were Alison Gordon's Kate Henry, a sportswriter who works with a Toronto police sergeant, starting with the baseball mystery *The Dead Pull Hitter* (1989) and Medora Sale, whose Harriet Jeffries, a photographer, shared her detection with a Toronto police inspector from *Murder in Focus* (1989).

A lively version was created in Sydney, in Marele Day's Claudia Valentine, tall, even sometimes elegant. Written with wit and style and resolving the problem of violence by making Claudia only use her long legs – to run or to kick – Day's novels did well in the USA, winning a prize with *The Last Tango of Dolores Delgado* (1992). There were other Australians like Jean Bedford with her sensible detective Anna Southwood, but their most striking contribution to the growing crowd of liberated women detectives was Kerry Greenwood's Phryne Fisher, starting in *Cocaine Blues* (1989), definitely a lady, but independent in terms of curiosity and sexuality, whose adventures are set back in the wealth and social mobility of 1920s Melbourne.

III FEMINIST DETECTIVES IN BRITAIN

Whatever moves Sayers and James had made towards an independent female detective, the establishment of the figure in Britain basically follows the powerful development made in America. But there is an exception: before Paretsky and Grafton made their moves Hilary Tamar appeared in *Thus Was Adonis Murdered* (1981) by 'Sarah Caudwell' (in fact Sarah Cockburn). A professor of medieval law at Oxford who solves crimes in a welter of literary reference and a somewhat mannered style, Hilary is the narrator, but never reveals her or his gender. Such an ambiguous name-game was a golden-age staple for a well-concealed criminal, but Caudwell ingeniously reverses its role and significance in an inherently feminist manoeuvre. It is a limited trick, but one that indicates that transatlantic borrowing may come with a crucial, and sometimes thought-provoking, difference.

Liza Cody had already turned from advertising work to crime fiction with *Dupe* (1980). Anna Lee is a strong-minded young woman working for a seedy detective agency; living in then unfashionable Notting Hill, not particularly fit or strong and relying on her wits rather than action or a gun, Anna, like Sharon McCone, is a friendly soul with a feminine first name. But she is strongly independent and without family or, usually, lovers, though she is (before the

Americans) equipped with a less than macho male neighbour – in this case an untidy poet with a rarely seen wife. The novels are consistently feminist in a reserved way: Anna faces male harassment and distrust in the office and on the job and, as Irons and Warthly-Roberts note, in all but one novel (*Stalker*, 1984) she deals with the 'murder or victimization of a young woman' (1995: 64). The tone is English understated realism and the action is limited in range and impact as Anna solves, without much sense of triumph, her cases. Irons and Warthly-Roberts saw a 'sense of emptiness at the desperate future faced by her clients and even by herself' (1995: 71), but British readers may see this as a fair account of a single woman's life in London in the period. *Stalker*, set mostly out of London and involving Anna both in robbery and a sudden love-affair, is a colourful book, but Cody herself moved on to more melodramatic and, in an indirect way, feminist stories in her series based on the unreliable first-person narration of a woman wrestler called 'Bucketnut'.

Joan Smith, a well-known serious journalist, started a short series based on an English lecturer, Loretta Lawson, in *A Masculine Ending* (1987). With wide references to culture and politics, especially feminism, the novels seem like a more radical version of Cross, and like hers they tend to be stronger in wit, references and colour than their actual mystery plotting: the most recent, *Full Stop* (1995), resolves this potential problem by moving towards the open form of postmodern crime fiction. Sarah Dunant, another journalist, influential in the early 1990s from a late-night cultural television programme, and with Peter Busby half of 'Peter Dunant', author of the radical ecological thriller *Exterminating Angels* (1983), began with *Birth Marks* (1992) a series focused on Hannah Wolfe, an intelligent feminist with a good line in ironic talk. The plots involve, more searchingly than most in the sub-genre, the constraints and distortions placed by social expectation on women's lives – through birth in the first novel and through the beauty business in the more energetic *Under My Skin* (1995). Witty and perceptive as they are, the novels are not as significant as Dunant's reason for abandoning them: she felt that using a series character meant she could not make her readers genuinely fear for the heroine's safety or sanity (2000: 19).

That seriousness about her project is characteristic of several British-based, but in fact international radical writers who use the feminist detective as a mouthpiece for strong statements about politics, whether feminist or not. Gillian Slovo, whose parents were leading anti-apartheid activists in South Africa, at the cost of her mother's life, created Kate Baeier in *Morbid Symptoms* (1984). Aware of gender issues – Kate is a mother as well as an investigative journalist – and also interested in the possibilities of psychoanalysis for both liberation and constraint, Slovo traces murder in multinational London out to its sources in the repressive, and male, agencies of totalitarian South Africa. Political in both a traditional and a feminist sense, and treating British social issues as well, notably in *Death by Analysis* (1986), Slovo, like Barbara Wilson (see pp. 175–6), helped to stiffen and sophisticate the thematic politics of the sub-genre: Pykett notes that Slovo 'takes for granted a radical, left-wing perspective' (1990: 58).

In the same spirit 'Hannah Wakefield' conceals two unidentified Americans in London, and their first novel, *The Price You Pay* (1987), uses Dee Street, a firmly left-feminist lawyer, as the focus of a story combining recent American radicalism with Cuban and Chilean politics. Their second book, *A February Mourning* (1990), turns to mainly British issues, political rather than merely criminal. Like Slovo, Wakefield combines feminism with radical politics, but lacks her consistent explorations of feminist issues through the plot and characterisation.

Only the broadest definition would find feminism in Antonia Fraser's series of novels about Jemima Shore, television star and amateur investigator – Pykett notes both the novels' 'preposterous plots' and their updated, designer-style connection to the golden-age tradition (1990: 49), but their reverse is found in Val McDermid's series, starting with *Dead Beat* (1992), about Kate Brannigan, a professional private eye working in the excitable gloom of modern Manchester. Dealing with realistic crimes – theft and blackmail as well as murder – and employing friends and assistants with special skills, Kate is witty, self-deprecating and a model of liberal probity among the young. More sociable and less attitudinising than Kinsey Millhone, her closest parallel, Kate's skilful compromises are summed up by her sex-life: her partner is a male disc jockey who lives in the house next door, access being provided by a rear conservatory open to both.

IV   THE LESBIAN DETECTIVE

Plain notes that Kate Brannigan is one of the few heterosexual women private eyes who succeed in 'negotiating the crisis' between sexuality and independence (2001: 164–5, n.3) and more generally asks whether such a figure can 'ever really threaten to destabilize a patriarchal system in which she is also profoundly implicated through structures of desire ?' (2001: 143). For many feminist writers the solution to this enigma is, in fiction if not also in life, to take desire out of gender-opposition by adopting a lesbian stance.

The earliest moves in this diversifying development were M. F. Beal's *Angel Dead* (1977), the first lesbian crime fiction novel, focused on radical feminist Kate Guerrara, followed by Eve Zaremba's Vancouver-based Helen Keremos, who comes out slowly in *A Reason to Kill* (1978), a novel Anthony Slide calls 'tightly worded and constructed' (in Winks, 1998: II, 1074) and Vicki P. McConnell's *Mrs Porter's Letters* (1982) with the detective Nyla Wade: Slide finds her 'plot-lines invariably silly and heavily influenced by Gothic romance' (in Winks, 1998: II, 1073). These initiators were followed by the contribution of Barbara Wilson. *Murder in the Collective* (1984) is a major novel in several ways. In addition to offering a well-crafted mystery where the amateur detective Pam Nilsen comes to recognise that her lesbian identity is as important and liberating a truth as the solution of the crime, Wilson also offers strategies to elude and redirect the inherent masculinism of the private-eye form. Pam is a twin, and this destabilises individuality, not gender, because her sister Penny remains heterosexual. Secondly, and with wider impact, the social and work context is collective: Pam manages a jointly owned and operated printing firm, with a large group of workers as well as friends and associates – the skill of managing a large cast is one of Wilson's less observed qualities. The novel also challenges the traditional individualistic and apolitical morality of the crime novel. The solution depends on Pam unravelling a complex chain leading back to American espionage and intervention in the Philippines; the murdered man is in fact a plant to spy on some of the printing workers. But Wilson goes further in subversion: the murderer is the man's wife. She has acted to protect herself and her friends, and Nilsen the evaluative investigator lets her go – but, unlike P. D. James with Cordelia Gray's similar sympathy, the murderer does not conveniently die.

Into this 'pointed critique of the genre', as Babener calls it (1995: 147), Wilson weaves a good deal of consciousness-raising, both feminist and more generally radical, through collective discussions and Nilsen's own thoughts. She pursued a more focused account of crimes against women in *Sisters of the Road* (1986), dealing with a wide range of male exploitations – financial and occupational as well as physical – in the central narrative about a murdered prostitute. The novel combines the intellectual feminist politics indicated in the title and the motive force of what Babener calls 'a sisterly consolation' (1995: 155) for the sorrows experienced throughout by women. This makes it in many ways a more satisfying, or at least more traditional, piece of fiction than *The Dog Collar Murders* (1989) in which Wilson, as Gorrara says 'engages directly in intellectual investigation of key issues in the lesbian community' (1998: 175), notably the right to practise sado-masochism.

With these three rather different novels Wilson made it clear that a lesbian detective was a credible and effective figure through which to identify crimes involving gendered as well as social oppression, and many writers have followed her. A strong move towards the mainstream of crime fiction was made by Katherine V. Forrest, an editor at Naiad, a specialist lesbian press, who in *Amateur City* (1984) created Los Angeles Detective Inspector Kate Delafield. This, described by Plain as 'a novel of office politics' (2001: 167), had limited action but the second, *Murder at the Nightwood Bar* (1987), plunges Delafield deep into urban violence and conflicts over lesbianism: Marchino describes her as 'a strong, hard-working homicide detective' and the novels as 'entertaining and believable police procedurals' (1995: 65). Forrest writes with some of Paretsky's strength and also her earnestness: Plain finds her 'somewhat didactic' (2001: 173). But she also has a substantial impact: Plain concludes that the first four novels are 'one of crime fiction's most sustained engagements with the politics of sexuality' (2001: 168), and Bertens and D'haen find *Apparition Alley* (1997) 'brilliantly succeeds in weaving lesbian and homosexual themes and issues into its plot' (2001: 80). Forrest's influence has been considerable, with lesbian police officers playing a leading role in Mary Morrell's *Final Solution* (1991), focused on Lucia Ramos, who separates her work and her personal life, and in Catherine Lewis's *Dry Fire* (1996), where policewoman Abigail Fitzpatrick is a focus for 'the whole range of power issues facing lesbian officers' (Betz, 1999: 91).

A quite different tone was maintained in the short but very well-known series by Mary Wings: though set in America, the first two novels were written when she was living in Holland and first published in Britain. Emma Victor leaves public relations in Boston for amateur detection in the challengingly titled *She Came Too Late* (1986), but moves to San Francisco in *She Came in a Flash* (1988).

There is a mystery involved and Victor is a competent, tricky detective, brave sometimes to the point of foolhardiness, but the dominant feature of the novels is their wit. Without using Kinsey Millhone's masculinist tough talk, Emma Victor is full of jokes, ironies and general *joie de vivre*. Liberating in Barthes's sense of *jouissance* as much as in terms of lesbian feminism, the novels brought real colour and humour to the new sub-genre that had so far been distinguished by serious, and occasionally ponderous, weight.

Through their strong public reception these writers established the lesbian detective, and many authors have exploited the breach they made in both conventional publishing and the traditional limits of crime fiction. Sandra Scoppetone's Laura Laurano, a New York private eye who specialises in listening to people, first appears in *Everything You Have Is Mine* (1991), a coherent and effective story which was, according to Walton and Jones (1999: 105), the first to be published in the mainstream. Sarah Dreher created the eponymous *Stoner McTavish* (1985), a travel agent turned detective and a determinedly serious character who, as Munt comments, 'battles against homophobia and misogyny' (1994: 96) and is also, as in *Gray Magic* (1987), a defender of native American rights. Laurie R. King's Kate Martinelli, first seen in *A Grave Talent* (1995), is a San Francisco police detective: as in *Night Work* (2000) the stories often combine her police work and emotional life with substantial amounts of information on women's issues. Martinelli's ethnic background is a minor element in the stories but, as will be discussed later, lesbian police detectives are also used by American writers who focus substantially on racial issues.

In Canada Lauren Wright Douglas uses Caitlin Rees, an ex-lawyer, to explore blackmail threats against a covertly lesbian television personality in *The Always Anonymous Beast* (1987), and Jackie Manthorne's *Ghost Motel* (1994) introduced Harriet (Harry) Hubley whom Melvin calls 'Harlequinesque ... albeit a tad didactic' (1996: 146). In Australia Claire McNab (first published in America with Naiad) deployed a lesbian police detective, Inspector Carole Ashton, as glamorous as the harbour-wide settings she enjoys, but more rigorous was Finola Moorhead's searching account of oppression within and outside the police in her prize-winning one-off novel about a lesbian police-sergeant in Sydney, *Still Murder* (1991). Rose Beecham presented in *Introducing Amanda Valentine* (1992) a former New York policewoman now acting as a private eye in Wellington, New Zealand. In Britain, Val McDermid produced the left-wing journalist Lindsay Gordon who, starting in *Report for Murder* (1987), specialises in crimes around the edge of union politics, while Rebecca O'Rourke, in the much admired *Jumping the Cracks* (1987), made her lesbian investigator Rats a working-class girl on the edge of social exclusion. Stella Duffy, like the Americans Sarah Schulman and Barbara Wilson herself with *Gaudí Afternoon* (1990), has taken lesbian investigations beyond the formal and thematic constraints of realistic fiction and they will be considered later with other post-modern versions of crime fiction. Appearing, succeeding, and becoming remarkably varied within 20 years, lesbian feminist detection has been one of the most striking signs that crime fiction is still capable of representing, in its apparently unending diversity, issues of real and new importance to its authors and readers.

V   MALE GAY DETECTION

Holmes and Watson may have been homosocial and the criminography of R. L. Stevenson and E. W. Hornung may have moved closer to actual homosexuality, but there seems to have been no identifiable male homosexual crime fiction before the 1960s and the beginnings of the gay liberation movement, not even in the crime novels Gore Vidal wrote in the 1950s under the pseudonym of Edgar Box.

In 1966 George Baxt made an innovative move in creating a police detective who was both gay and black with an exotic name, Pharoah (*sic*) Love and an only lightly coded title, *A Queer Kind of Death*. But Love is tough as much as gay: as Pepper comments, he is no victim (2000: 97–8) and ends by propositioning the villain in return for immunity. Rich in dialogue and dealing little with the colour issue, there is not much emphasis on homosexuality either – the novels are camp rather than gay. There were two more novels in the 1960s, but Anthony Slide, writing about gay mysteries, finds them 'frankly ridiculous' (in Winks, 1998: II, 1077) and Baxt turned to non-series thrillers about Hollywood stars of the golden age. Decades later, when homosexual detectives were more widely known, he resumed Pharoah Love with *A Queer Kind of Love* (1994), but the style and the approach seems now unconvinced and unconvincing – Jeff Baker and Don Sandstrom find the recent work 'trite and tired' (in Pederson, 1996: 53).

The other early figure in male gay detection is parallel to (at some distance) rather than influenced by Baxt. Though Joseph Hansen's

Fadeout appeared in 1970, it was rejected by publishers for two years
(Hansen, 1986: 116–18). His detective is the southern Californian
Dave Brandstetter, who works as an investigator for his father's
insurance company, specialising in what the second novel calls
Death Claims (1973). The approach is also much like Ross Macdonald –
Brandstetter visits people's homes, follows up leads, traces missing
people and the connections between them. Violence, as Cobley
notes, is at 'an absolute minimum' (2000: 69), but driving long dis-
tances and conducting lengthy discussions, both techniques familiar
from Macdonald, move the novels along smoothly, if rarely excit-
ingly, though Newton Baird has praised their 'beautifully styled
description and dialogue' (in Pederson, 1996: 483).

The hero is far from tough – Plain calls him 'medium-boiled'
(2001: 97) – and has a rather quiet personality: Symons thought him
'a dull and sentimental fellow' (1992: 240). There is certainly none of
Wings's celebration of homosexual difference in his life, nor even
Wilson's thoughtful arguments for the validity of such a position
but, as Slide comments, 'homosexuality, often closeted, is a primary
focus of the plotlines' (in Winks, 1998: II, 1070). Brandstetter usually
has a lover, though as his long-term partner has died before the first
story, his emotions are often mournful, and while he encounters several attractive men in the course of the stories, romance and delight
seem at best replaced by comfort and tenuous security. The normalcy of the homosexual male detective is a central point, and
the novels include a good deal more real detection and explanation of crimes than is usual in the male private-eye tradition. The
plots are detailed and neatly-fitting, in some ways closer to clue-
puzzle rigour than the private-eye flexible plot style: Hansen is not
above including clues and he specialises in constructing, much like
Christie, highly complicated scenarios at the murder scene.

Though the positioning is homosexual, it is a very masculine
world: where the lesbian writer's characters have to confront male
power in many forms, in spite of their separatist emotional position,
the gay detective can operate along the channels of traditional male
power with only occasional recognitions of his role outside it. This
extends to the choices Hansen makes about plot: Bromley has noted
that 'the death or disappearance of a father, son or husband is almost
always the precipitating moment of the text' (1989: 103) – a feature
shared with many nineteenth-century women detectives. But the
maleness of the stories is not a simply moralised straight-gay divide:
in *Death Claims* it is an overlooked covert gay lover who has killed

the missing father. Yet this one-sided account of gender is a limitation of interest in the text, and indeed the fact that, as Plain comments, 'in the world of Dave Brandstetter women simply do not signify' (2001: 101) transmits a restricted view of real male homosexual life.

Highly competent, genuinely interesting about the crimes they choose to explore, and increasingly committed to a gay stance (*Early Graves*, 1987, deals with the AIDS epidemic), the Brandstetter series seems to have had less impact than it deserves. There has not been as large a following for Hansen's initiative as there was after Wilson in lesbian crime fiction. The prolific Canadian writer Edward Phillips wrote a sharp and stylish series of gay crime novels – not detective stories – focusing on a Toronto lawyer, starting with *Sunday's Child* (1981); 'Richard Stevenson', in fact Richard Lipez, created Don Strachey, dealing overtly with gay issues in a series starting with *Death Trick* (1981), and 'Nathan Aldyne' (Michael McDowell and Dennis Schuetz) contributed to the emergent sub-genre with *Vermilion* (1980). Michael Nava's Henry Rios, first appearing in *The Little Death* (1986) and developed in the widely successful *Goldenboy* (1988), is a Mexican-American gay lawyer turned detective; combining forms of marginality and also being successful in detection as he does, Pepper felt Rios was 'too good to be true' (2000: 158), but Slide calls Nava 'a sensitive and inventive novelist' (in Winks, 1998: II, 1071). Berten and D'haen find Nava's work 'particularly interesting' (2001: 185), along with the novels of John Morgan Wilson, who presents 'a heartbreaking picture of the gay community of Los Angeles' (2001: 187).

In Britain the much-admired novelist Julian Barnes wrote three books as 'Dan Kavanagh' about Duffy, a mostly gay semi-criminal London investigator, but though they have wit, irony, and a constantly interesting style, they never had much success. The specialist GMP (Gay Men's Press) has published two novels by Jeremy Beadle, *Death Scene* (1988) and *Doing Business* (1990) and W. Stephen Gilbert's *Spiked* (1991): set in the seedy and excitable world of 1980s London these tend to be wordy – though *Spiked* is also witty – and lack Hansen's ability to mould gender issues into both the plot and the values of the investigator. Even Sydney, with a major gay culture, many aspiring writers and a long tradition in crime fiction, has not produced the male gay equivalent of either Kate Delafield or Emma Victor, despite attempts by Dennis Freney in *Larry Death* (1991) and John Dale in *Dark Angel* (1995) to open up the market: the main Australian contribution in this field is Roger Raftery's stark *The Pink Triangle* (1981), set in Adelaide and based on a real gay-bashing murder by the police.

It may be simply that the image of the macho detective, ready for action and violence, equally tough of talk and hide, is one with which the male gay community is reluctant to identify, and it is noticeable that the best of the writers, like Hansen, Barnes, Nava and Phillips, have distinctly moved away from the private-eye tradition. It is, though, also possible that this sub-genre has lacked potent initiators: neither Baxt's complex camp stance nor Hansen's high but unexciting competence had an imitation-compelling power. The early lesbian thrillers are themselves fairly unconvincing both as crime stories and as gender politics: it may be that much is owed in that sub-genre to the skills and leadership of Barbara Wilson, and these have not yet appeared in the male equivalent.

9

Diversifying the Viewpoint: Race

I AFRICAN–AMERICAN CRIME FICTION

Crime writers have long made at least some variations across the borders of gender and class, but to make the detective anything but a Caucasian has been most unusual – in *The Moonstone* Ezra Jennings is a racial hybrid who does not survive, while both Fergus Hume's Hagar of the Pawnshop, a gypsy and 'Eastern beauty' (1898: 9), and Earl Derr Biggers's Charlie Chan were exotics whose exceptionality confirmed the whiteness of the power to detect – and they were not black. There were some early real exceptions in the confines of African-American culture: Pauline Hopkins's *Hagar's Daughter* and *The Black Sleuth* by the slave-born writer and historian John Edward Bruce, which includes scenes set in Africa, appeared in periodicals for black readers as early as 1901–2 and 1907–9 respectively: as Stephen Soitos comments, in a full discussion of these striking predecessors, they 'used the formulas of detective fiction to contrast this Afrocentric worldview with a racist Euro-American hegemony' (1996: 221). A dubious contribution, not unlike a black version of the Charlie Chan stories, were the stories serialised in the *Saturday Evening Post* in the 1920s and 1903s about Florian Slappey, by the white southerner Octavius Roy Cohen, first collected as *Florian Slappey Goes Abroad* (1928). A more valuable and conscious intervention in crime fiction was made by the Harlem renaissance writer Rudolph Fisher in *The Conjure-Man Dies* (1932), a police mystery in 'golden age' manner with 'a completely black environment with an all-black cast of characters' (Soitos, 1996: 93), including four detectives. Fisher brings substantial power to this initiative, as he 'infuses the detective formula with his concerns as a black American modernist writer' (Gosselin, 1999: 326).

Foregrounding the language, culture and social critique of a black viewpoint, *The Conjure-Man Dies* remained a bold predecessor until Chester Himes made literal the French phrase 'Serie Noir' and started a series of ten novels about the Harlem-based police detectives 'Grave Digger' Jones and 'Coffin' Ed Johnson with the prize-winning *La Reine des pommes* (1958; translated into French from Himes's *The Five-Cornered Square* and then appearing in the USA as *For Love of Imabelle*, 1959, and also as *A Rage in Harlem*, 1965). Himes's titles are only part of his imaginative energy: his heroes use both words and guns as brutal weapons in what Schmid calls 'an exercise in mayhem' (1999: 286). They exhibit rage more than probity and method, and Pepper argues this derives from their sense that they and the people they police are trapped in 'an exploitative and racially oppressive system' (2000: 113). In spite of the 'absurd humour' (Soitos, 1996: 152) these comedies are very dark and Soitos also identifies in them 'the pessimistic world-view that colours the last half of Himes's autobiography' (1996: 153). It is not a passive pessimism: Jones and Johnson are vigorously male chauvinist and anti-homosexual and can even seem racially negative. Mandel feels they 'operate mainly against blacks, upholding white law' (1984: 57) and Pepper sees 'their conflicted status as defenders of a law that does not represent black interests' (2000: 114). With similar complexity, the crimes of murder, theft and extortion are not simply committed by bad whites against an innocent coloured underclass: in this world black is set against black, whether criminal or detective. Soitos sums up by referring to another major and disturbingly veracious black writer: 'There is little moral ground to stand on for African Americans in these novels. Like Ralph Ellison's Rinehart in *Invisible Man*, they have lost themselves in a maze of contradictory possibilities' (1996: 153).

Comprehensible in terms of postcolonial criticism, the novels create the consciousness of the black oppressed through the jazz, food, street-life, and historical awareness that are central to black American experience, and they use vernacular language as a weapon of challenge to white normalcy – 'abrogation' is the term used by postcolonial analysts. Like most potent colonised self-expressions, the novels are steeped in a sense of complicity and also express their full meaning through allegory. This may be primarily positive in its surreal power, as in the dynamic myth in *Cotton Comes to Harlem* (1965), where the slave experience is appropriated through a literal and also symbolic bale of cotton appearing in the city, as well as a scam to repatriate American blacks to Africa; or it may be darkly negative as in the final volume, *Blind Man with a Pistol* (1969), where the detectives fail to restore any kind of order, white, black or complicit, and their Ellison-like impotence is symbolised in the bleak title. The Harlem series is a major event in the history of crime fiction and Himes, through the imaginative power and the austere vision that led French commentators to see him as a true existentialist, broke the white mould of the detective novel and made it possible for others to follow in less challenging and more politically assimilable ways.

The work has been described in a general way by Paula L. Woods in *Spooks, Spies and Private Eyes* (1995) and with a more political and influential emphasis by Stephen F. Soitos in *The Blues Detective* (1996): it is a rich and varied story line. The first quasi-conventional channelling of the energies of black crime fiction was John Ball's *In the Heat of the Night* (1965), which won prizes in both the USA and Britain as a first crime novel. Responding to the civil rights movement in the American South, he created a black police detective in Virgil Tibbs, who both solves a racial murder and, like many black activists of the time, coolly outfaces everyday colour-based hostilities in a harshly racist southern town. Both a highly competent mystery and a timely political statement, the novel was powerfully filmed with Sidney Poitier as the aspirational hero. Ball continued with Tibbs detecting back home in Pasadena, as in *Johnny Get Your Gun* (1969; republished as *Death of a Playmate*, 1972), yet in publishing, as in social history, racial liberation was slow, and there was no rapid follow-up to Ball's important initiative until the early 1980s.

George Baxt's gay detective Pharoah Love, discussed above, is a diversion from Ball's seriousness and another ironic response was by Ernest Tidyman, a journalist and editor who created in *Shaft* (1970) an African-American version of the swinging private eye, with some borrowing from James Bond. Not as self-parodic as the film, the novels, seven by *The Last Shaft* (1975), offered through Shaft's confident style and sexuality a resistance to white supremacy that is both fantasised and sentimental, as if Himes had gone in for integration on Madison Avenue. Essentially unserious as he was, Tidyman nevertheless marked the growing confidence of black crime writing, which reached a major new stage in the work of Walter Mosley.

Pepper (2000: 123) has related the rage of Himes's work to the mood of the Watts riots in 1965, and he also links the impact of

Walter Mosley to the widespread revulsion over the beating of Rodney King in Los Angeles in 1992. With a black private eye working in Los Angeles, the reversal of tradition is clear, and the opening scene of the first novel, *Devil in a Blue Dress* (1990) deliberately reworks the start of *Farewell My Lovely*: a white man enters a black bar, but the viewpoint is with the normal occupants, including the detective, Easy Rawlins (really Ezekiel, an elegant combination of demotic casualness with prophetic potential). An immigrant from impoverished West Texas, an ex-GI who has sought not a fortune but a decent modest living in California, his inquisitive and intelligent character leads him into freelance detecting, at first for a white man but eventually in cases, including murder, that belong to and spread through the black community. Mosley's world is a diluted and calmer version of Himes's dark vision and it locates black crime fiction firmly in the literary mainstream.

Though the setting is consistently in African-American Los Angeles, the timing of the novels is wide-ranging: Mosley starts in the post-war period, realising its failure to distribute boom wealth across both class and colour, moves on in *A Red Death* (1991) to the McCarthy period – though its politics hardly touch Easy's world, then to the late 1950s in *White Butterfly* (1992) and then to the political turmoil of the early 1960s in *A Little Yellow Dog* (1996). As Haut comments, he reconstructs 'the lost narrative of black Los Angeles' (1999: 106) – another crucial manoeuvre in postcolonial discourse. He also shapes in Easy a modest and uncertain move towards citizenship: not being, like Marlowe or Spade, 'a free economic soul' (Pepper, 2000: 126), he has to work – in a factory, for an estate agent, as a school janitor – and buying a small house in Watts is his most cherished and sometimes perilous achievement. It can seem an improbable and less than radical idyll, as when in *Black Betty* (1994) two kindly white neighbours baby-sit his two adopted children, and this may make the novels more acceptable in a white liberal world, but Mosley creates, for the most part credibly, a hero whose difficulties and determination realise the strains of an America where wealth and power remain inherently white.

Easy, like most detectives, whatever their gender or colour, is often unduly fond of drink and sex and, as with Warshawski, his single-mindedness can be damaging – many of his black friends die in the course of his complex adventures, and this enacts complicity of a more profound kind than Warshawski's collateral damage. Although his aspirations and skills are in part like those of whites, he retains many of the features inherent to the black experience: in *Devil in a Blue Dress* he describes himself as 'invisible' (1990: 135) and Grierson (1999) saw his work in the tradition of what Henry Louis Gates and Houston A. Baker have identified as 'signifyin', the coded and trickster-like ironic response of the black oppressed in America: Pepper explores this theme more fully (2003).

The novels are rich in black language, often suggesting a milder form of Himes's abrogation, and they can also claim some allegorical power, not only in their historical sense and their frequent awareness of the oppression of other races, notably Hispanics and Jews, but also in their presentation of a master narrative, a black aspirational story in which Easy symbolises an upwardly mobile African-American whose story has rarely been told. But the move is made without losing touch with the possibility of recidivist violence, memorably realised in the id-like figure of Easy's boyhood friend Mouse – who may die at the end of *A Little Yellow Dog* – or may not. Mosley's series has a yet uncompleted potential and also, through its recurrent seriousness, sheer literary quality and market success, provides a model that other authors and publishers have been tempted to imitate and even rival.

Gar Anthony Haywood followed Mosley with another black private eye working in Los Angeles, starting with *Fear of the Dark* (1988); Aaron Gunner, like Easy Rawlins, is an ex-soldier with an Old Testament first name. Sacked as a Los Angeles police recruit, he is both a private eye and an electrician and becomes involved in the mysteries that link the black guerrilla movement to the white professional world: a serious and thoughtful creation, Landrum calls Gunner 'a sort of anti-John Shaft' (1999: 174). Gary Phillips created a black detective in the Hammett tradition with *Violent Spring* (1994), with Ivan Monk, a 'socialist private eye', as he is described in the novel. Not only concerned with black issues – Monk has a Japanese-American girlfriend – Phillips makes a range of social threats both substantial and political, disrupting, as Pepper comments, 'the basic premise of the genre: that individual solutions to larger social problems can be achieved' (2000: 93).

A less collective account of the black detective emerged when James Sallis, a white writer and Himes's biographer, created the adventures of Lew Griffin, who acts as, rather than is, a private eye in New Orleans, starting in *The Long-Legged Fly* (1992). Pepper sees Sallis as a 'descendant of Himes', aware of the double-consciousness and masking that are central to black life (2003), but though they are highly excitable and violent, the novels lack the communal and socially critical edge of the black writers. They tend towards white crime fiction like Crumley's in Griffin's obsessive self-concern and his fully privatised role, which is, in Willett's account, to 'prevent individuals, including himself, from sinking into an abyss of drink, self-loathing and despair' (1996: 126).

This redirection of the black detective towards individualism and the traditional concerns of the private-eye novel is not only a containment but also a testimony to the eventual – though slow, compared to women detectives – growth of this sub-genre towards a strong and acknowledged place in the world of crime fiction. There have been some international moves in the same direction. Mike Phillips's Sam Dean is a London-based journalist and researcher of Caribbean origin whose investigations lead him into murder cases. One of the few writers to locate the private-eye – albeit basically amateur – form in Britain, Phillips's closely plotted and well-written novels, mostly using Dean as the focal figure, deal with a wide range of crimes and dishonesties, rather than focusing on black oppression as the Americans tend to do. *An Image to Die For* (1995) is a fairly traditional mystery – the posh sexy blonde does it, just as in Chandler – but is rich with the multi-class multiracial sociology of modern Britain. Phillips shows his range in *Point of Darkness* (1994) by taking Dean to New York where, among friends and relatives, he is rapidly involved in a complex international and Africa-related business scandal, but his work has had few parallels in Britain. Quite different is Victor Headley's vivid series, starting with *Yardie* (1992), which are effectively crime novels exploring the crime and drugs culture among some British Caribbeans. Less effective has been the attempt by the white writer Reginald Hill to diversify his output with Joe Sixmith, a black private eye from unfashionable and unexciting Luton, starting with *Born Guilty* (1995). This and its successors seem more like comic, even condescending, novels about lower-middle-class life than crime-focused accounts of multiracial Britain.

Australia's growing awareness of aboriginal cultural identity and social oppression has led to the ironic triumphs of 'Detective Inspector Watson Holmes Jackamara of the Black Cockatoo Dreaming' in some short stories by the well-known writer Mudrooroo Narogin (1990, 1993), and some more realistic and tragic detective-free crime stories by Archie Weller (1990, 1993). An aboriginal police procedural by Philip McLaren, *Scream Black Murder*

(1995), explored crime and racial tension in Sydney very effectively: it is striking that the most interesting police stories in Australia have been written from an indigenous viewpoint. In New Zealand Laurie Mantell included among her English mysteries a Maori policeman named Steven Arrow in *Murder and Chips* (1980), Gaelyn Gordon, from *Above Suspicion* (1990) on introduced in somewhat procedural mode Maori Detective Sergeant Rangi Roberts, and Paul Thomas has created vigorous and witty accounts of what Terry Sturm calls the 'renegade Maori detective Sergeant Tito Ihaka' (1998: 624), start-ing with *Old School Tie* (1994; published in London as *Dirty Laundry*, 1997). In spite of these lively international contributions, it has been the riches of population and talent among African-Americans which have been central to the substantial achievements in black crime fiction.

II   BLACK WOMEN DETECTIVES

The racially conscious detective was not only a man: the sub-genre has been considerably strengthened by finding a place in the sub-stantial world of women writers and readers. When feminist private eyes were well established, but before Mosley's first novel, Dolores Komo produced the first black woman detective in St Louis-based *Clio Brown, Private Investigator* (1988). Described by Munt as 'fiftyish, fat and folksy' (1994: 111), her colour is more significant than her gender as an innovative feature. Soitos calls it 'a rather mundane mystery novel' (1996: 229) and the difficulty of combining innova-tive characterisation with a real mystery is never fully resolved. In 1991 Nikki Baker published *In the Game*, and followed this up with *The Lavender House Murder* (1992) and *Long Goodbyes* (1993), using Virginia, or Ginny, Keely, a sympathetically presented black lesbian amateur detective from the professional class: as Bertens and D'haen note, Baker's novels are 'stylistically so much better than most crime writers' (2001: 202). In 1992 Eleanor Taylor Bland produced *Dead Time*, starring Marti MacAllister, a lesbian police officer known as 'Big Mac'. Valerie Wilson Wesley continued the development in 1994 with *When Death Comes Stealing*: Tamara Hayle, a single mother who has left the police because of racist treatment of her son, is a private eye dealing with tensions inside black families, including her own. The now active sub-genre was deployed in 1997 by Charlotte Carter with *Rhode Island Red*: detective Nanette Hayes, in manner like a female Shaft, has a BA in French from the prestigious Wellesley College and the novel is accordingly sophisticated, with what Pepper calls a 'fluid be-bop style and open-ended structure' (2000: 90) – Reddy sees the effect as postmodern (2003). These novels varied and disseminated the idea of a black woman having the power to investigate disorder, and all bore to some degree a political message as well as a criminographical pattern, but, as Soitos notes, they tend to be 'more concerned with female identity' than racial politics (1996: 223). This is not the case with the writer who has emerged as the leader of this group.

BarbaraNeely (she prefers no space between the words, like bell hooks disrupting patriarchal tradition at the level of the signifier to start with) produced an unusually rich and challenging version of black women's crime fiction with *Blanche on the Lam* in 1992. Her detective's name has the parodic grotesqueness characteristic of postcolonial writing: this big, very black woman with unstraightened hair is called Blanche White. Unlike most detectives, with the probably influential exception of Easy Rawlins, she is also working-class, in her case a housemaid – with strong historical suggestions of slavery. Although she works alone, she is constantly aware of her family and also the black community through time. Blanche is an amateur detective, tracing mysteries that just occur in her ambience, and Neely makes use of clues, suspects and a final revelation of a clue-puzzle kind. Pepper suggests that this traditionalism muffles Blanche's subversive politics (2000: 87), but Neely successfully uses the close observation and the lengthy reflections characteristic of that sub-genre to develop her racial critique as much as the mystery itself.

In *Blanche on the Lam* Blanche has just escaped from a North Carolina court after being jailed for passing bad cheques; she takes refuge in a large house by impersonating an expected housekeeper – the invisibility of the black to the white is again a mechanism of secret resistance. An excellent worker, she is also a woman of feeling, and sympathises with white victims of patriarchal white culture, including most of the women and a retarded young man. But her power to empathise with intra-white oppression does not reduce her racial sensitivity and Neely realises in penetrating detail what Pepper calls 'ways in which the interlocking and yet diverging forces of race and class operate to subjugate and dehumanise poor black subjects' (2000: 88). Soitos sees her as another exponent of the 'signifyin' trickster role and a powerful focus for that other main feature of black response, the 'double consciousness' (1996: 35–6) which combines self-awareness with knowledge of how the black self is seen from a white position. Blanche though, as Easy Rawlins partly could and Himes's detectives never tried to achieve, is able to avoid the disabling impact of 'double consciousness' and uses her tricksterism to provide consciousness-raising for her audience as well as many minor vengeances and satisfactions for herself – like feeling she bosses the house, singing Nina Simone songs and always spitting at a statue of a confederate leader. Aware of many threats – all of the USA was 'enemy territory ... for someone who looked like her' – she is also a resister 'capable of negotiating every territory' (1992: 215).

Blanche's methods, while including close observation, innate shrewdness and a trace of psychic insight, also relate to her political position and knowledge – she has taken a course in African history and culture. This novel targets white criminality and oppression, but Neely went on to subject attitudes within the black community to her critique. The title of *Blanche and the Talented Tenth* (1994) isolates the belief of the early twentieth-century black thinker W. E. B. Du Bois that the black community should cultivate its gifted fraction as leaders to bring about social reform. In the north-east now, Blanche visits a social club primarily for wealthy professional blacks. There is a murder, and she investigates again. Though white oppression remains firmly in her mind, Blanche recognises the many ways in which the 'talented tenth' have become fully incorporated in the white way of life and its values: the murder comes out of their borrowed hatreds and mendacities. In more recent novels Neely continues to vary the context and role of her detective: in *Blanche Cleans Up* (1998) she is in Boston encountering urban corruption – as Bertens and D'haen comment, this novel is 'far more consciously political' than her others (2001: 196). In *Blanche Passes Go* (2000) she is back in the south and the main challenge is male violence against women. Flexible and with varying targets, as well as serious and compellingly written, Neely's novels have created a major figure in crime fiction.

There has been some international extension of black women detectives. In England a young woman of Caribbean origin was one of the amateur detecting pair in Barbara Machin's *South of the Border* (1990), a realistic novel (and before that television series) about crime and disorder in 1980s South London. A far more lightweight contribution is the series by Susan Moody, starting with *Penny Black*

(1984), featuring Penny Wanawake, a six-foot glamorous aristocrat who happens to be black and romps through a basically comic series of detective adventures among the well-heeled; but Lisa Fuller, the aboriginal police detective in Philip McLaren's Sydney-based *Scream Black Murder* is much more radical in terms of both gender and race.

III OTHER AMERICAN ETHNICITIES

The best-known author of racially focused crime fiction outside the African-American world is Tony Hillerman. Long resident in the south-western Navajo region, he has produced a widely acclaimed series using detectives of the Navajo Tribal Police. He started in *The Blessing Way* (1970) with Sergeant Joe Leaphorn, a mature, shrewd man who combines deep knowledge of the region and native tradition with determination and thoughtful detection to unravel sudden irruptions of murder into the normally harmonic Navajo way of life. Hillerman's novels combine capably developed mysteries with the context of magnificent settings and a complex and subtle native culture. Symons found them 'essentially unexciting', though he did add 'for a British reader anyway' (1992: 240) – but Willett, also British, found 'grandeur and intensity' in the books (1992: 48) and most American commentators, and many international readers, have found them impressive both in local context and overall political positioning.

Hillerman varied the somewhat cool and settled tone deriving from Leaphorn by introducing the much younger Jim Chee in the fourth novel, *People of Darkness* (1980): Chee combines his police work with aspirations of becoming a shaman, and the rich Navajo magical world of traditions, hauntings by the dead and the malign activities of witches is always close to his mind. But it is he, not Leaphorn, who contemplates moving away, first through his liaison with a white girlfriend and then with a city-based Navajo woman lawyer. This cultural conflict is resolved in terms of staying at home, and some critics have seen a Native American essentialism as being a conservative element in Hillerman's work: Pepper finds it disappointing that Hillerman does not give mythic forces any actual role either in crimes or resolutions (2000: 165) while Murray feels that Native American grievances and resistance are not adequately presented (1997: 138–9). It is true that, as Templeton comments, Hillerman 'tends occasionally to romanticise the Navajo' (1999: 45) and his local rather than global view of the situation avoids the larger politics of American colonising racism. But the history of the white extermination and oppression of people like the Navajo is often remembered, especially through the meanings of the landscape. Many of the crimes are in fact the result of continuing white incursion, either continuous with the past, as in *Coyote Waits* (1990), where money stolen by ancient outlaws (surprisingly, Butch Cassidy and his gang) is sought with murderous results, or painfully modern as with the multiple murders in *Dance Hall of the Dead* (1973), where an incursive anthropologist kills local people in his quest to be a hero of white academic culture. While this inculpation of the whites could be held to obscure possible tensions among the natives – the sort of essentialism Himes above all avoided – Hillerman is also well aware of strains both within Navajo culture and between them and the other native peoples in the region, notably the Zuni and Pueblo Indians.

Neither Leaphorn nor, for the most part, Chee, can be classed as tricksters – their police identity makes that a difficult manoeuvre – but wise men and women and indigenous skills are often used in the detecting, and there is a strong element of a Native American version of 'double consciousness', especially realised through the trials of Jim Chee. Templeton has argued that in Hillerman murder itself 'becomes a post-colonial metaphor for cultural genocide, as does the destruction of the environment by mining companies, the military, or by hydroelectric companies' (1999: 44) and while the texts do not always operate at this level of intensity, sometimes slipping towards touristic travelogues, the best of them, and all of them to some extent, explore through the crimes done in fiction the crimes done in history and continuing in the present against the Native American people.

Under Hillerman's influence there have been many re-formations of the idea of an ethnic detective operating in some way against the power of the white majority – equally but more successfully ethnic. Aimeé and David Thurlo have also used a Navajo detective, but a woman, Ella Clah. More distantly related to Hillerman are Linda Hogan's Lakota Sioux Stacey Red Hawk, an FBI officer working in the 1920s among the Osage people in Oklahoma, starting with *Mean Spirit* (1990), Louis Owens's Choctaw-Cherokee Deputy, Munro Morales, starting with *The Sharpest Sight* (1992), Carol Lafavor's more earnestly radical amateur investigator Renée La Roche, a lesbian Ojibwa in *Evil Dead Centre* (1997), Jean Hager's detectives,

Chief Bushyhead and Molly Bearpaw, as in *Spirit Caller* (1997). Far from Hillerman's south-west is Dana Stabenow's Kate Shugak: Landrum describes her as 'a tough independent Aleut working in the Anchorage district attorney's office' (1999: 178). She first appeared in *A Cold Day for Murder* (1992) and Stabenow has achieved a substantial following for her combination of interesting mystery, liberated spirit and solid contextual realisation. In a similar context the Canadian Scott Young created an Inuk Mountie, Inspector Matteesie Kitologitak, in *Murder in a Cold Climate* (1990).

The non-WASP model has diversified. S. J. Rozan (discussed in some detail by Bertens and D'haen, 2001: 206–14) has created with sociocultural depth Lydia Chin, an Asian-American private eye, in *China Trade* (1994) and Chang-Rae Lee uses Henry Park, a Korean-American surveillance agent, as the focus of the widely praised exploration of modern multiculturality, *Native Speaker* (1995), which Pepper regards as 'spectacularly innovative, startlingly fresh' (2000: 167). Japanese-American detection has also appeared: 'E. V. Cunningham' (in fact the well-known leftist writer Howard Fast) started with *Samantha* (1967) a series about Masao Masuto, a police detective in Beverly Hills, and more recent has been Dale Furutani's Ken Tanaka, who makes, as Izzo notes (2000: 227), 'explicit discussion' of his hybrid world. Bertens and D'haen describe his work as 'one long meditation on what it means to be a Japanese American' (2001: 184).

A substantial number of racially focused crime stories have risen from the Hispanic community in America. Marcia Muller started her Elena Oliverez series with *The Tree of Death* (1983) and, as Libretti discusses (1999), Lucha Corpi in *Eulogy for a Brown Angel* (1992) uses Gloria Damasco to investigate the murder of a child during the Chicano Moratorium march in East Los Angeles in 1970, and in *Cactus Blood* (1995) the crime – which turns out not to be murder – is set in the Chicano farmworkers' strike of 1973. Alex Abella's Charlie Morell, a Cuban-American court investigator, first appeared in the richly elaborated *The Killing of the Saints* (1992). Michael Nava, discussed above as a gay writer, has gained considerable notice with his Hispanic lawyer-detective Henry Rios and Izzo (2000) discusses a range of Hispanic women detectives, including Gloria White's Ronnie Ventura and Edna Buchanan's Britt Montero.

A strong ethnic group which has not had, recently at least, so much cause to oppose oppression in America, but has still used crime fiction to some degree to explore tensions around its identity, is the substantial and in many ways strongly integrated Jewish community. Ironic crime writers like Roger L. Simon and Andrew Bergman (see p. 138) occasionally played with Jewishness as an element of difference, and Kinky Friedman, starting in *Greenwich Killing Time* (1986), made Jewish wit an element in his bravura New York investigator, himself called Kinky Friedman and former leader of a music group called 'The Texas Jewboys' (which had actually existed). Without this sense of burlesque, Harry Kemelman's successful series starting with *Friday the Rabbi Slept Late* (1964), drew usually gentle attention to ways in which covert discrimination could turn into a destructive force. Something more like the critically self-conscious tone of the black and Native American crime fiction appeared in the work of Faye Kellerman – with her husband Jonathan, and like Ross Macdonald and Margaret Millar, one of the very few husband-and-wife teams to succeed separately in the genre. In *The Ritual Bath* (1986) Rina Lazarus, an orthodox Jew, works as an amateur alongside police detective Peter Decker, described by Lawrence Roth as a 'noir-tough Jewish cowboy type' (1999: 187). There are procedural elements, but as the crime is focused in a strongly Jewish environment Decker is increasingly drawn into the significance, including for himself, of the orthodox religion and identity. Kellerman's use of the mystery to explore the role of religion in contemporary identity is the serious side of modern Jewish crime fiction. Jerome Charyn's novels are highly comic, as well as probing, but they are, as Haut comments, 'more interested in magical realism than verisimilitude' (1999: 197): in *The Good Policeman* (1990) chief of New York detectives Isaac Sidel identifies with more than merely Jewish themes, though his internationalist wisdom is also seen as having diasporic Jewish roots. But Charyn's ethnic focus has less impact than his surreality in form and theme, and the novels are best considered as an example of another category of radical crime fiction, one which generates a postmodernist critique of the underlying authority of modern ideas of subjective consciousness.

10
At the Cutting Edge

I POSTMODERN CRIME FICTION

Postmodern fiction, including crime fiction, is sometimes held by conservatives to be without coherence or identifiable meaning – Symons judged Paul Auster's *City of Glass* (1985) 'a clever, sterile book' (1992: 332). But postmodernism is a form of resistance with its own version of politics, rejecting what are seen as the invalid and deforming concepts of consistency and subjective identity as being based on unduly constraining rational and aesthetic systems, whether of classical realism or modernism. In postmodern fiction coincidence, overlapping accounts, indeterminacy are the plot motifs and parody, irony and inconsequence are technical tools to dislodge the idea of a single knowing and moralising subject, operating in ordered time and with purposive function. Postmodern crime fiction has a special importance because major early postmodernists employed the genre to establish their positions against rationality and humanism. As Michael Holquist argued in an influential essay (1971) and Stefano Tani outlined in detail in *The Doomed Detective* (1984), Borges, Butor and Eco in particular showed how crime fiction can, by being less determinate and simplistic than usual in its processes and outcomes, be a means of questioning certainties about the self, the mind and indeed the ambient world. The discussion has been reopened in a recent essay collection (Merivale and Sweeney, 1999).

The political edge of postmodern crime fiction is confirmed by the fact that some early examples came out of the black movement. Soitos calls Chapter 6 of his book 'Black Anti-Detective Novels' and deals closely with Ishmael Reed's *Mumbo Jumbo* (1972) and Clarence Major's *Reflex and Bone Structure* (1975). Frank Campenni (in Reilly, 1980: 1247) describes Reed as 'primarily a satirist and parodist' and *Mumbo Jumbo*, set in the 1920s, is in part a mystery focused on a 'double conscious trickster detective' (Soitos, 1996: 183) named PaPa

La Bas, who runs a detective agency called the Neo-Hoodoo Kathedral. The novel is a freewheeling fantasy, but a serious one with a bibliography and a recurrent commitment to black issues. Major's novel makes frequent reference to crime fiction practices, and there is a strong sense in *Reflex and Bone Structure* that fantasy and the deconstruction of the traditional novel are meant to ridicule and criticise the white tradition in a politicised postmodernism.

Thomas Pynchon's ground-breaking postmodern novel *The Crying of Lot 49* (1966) is in many ways an irrational and unresolved detective quest and it seems to have been a major stimulus for Paul Auster's detecting without outcomes beyond the positive power of uncertainty, as shown in his *New York* trilogy, though connections can also be seen with critical theorists such as Maurice Blanchot (Nealon, 1996). In the first novel, *City of Glass* (1985), well analysed by Malmgren (2001: 122–31), a poet and detective writer named Quinn impersonates a private eye named Paul Auster and undertakes a quest for a mad scientist who, it transpires, walks through New York to trace out letters which will eventually provide the Borgesian phrase 'The Tower of Babel'. Both the cleverness and the sterility which Symons deplored are in fact central to the message about the randomness of knowledge and identity in mass-mediated, commodity-oriented, identity-fragmented modern society, and this is pursued in the rest of Auster's *New York* trilogy, *Ghosts* (1986) and *The Locked Room* (1986), which both diverge from and eventually, obscurely, relate to the first novel, as Bernstein has indicated (1999).

Auster is not alone. Some of the most investigative and formally aware of recent writers move on from radical crime fiction to patterns which are essentially and dissentingly postmodern. After three powerful expositions of crime in the context of gender, Barbara Wilson produced *Gaudí Afternoon* (1990), in its title a respectful reference to *Gaudy Night* but in its themes of gender-choice and gender-change relating to the work of Judith Butler (1990) on ways in which gender is a performance that, like the body itself, can be radically varied at will. The story starts as a standard amateur detective quest for a missing husband but, as Gair comments, it will be 'only peripherally concerned' with crime (1997: 111). Indeterminacy is all: Cassandra Reilly, the quasi-detective, has chosen her own name, and the leading characters shift genders and familial roles playfully and liberatingly. Sweeney finds the book 'witty, exuberant, delightfully self-reflexive' (1999: 127), but it is also a serious critique, and both its tone and theme are parallel to Sarah Schulman's work. Starting with

The Sophie Horovitz Story (1984) she presents lesbian detection in a form which is, as Munt comments, 'unrelentingly metafictional' and 'a parody of "types"' (1994: 176, 174). Mixing radicals, lesbians and revolutionaries with typically postmodern effrontery – a sleuth is called Mrs Noseworthy – Schulman reads like a droll and unpretentious version of Auster. Like Wilson, her later novels move away from crime fiction, as the generic model is primarily used as an instrument to parody quests for knowledge.

Schulman's playful interrogations and Wilson's serious game seem to combine in the feminist revenge fantasy *Dirty Weekend* (1991) by Helen Zahavi. In Brighton, an English town notorious for weekend sexual adventures, she sets a set of spree-killings in reprisal for generalised male oppression by Bella – her name being the Latin for both 'beautiful woman' and 'battles', as Harris and Baker note (1995: 599). Victimised for all her young life, she has escaped to Brighton. A stalker terrifies her, and, deciding to be butcher rather than lamb, she breaks into his flat and beats him to death with a hammer. Personal anti-male vengeance becomes a crusade, and finally, in a liberating allegory that makes this a form of postcolonial discourse, she stalks a modern 'Jack the Ripper' and stabs him while humming an old-fashioned popular dance song. The events of the novel shocked readers, women as well as men, but worse yet was the cheerfully comic tone of Bella's discussions with the reader of her plans and their achievement. While some might think that Zahavi uses a comic form to sugar the pill of a ferocious feminist message, it seems rather that this is a postmodern move to disrupt textual certainties as much as masculine poise, and in its success, not repeated in her more serious and less fanciful later novels, Zahavi has created one of the real originals of crime fiction.

Postmodern crime fiction, with its tonal complexity and its rejection of ancient traditions of certain knowledge, assured identity and detective-centred moral authority, seems at present an exotic part of the genre, but it has recurred around the world. The Australian Jan McKemmish's first novel *A Gap in the Records* (1985) is a well-sustained critique of over-certainties, thematic and formal, as a group of middle-aged women explore lacunae in the national, and masculine, psyche. Malcolm Pryce's *Aberystwyth Mon Amour* (2001), with its reference to Marguerite Duras's important early postmodern novel (and film) *Hiroshima Mon Amour*, is a highly comic private-eye parody that also pillories fantasies of Welshness past and present. Playfulness is part of the seriousness in postmodernity and crime fiction has long accommodated literary parodies and self-aware extrarationality like the Detection Club: it may be that postmodern crime fiction has, implicitly at least, longer-standing roots than the other forms of critique and resistance, focused on gender and race, that have so strongly and positively developed in recent decades.

II GENERIC VIOLENCE

Genres and sub-genres can depend for identity not only on plot structure and content, but, like the difference between comedy and farce or tragedy and melodrama, they can also rise from the emphasis laid on events and reactions to them. In the last two decades some writers have made violence so central a feature of their texts that it appears to have taken on a generic force and expresses, explores and even exploits concerns that are newly evident in the social and cultural context.

Crime fiction has long been familiar with violence. It is basic to the clue-puzzle, but covert, contained as part of the sub-genre's euphemistic meaning. Variations of violence signify throughout the private-eye form, not only in the central and often explicit deaths but also through characters – the head-contused but unbleeding male private eyes who suffer assaults only on their consciousness, and the incised and relished wounds of the body-opened female victims; while the feminist private eyes receive abraded wounds, both contused and bleeding, to reveal their combination of hero and victim. But that signifying violence was non-generic, intermittent even in Spillane, and could be absent as sometimes in Ross Macdonald.

To a regular reader and reviewer of crime fiction it became clear, in the mid-1980s, that something was changing, violence was being foregrounded. The never reticent McBain's *Widows* (1991) opens with a young woman repeatedly ripped with a knife, while in *A Taste for Death* (1986) P. D. James, previously following the clue-puzzle's bloodless model, offers a spectacularly gory start. Since then the bloodstains have spread, and a sub-genre has formed where violence is necessary, central and a thematic focus.

Knight pointed out (1991) that ferocious violence existed as long ago as *The Newgate Calendar* – Dick Turpin is illustrated burning an old woman on the fire to make her reveal her savings – but this was by no means regular and so was never generic. Growing and emotively charged violence unmediated by a deploring detective is found in the crime novel, with Chase and Thompson as clear examples, but both there and in the more detailed realism of the police procedural form, and notably in the 'True Crime' genre, there remains a moral evaluation of the evil of such relished mayhem. It remains unclear whether this officially deplored violence is enjoyed in terms of fantasy commitment, as alarmists usually think, or more complex and defensive reasons: the fact that the audience for 'True Crime', especially on television, is predominantly female and mature suggests it may be a defensive consideration of the possibility of physical harm. However, the ways in which in modern media violence is both emphasised (the crashes in Formula One racing, the harm done to boxers) and emotionalised (the flowers left for a rape-murdered child) have certainly led to wider awareness of brutality, especially serial killers. It was the cheap newspapers of the day which made Jack the Ripper a domestic monster and in recent years it was publishing in newspapers and book form that made the serial killer as a literary genre into what Priestman calls 'a fixture' (1998: 33): in 1994 Joyce Carol Oates wrote a major essay in *The New York Review of Books* on no less than ten recent accounts of serial killers.

These ferocious recent representations seem not just demonisable media exploitation but a coherent form of contemporary anxiety. In art and theatre, as well as in critical theory and the previously calm pastures of literary criticism, the pains, distortions and potential fragmentations of the human body have become a central, even obsessional topic. Recurrently there is expressed both a fascination and an anxiety about the human envelope that once was a temple of identity but is now, as posthumanist criticism explains (Badmington, 2000), a fragile physical reification of the idea that human subjectivity is itself no more than a fragmentable construct. What Joel Black describes as 'the aesthetics of violence' (1991) may in the hands of the newly and generically violent crime writers be expressing in vivid form a new range of anxiety about personal and, by extension, social disorder.

Some of the new moves were still, in spite of their intensity, contained within forms of exculpating moralism. McBain's much incised woman in *Widows* turns out to have been a blackmailing mistress; James's blood-spattered church vestry will assume the aura of sanctity and sacrifice. Andrew Vachss's novels, starting with *Flood* (1985), use a Spillane-like vigilante moralism to justify what Willett describes as 'brutal nightmare visions of garbage and graffiti, violence and drugs in the desolate waste of New York city' (1992: 57). But among the most forceful authors of generic violence – who are not accidentally the best-sellers among them – there is an indeterminate, even postmodern, stance on the morals of violence, and the reader is left to encounter it with much diminished or even absent agencies of disapproval and containment.

When James Ellroy, with a difficult personal background that included petty crime and his mother's murder, turned to fiction he wrote one private-eye novel and then three tough-cop stories in the Lloyd Hopkins series about what Bertens and D'haen call 'a racist, sexist and violent police officer' (2001: 98). In *The Black Dahlia* (1987) he began the immensely successful 'L. A. Quartet'. Using police detectives, including some procedures, recognising racial tensions and making corruption in big business, politics and the police themselves central themes of his highly complex plots, Ellroy's enterprise is a much more credible account of crime in southern California than was provided by the private-eye writers, including Hammett: a reclamation of a multi-criminal white history in some ways parallel to Mosley's black-focused recovery of the place and the past.

Physical violence is central from the start: *The Black Dahlia* begins with the brutal 'Zoot-suit Riots' where police and white servicemen viciously fought Hispanics in the streets of Los Angeles. The friendship formed there between detectives Bleichert and Blanchard is sealed in blood and pain in their ferocious boxing bout. The sound, smell, and most of all the anguish of wartime Los Angeles is potently well realised and climaxes with Elizabeth (Betty) Short's body, naked, disfigured, eviscerated, and cut in half, lying in the city. The reasons for her death are the core of the ramified plot: the murder will be traced to a savagely dysfunctional family whose corrupt patriarch was directly involved in the Hollywood land scandals. Sociohistorical symbolism lies heavily on the fact that the murder and the pornographic film that was part of Betty Short's fall were both set in a house beneath the famous hillside letters that name Hollywood.

Betty's dismembered body is a semiotic sign for the unhuman, or posthuman, practices of the city, and Bleichert's obsession with her is his own psychically fragmenting force. Never a secure hero – he is less than brave, his boxing career included fixes and his father was a Nazi sympathiser – he comes close to derangement in his obsessive quest after his colleague and close friend Blanchard disappears. Approaching the psychic abyss, he encourages a Short lookalike to dress like her for sex, though this in itself turns out to be part of the plot: she is the daughter of the murderous Sprague family.

Masculine certainty is one of the many casualties in this world, but it is not a simple demise: Cohen links this failure in identity with the spectacle of the city and a general 'crisis of urban subjectivity' (1997: 171) and Horsley sees 'the strength of the bond between the money-makers and the myth-makers' (1998: 152) as a inculpating force behind both the Sprague household and the multiply-criminal police force. A strident evocation of the darkness of American socio-cultural history and also an exploration of collapsing identity and its physical detritus, *The Black Dahlia* nevertheless can seem less rigorous: the core plot is in fact curiously like Chandler in that a deranged woman did the murder, and the noble friend – Blanchard is a double for Rusty Regan – was killed in the same way, but this time by her daughter, the Betty Short lookalike. In keeping with that masculinist theme, women are treated consistently as objects of desire and dismissal, with the eventual exception of Kay Lake, lover first of Blanchard then of Bleichert, herself a former torture victim with the marks to prove it. Becoming a schoolteacher and always an implausibly sweet person, she enables the regrettably positive ending where Bleichert, returned from the edge of disintegration, flies to meet her as she is to bear their child.

Such uncharacteristic optimism and Chandleresque moral simplicities aside, *The Black Dahlia* is a major text, amplifying and modernising crime fiction and shaping violence as a central force and medium of meaning. That position was developed, though never more sharply focused, in Ellroy's later books – *L.A. Confidential* (1990) reworks the theme of Hollywood myth and Los Angeles corruption, this time showing more clearly how patriarchy appropriates and deforms women as prostitutes are made by plastic surgery to look like film stars, and also developing much more fully the processes of corruption and real crime among the police. *The Big Nowhere* (1988) engaged with the politics of the McCarthy period but also more focally extended shock and violence into homosexual incest, and *White Jazz* (1992) takes this ultimate sexual taboo further across several families. These novels develop the tendency, evident in *The Black Dahlia* through both Bleichert and the Sprague family, to find crime ultimately a matter of personal moral collapse, though they never defer social corruption to the sidelines: it is a mark of Ellroy's range and imaginative breadth that he has maintained a consistently social view and sees a collapse of the authentic identity of the city as well as the person in the world of signifying violence.

A smaller canvas than Ellroy's, but a similar intensity of detail and plot, as well as a greater impact through one particular image, has been the achievement of Thomas Harris. After a competent terrorist novel, *Black Sunday* (1975), he produced the serial-killer story *Red Dragon* (1981). The multiple crimes of Ted Bundy, Ed Gein and Jeffry Dahmer had, especially in their much-mediated form, made Americans aware of a new threat: Selzer reports that the term 'serial killer' itself was coined in the mid-1970s (1995: 93) and the growth of the literary phenomenon is treated by Malmgren (2001: 172–9). The terrorists of their day, serial killers were widely discussed and rapidly fictionalised. In *Red Dragon* vivid detail grimly realises the crimes as families are attacked, brutalised, lined up for photographs – the killer is himself a mediator. Crazed into thinking himself a version of William Blake's Red Dragon, he is tracked down by the FBI agent who has previously caught the deranged psychiatrist Hannibal Lecter. While the violence is much relished, especially the burning to death of an annoying journalist, and Lecter's cannibalism is teasingly mentioned, the novel does not make violence generic: it recognises a growing interest in brutality, but the form is no more than a success-ful mainstream detective chase to extirpate the violent, as is the first film made from it, *Manhunter*.

But this changes in the succeeding novel, *The Silence of the Lambs* (1988), an international standard of crime fiction and a massive suc-cess as a film. In terms of crime fiction norms this is a much less well-organised book than *Red Dragon*: it does not even introduce the villain until almost a third of the way through and uses a late and tricky device – the dressmaker's darts that reveal his purposes – to bring detective Starling coincidentally to the killer's house. The novel spends much time and focus on another character who is nei-ther killer nor detective, Hannibal Lecter. A good fiction editor might have tidied this up, and in so doing destroyed the novel's impact: these curious structural motifs make the novel generically and thematically focused on violence and the accompanying con-cerns with identity and subjectivity.

Jame Gumb's violence against women is never described in the forensic detail that was central to *Red Dragon*: the real horror of his crimes is the idea, not the reality, of skinning women to make a suit of clothes, focusing on disassembling the body in order to reshape another. The novel's image of an insect emerging from a cocoon fore-grounds the concept of reidentification of the self through violence, and it is as a form of insect, wearing huge-lensed goggles, that he is finally killed by Starling. The idea of posthuman metamorphosis is imposed on the simplistic concept of gayness as the motive for murder.

Lecter represents another stage in purposive violence: he likes eating people, but the fact that he is also a genius psychiatrist conveys some higher authority onto this breach of the ultimate human taboo. He also uses self-transforming violence when he not only murders two police to escape but cuts off a face and places it over his own in disguise: the exotic and compelling nature of the image has overridden the ludicrous suggestion that an ambulanceman could intubate such a face without noticing its impermanence. Yet Lecter's relation with Starling indicates that his role is positive. Though he is first imagined as a Gothic monster, encaged and, as the police later discover, terribly dangerous, he is courteous to her and in fact comes to play the highly artificial role of expert adviser, the genius detective who needs nothing but his thoughts to solve a case. Though again, the improbability that he actually knew Jame Gumb is elided by the charm of the idea: his extra-human behaviour is condensed with his super-human detection. As Clarice's real mentor he minimises the police effectively and the plot pursues this anti-procedural theme – as in a private-eye novel they have rushed off in the wrong direction when Clarice triumphs bravely and alone at the end.

Braving Gumb's disembodying violence, she is in part traditionally identified as a Gothic heroine and will also be what Clover (1989) has influentially described as 'the final girl', the brave young woman who is not killed and finishes off the destroyer of women. But this success comes because Starling herself has undergone physical changes of identity. She has the gun-speed to out-shoot Gumb because she has exercised long to strengthen her hand to masculine standards at FBI school. In dress and physique she is never feminine, and in the film Jodie Foster caught well her grave androgyny. Herself a physical and social construct, an upwardly mobile professional masculinised woman, she is also haunted, as the bestialised human Lecter brings out, by nightmares of violence to animals on the farm of her parentless youth: the silence of the lambs relates both to their killing and also to a prospective exorcising of her anxieties when she has sufficiently reconstructed herself. This may go further than humans merely escaping animal-based phobias: Wolfe and Elmer have suggested that 'cross-species identification' (1995: 144) is a central feature of the film and it is implied in the novel through the title, Starling's surname, the bestial imagery around Jame Gumb, as well as Lecter's power of smell, animal-like caging and, of course, eating habits.

The vulnerability of the human body and the transformations of gender and class that are clearly focal themes in the story also extend to a 'posthuman' speculation about the invalidity of our separation from the animal regime, which makes the fascinating nature of Lecter's cannibalism all the more explicable. It was emphasised in the film to the cost of Starling's character: where the novel ends with her comfortably in bed with a man – and some dogs, admittedly – the film ends with Lecter raising a uniform laugh with the ambiguity of saying he is 'having a friend for lunch': on the menu is Dr Chilton, the weak all-too-human gaoler of the free, supremely animalised mind that Lecter symbolises.

Symons thought *The Silence of the Lambs* was 'the literary equivalent of a video-nasty' (1992: 322) and he was right to suggest a new generic formation parallel to the teenage fascination with body-dismantling horror movies and the physical fetishisation of pornography: there is even a horror fiction sub-genre called 'splatter'. The violence is central to the impact of the novel, and to support it Harris has eclectically gathered disparate sub-generic features – proceduralism, feminism, the Gothic, the heroic criminal in a book as inventive and rich as *The Woman in White* (Lecter and Fosco have many similarities), and a focal text of the new sub-genre of violent crime fiction.

It has not been successfully imitated – the third novel *Hannibal* (1999) seems a strained attempt to renovate the characters and especially to heroise Lecter as a consequence of the film treatment of him. He rescues Starling from his own former victim, who is himself moralised by having deserved his fate at Lecter's hands, then and now, by being a corrupt and cruel billionaire. Harris also bathetically explains Lecter's otherwise enchanting cannibalism by relating it to the Nazi brutalisation and murder of his beloved little sister. Plain has argued that Harris ironises the voyeuristic desires of the reader and represents Lecter as a Satan-like 'fallen angel' (2001: 226), but even this praise sees the novel as being in the shadow of the potent and violence-focused inventions of *The Silence of the Lambs*, which remain in their effect ambiguous: Malmgren pointedly asks whether the Harris books act towards ultra-violence as 'vaccine or virus' (2001: 190).

Other authors have responded to the concept of centralised violence and threat to identity through the medical brutality permitted a forensic specialist. The leader has been Patricia Cornwell, a journalist who gained experience with a medical examiner, and who with *Post-Mortem* (1990) started a successful series based on Kay Scarpetta, chief medical examiner in Virginia. With feminist crime fiction as a point of departure, the novels involve Scarpetta in tension with men who resent her authority. A single woman, like V. I. and Kinsey, she lives unlike them in consumerist style with fine cars, kitchens and restaurants, but this comfort is contrasted with the austere and starkly realised details of the dissecting room: body parts, techniques of autopsy, recurrent treatment of physical dysfunction all make these novels into celebrations of the dismantling of the human envelope. *The Body Farm* (1994) involves a research establishment where human parts are exposed to verify their rate and kind of decay.

Fascination with the results of violence is a major feature of the novels, but in company with it goes an insistence that Scarpetta's identity is under threat, psychic as well as physical. She is pressured as a woman, rather than a scientist: her love-life is intermittent and mostly miserable and she is consistently challenged as a person with authority and pressed towards an anonymous abyss. Her lesbian niece is an IT expert, more wedded to machines than to a woman: her gender choice seems insignificant. Messent notes the 'deep ambivalence about identity, the social order and their ability to sustain each other that runs through all of Cornwell's writing' (2000: 134). This incipient posthumanism never attains the imaginative power of *The Silence of the Lambs*, in part through Cornwell's often leaden prose style and what Ellen Bleiler calls her 'increasingly formulaic' plots (in Winks, 1998: II, 245), and in part through Scarpetta's somewhat smug and self-concerned persona. The pressure on Scarpetta's identity is also weakened as later novels slip into what Bertens and D'haen call 'a frenetic straining for effect' (2001: 172) within melodramatic plotting based on series villains like Temple Gault and, later on, Jean Baptise Chardonne, a French werewolf. Diluting the deconstructive power of a violence-focused narrative, Cornwell's novels, as Tomc comments, 'combine an aggressive critique of "patriarchy" with a narrative that highlights the varieties of submission and conformity' (1995: 47). She brings back towards the mainstream the initiatives of Ellroy and Harris, and in doing so shows the contemporary power of the sub-genre of violent crime fiction.

There have been followers of Cornwell like Kathy Reichs, starting with the Montreal-set forensic mystery *Déjà Dead* (1997) – Reddy finds her less 'conservative' and 'self-indulgent' than Cornwell (2003) – and Mary Willis Walker, with her 'Molly Cates' series starting with *The Red Scream* (1995), is discussed at some length by Berten and D'haen. They find her work, like Cornwell's, belonging 'to the illiberal, strongly gendered world of the thriller' (2001: 169). A more genre-testing thriller of violence, and response to Harris, is by Val McDermid. Well established in both lesbian and heterosexual feminist crime fiction, in 1995 she produced *The Mermaids Singing*, which seems in many ways to rework *The Silence of the Lambs*. In a gloomy northern English setting, a serial killer is at work, dumping sexually brutalised dead young men. A profiler is brought in to work with Carol Jordan, a police detective. But intercalated with their inquiries are the killer's memoirs, starting with a pleasurable visit to a torture museum in Italy. It soon becomes clear that the killer is selecting men and torturing them to death with ingenious machines when they fail to deliver the required emotional and sexual commitment. Skilled with the machinery, and also an expert with IT, the post-human killer is an aesthetician of violence, and McDermid provides well-chosen quotations from De Quincey as epigraphs to each chapter of detective operations.

The broken male bodies match the diminished masculine identity of Tony Hill, the profiler, who is impotent, can only achieve orgasm through telephone sex, with one favourite caller, and cannot respond to the attractive companionship of Carol Jordan. Gender tensions multiply: Carol is herself harassed by sexist police, but women are not exculpated – a journalist exercises female rapacity in her informational inroads into the police. Male detectives, thinking they are looking for a deranged homosexual, have to pose as gay in their inquiries, much to their confusion and re-education. But neither the wrongly arrested gay man – who hangs himself in gaol – nor the eventually imagined woman serial killer is in fact the murderer. The murderer is finally revealed as a gender-changing man who has – this device is fairly well explained – been Hill's telephone lover. In a chase-style ending, with Carol Jordan ultimately to the rescue, Hill himself is his/her last victim – and so a male 'final girl' (Plain, 2001: 225–6) – who manages to kill the killer by feigning a false desire, ending as both a criminalised detective and a fabricated sexual identity.

A sustained piece of powerful writing, *The Mermaids Singing* is also an exploration of violence both external to the tragically vulnerable body and internal as human consciousness fragments. Though it could be seen as finally a refusal to imagine a female serial killer – something of a taboo in modern media, and touched on in films like *Black Widow* and *Basic Instinct* – the novel is more fairly seen as a realisation of the notions of performative gender and an example of how the sub-genre of violent crime fiction, when imaginatively empowered and technically sustained, can deliver compelling accounts of contemporary crime. Something of the same position is arrived at in Stella Duffy's *Fresh Flesh* (1999) when, after a slowly developed mystery for Saz Martin, her cheeky South London lesbian investigator, her already scarred body is almost torn apart. Violence becomes the climax of the novel, thematic as well as structural, as in McDermid.

Brett Easton Ellis's controversial *American Psycho* (1991) is in form a crime novel recounting the experiences – or the fantasies – of a Wall Street yuppie in both his obsessive quest for the perfect lifestyle and his increasingly violent attacks on woman. Famously, Patrick Bateman, wealthy and well-educated, graduates through simple murder and mutilation to killing a woman by forcing a rat up her vagina and dismembering another with a chain-saw. Widely reviled by feminists and many others when it appeared, as in Naomi Wolf's angry review (1991), and to many seeming like a deliberate celebration of gendered sadism, the novel has had a less negative ultimate acceptance on the basis of posthumanist theory. There are internal clues that suggest the whole is a deranged fantasy, a feature more strongly suggested by the film (directed by a feminist). The novel is now widely seen, like *The Mermaids Singing* and the strongest examples of the modern sub-genre of violent crime fiction, as being a satirical rhapsody on the implications of gender and identity under pressure in a world where meaning is born by surfaces and commodities, identity is transitional and reconstructable, and emotions may only be seen as valid when they, and behaviour, become extreme. Novels of this kind have been produced by the major French theorist Julia Kristeva: *The Old Man and the Wolves* (1994) and *Possessions* (1998) deal with crimes set in a Southern Californian nowhere, called Santa Varvara, and they explore ways in which in contemporary society and the age of the holocaust people are reduced to the level of what, as Plain discusses (2001: 9–11), Kristeva has in *Powers of Horror* (1982) described as the 'abject', a human entity, rather than a person, who is powerless, connectionless, in both thought and action, a terrible threat to others, and so a natural topic for crime fiction.

* * * * *

Through socially shared morality and through a sense of personal identity the detectives of the clue-puzzle and the private-eye forms kept at bay their sense of collapsing values and threats to the personal psyche as well as the body. The radical rewriters of the form, whether using gender, race or, more rarely, social politics as their field of value, also could (except the rigorous-minded Himes) usually find positive formations, domains of hope which were illuminated by the resolution of the mystery. But in postmodern crime fiction and the new, related, sub-genre of violence, such consoling certainties – while still available in the other sub-genres – are not to be identified.

After two centuries of crime fiction the uncertainties, formal and thematic, that dominated *Caleb Williams* and the fiction of Charles Brockden Brown are visible again. Through faith in a detective who represented some form of value – disciplinary, rational, psychological, imaginative or simply physical – the massive genre of crime fiction was able to shape forms that both recognised and offered at least passing resolutions to contemporary anxieties, especially the displaced fear of death. It is a matter for conjecture, and even doubt, whether crime fiction, a form that in the latest manifestations of its diversity has re-established uncertainty as a dominating principle, will ever again be able to provide, except in retrospective mood and mode, easy confidences.

A Chronology of
Crime Fiction

1773 *The Newgate Calendar*: first major collection of crime without detectives

1794 William Godwin, *Caleb Williams*: first moves towards detection

1798 Charles Brockden Brown, *Wieland*: first American novel of crime and mystery

1827 Thomas Gaspey(?), *Richmond: Scenes from the Life of a Bow Street Runner*: the adventures of a proto-detective

1827–8 Eugène François Vidocq, *Mémoires*: real-life detection (and some fiction) from the former head of the Sûreté; translated into English in 1829

1828 Edward Bulwer, *Pelham*: first move towards the gentleman-detective

1830 Samuel Warren, *Passages from the Diary of a Late Physician* begins in *Blackwood's Magazine*: crime and punishment seen through the eyes of a disciplinary specialist

1838 Charles Dickens, *Oliver Twist*: Bow Street Runners and the Hue and Cry – crime before detection of any intensity

1841 Edgar Allan Poe, 'Murders in the Rue Morgue': the debut of C. Auguste Dupin, the first intellectual detective

1842/3 Edgar Allan Poe, 'The Mystery of Marie-Rogêt': Poe's partially successful attempt to turn real crime into fiction

1844 Edgar Allan Poe, 'The Purloined Letter': mystery so obvious no one can solve it – except Dupin

1849 William Russell, *Recollections of a Police Officer*: stories about Waters, the first plain-style police detective, set in London, first appear in magazines

1852 William Russell, *Recollections of a Policeman*: first anthology appears in America

1853 Charles Dickens, *Bleak House*: Inspector Bucket plays a large, but not thematically central, role as detective in this great sociopolitical novel

1856 William Russell, *The Recollections of a Detective Police Officer*: Waters published in book form in England

1860   Wilkie Collins, *The Woman in White*: first major 'novel of sensation' with important women characters, aristocratic criminals and some amateur detection

1861   Ellen Wood, *East Lynne*: more sensation, with a misled woman, another fiendish gentleman and some amateur detection

1862   Mary Elizabeth Braddon, *Lady Audley's Secret*: a woman criminal, with amateur detection

1864   Andrew Forrester Jun., *The Female Detective*: first woman police detective – long before they really existed

1864   W. S. Hayward(?), *Revelations of a Lady Detective*: Mrs Paschal of the detective office

1865   'Charles Felix', *The Notting Hill Murder*: the first English murder mystery with detection throughout

1865   'John B. Williams' (ed.), *Leaves from the Note-Book of a New York Detective*: the exploits of Jem Brampton, the first all-American detective

1866   Émile Gaboriau, *L'Affaire Lerouge*: the first French detective novel, starring Tabaret

1866   Mary Fortune, as 'W.W.' in *The Australian Journal*, may be the first woman writing self-conciously detective fiction

1867   'Seeley Regester', *The Dead Letter*: the first American murder mystery by a woman author (Metta Fuller), with detailed detection throughout

1868   Émile Gaboriau, *M. Lecoq*: the first appearance of the great French police detective

1868   Wilkie Collins, *The Moonstone*: mysterious theft eventually solved by an exotic amateur detective after failure of the professionals; multiple viewpoint a marked feature

1870   Charles Dickens, *The Mystery of Edwin Drood*: Dickens's last and unfinished novel was to involve mystery, disguise and – it seems – some detection

1874   Allan Pinkerton, *The Expressman and the Detective*: first in a series of realistic private eye stories

1878   Anna Katherine Green, *The Leavenworth Case*: first of a long series of New York-based detective mysteries

1881   Emile Gaboriau novels translated into English and published by Vizetelly in London

1886   Fergus Hume, *The Mystery of a Hansom Cab*: written and set in Melbourne, the first crime best-seller when reprinted in London in 1887

1887   Arthur Conan Doyle, *A Study in Scarlet*: first Sherlock Holmes novella

1891   Arthur Conan Doyle, 'A Scandal in Bohemia': first Sherlock Holmes short story, in *Strand Magazine*

1892   Arthur Conan Doyle, *The Adventures of Sherlock Holmes*: twelve *Strand* stories in collected form

1892   Israel Zangwill, *The Big Bow Mystery*: the first locked-room mystery novel

1894   Arthur Morrison, *Martin Hewitt, Investigator*: first of the 'plain man' alternatives to Holmes

1894   Arthur Conan Doyle, *The Memoirs of Sherlock Holmes*: more stories, but Holmes dies in the last, 'The Final Problem'

1901–2 Arthur Conan Doyle, *The Hound of the Baskervilles*: Doyle is persuaded to resume Holmes in *The Strand*, but sets story back before his death

1902   Arthur Conan Doyle, 'The Empty House': Doyle revives Holmes in *Strand Magazine*

1907   Maurice Leblanc, *Arsène Lupin: gentleman-cambrioleur*: imaginative French response to Holmes, trans. as *The Exploits of Arsène Lupin*, 1909

1907   Gaston Leroux, *Le Mystère de la Chambre Jaune*: first elaborate locked-room mystery, trans. as *The Mystery of the Yellow Room*

1907   Jacques Futrelle, *The Thinking Machine*: first collection of major genius detective stories

1907   R. Austin Freeman, *The Red Thumb Mark*: first appearance of the forensic-scientific detective Dr Thorndyke

1908   Mary Roberts Rinehart, *The Circular Staircase*: the first of many mysteries by an early American woman writer

1911   G. K. Chesterton, *The Innocence of Father Brown*: stories at least as subtle as Doyle's, but very differently focused

1913   E. C. Bentley, *Trent's Last Case*: often seen as the first 'golden age' novel

1913   Carolyn Wells, *The Technique of the Mystery Story*: first extended discussion of the genre

1920   Agatha Christie, *The Mysterious Affair at Styles:* first Poirot story

1920   Freeman Wills Crofts, *The Cask*: start of a series of detailed, plain detection

1923   Dorothy Sayers: *Whose Body?*: the start of Lord Peter Wimsey's career

1923   Dashiell Hammett starts publishing tough detective stories in *The Black Mask*: flowering of the American private-eye tradition

1925   Earl Derr Biggers, *The House without a Key*: the first Charlie Chan and the start of multicultural detection

1926   Agatha Christie, *The Murder of Roger Ackroyd*: the mystery which established Christie at the top of the profession

1926   'S. S. Van Dine', *The Benson Murder Case*: Philo Vance makes his debut in New York

1928   Arthur Upfield, *The House of Cain*: first novel starring the Australian aboriginal detective 'Boney'

1928   Patricia Wentworth, *Grey Mask*: Miss Silver, first woman detective in a novel engaged in full-scale detecting

1929   Dashiell Hammett, *Red Harvest*: first of the novels that were to influence so much in crime writing

1929   Gladys Mitchell, *Speedy Death*: Adela Bradley, most formidable of the early woman detectives, makes her appearance

1929   'Ellery Queen', *The Roman Hat Mystery*: first appearance, in New York, of the most complex of all the clue-puzzlers

1929   W. R. Burnett, *Little Caesar*: the first major American crime novel

1929   Mignon Eberhart, *The Patient in Room 18*: beginning of a long career in woman-oriented crime fiction

1930   Margery Allingham, *Mystery Mile*: the first substantial detecting by Albert Campion

1930   Dorothy Sayers, *Strong Poison*: Sayers first develops characterisation as much as mystery

1930   Agatha Christie, *Murder at the Vicarage*: Miss Marple joins the other new women detectives

1931   'Francis Iles', *Malice Aforethought*: first of A. B. Cox's psychothrillers

1932   Raymond Chandler publishes his first private-eye story in *Black Mask*

1932   Rudolph Fisher, *The Conjure-man Dies*: first black detective novel

1933   John Dickson Carr, *Hag's Nook*: first Dr Gideon Fell mystery

1933   Erle Stanley Gardner, *The Case of the Velvet Claws*: Perry Mason's first case

1934   James M. Cain, *The Postman Always Rings Twice*: first novel by the major American crime novelist

1934   Ngaio Marsh, *A Man Lay Dead*: first Inspector Alleyn mystery

1934   Rex Stout, *Fer de Lance*: Nero Wolfe's first appearance

1939   Raymond Chandler, *The Big Sleep*: first novel starring Philip Marlowe

1939   'James Hadley Chase', *No Orchids for Miss Blandish*: English writer imitates and exceeds the American tough crime novel

1940   Cornell Woolrich, *The Bride Wore Black*: start of a career in American Gothic crime novels

1943   Margaret Millar, *Wall of Eyes*: first American psychothriller

1945   Lawrence Treat, *V as in Victim*: first consciously procedural novel

1947   Mickey Spillane, *I, The Jury*: first appearance of Mike Hammer

1949   'Ross Macdonald' (as John Macdonald), *The Moving Target*: first appearance of Lew Archer

1950   Julian Symons, *The Thirty-First of February*: Symons's first psychothriller

1952   Hillary Waugh, *Last Seen Wearing...*: first high-quality American procedural

1955   'J. J. Marric', *Gideon's Day*: first major British procedural

1955   Patricia Highsmith, *The Talented Mr Ripley*: start of the major psychothriller series

1956   'Ed McBain', *Cop Hater*: start of the major American procedural series

1959   Chester Himes, *For Love of Imabelle*: first in the Jones and Johnson Harlem detectives series (appeared in French in 1958)

1962   P. D. James, *Cover her Face*: first case of Adam Dalgliesh, by the major post-war British clue-puzzler

1964   'Amanda Cross', *In the Last Analysis*: first American move towards feminist detection

1964   Ruth Rendell, *From Doon with Death*: first case for Inspector Wexford

1965   Ruth Rendell, *To Fear a Painted Devil*: first of Rendell's non-detective psychothrillers

1965   John Ball, *In the Heat of the Night*: first modern black detective novel

1966   George Baxt, *A Queer Kind of Death*: first gay male detective novel

1968   Dorothy Uhnak, *The Bait*: first of the woman police detective series

1970   Joseph Hansen, *Fadeout*: start of series about the major gay detective Dave Brandstetter

1970   Tony Hillerman, *The Blessing Way*: first in the long series of Navajo crime fiction

1972   P. D. James, *An Unsuitable Job for a Woman*: first English move towards feminist detection

1973   Robert B. Parker, *The Godwulf Manuscript*: first in the Spenser series, continuing the private-eye tradition in the present

1977   Marcia Muller, *Edwin of the Iron Shoes*: first real feminist detective novel, starring Sharon McCone

1977   'Ellis Peters', *A Morbid Taste for Bones*: start of the major historical mystery series featuring Brother Cadfael

1980   Liza Cody, *Dupe*: first British feminist detective Anna Lee

1982   Sara Paretsky, *Indemnity Only*: start of the major series starring V. I. Warshawski

1982   Sue Grafton, *A is for Alibi*: first appearance of Californian feminist detective Kinsey Millhone

1984   Barbara Wilson, *Murder in the Collective*: first major lesbian detective novel

1985   Paul Auster, *City of Glass*: first of the *New York Trilogy*, the major postmodern crime novel

1986   'Barbara Vine', *A Dark-Adapted Eye*: start of the major sequence of British psychothriller novels

1987   James Ellroy, *The Black Dahlia*: start of the major *L.A. Quartet*

1988   Thomas Harris, *The Silence of the Lambs*: first classic in the sub-genre of violent crime fiction

1990   Patricia Cornwell, *Post-Mortem*: start of forensic detective Kay Scarpetta series

1990   Walter Mosley, *Devil in a Blue Dress*: first in the influential black detective series starring Easy Rawlins

1991   Brett Easton Ellis, *American Psycho*: central and ambiguous text in new thriller of violence

1992   BarbaraNeely, *Blanche on the Lam*: first of the major black woman detective series

1995   Val McDermid, *The Mermaids Singing*: major British thriller of violence

1999   Stella Duffy, *Fresh Flesh*: feminism, postmodernism and the thriller of violence combine

References

PART I   DETECTION

Primary

Ainsworth, W. Harrison, *Jack Sheppard: A Romance*, 3 vols (London: Bentley, 1839).

Anon., 'The Diary of a Philadelphia Lawyer: I The Murderess', *Gentleman's Magazine* (Philadelphia), II (1838), 107–12.

Anon., *The Newgate Calendar from 1700 to the Present Time*, 5 vols (London: Cooke, 1773).

Anon., *The Malefactor's Register or the Newgate and Tyburn Calendar*, 5 vols (London: Hogg, 1779).

Anon., *The New and Complete Newgate Calendar*, 6 vols (London: Jackson, 1795).

Baldwin, William *see under* Knapp, Andrew.

Balzac, Honoré de, *Père Goriot* (Paris: Werdet, 1835), trans. as *Old Goriot* in *Collected Works* (London: Dent, 1897).

Balzac, Honoré de, *Illusions Perdues* (Paris: Furne, 1843), trans. as *Lost Illusions* in *Collected Works* (London: Dent, 1897).

Barrington, George, *Barrington's New London Spy* (London: Tegg, 1805).

Braddon, Mary, *Lady Audley's Secret*, 3 vols (London: Tinsley, 1862).

Brown, Charles Brockden, *Wieland* (New York: Caritat, 1798).

Brown, Charles Brockden, *Edgar Huntly, or the Memoirs of a Sleep-Walker* (Philadelphia: Dobson and Dickins, 1799).

Brown, Charles Brockden, *Arthur Mervyn*, part 1 (Philadelphia: Maxwell, 1799).

Brown, Charles Brockden, *Arthur Mervyn*, part 2 (New York: Hopkins, 1800).

Bulwer, Edward, *Pelham*, 3 vols (London: Colburn, 1828).

Bulwer, Edward, *Paul Clifford*, 3 vols (London: Bentley, 1830).

Bulwer, Edward, *Eugene Aram*, 3 vols (London: Bentley, 1832).

Cassiday, Bruce (ed.), *The Roots of Detection* (New York: Ungar, 1983).

Clive, Caroline, *Paul Ferrol* (London: Saunders and Otley, 1855).

Collins, Wilkie, *Basil*, 3 vols (London: Bentley, 1852).

Collins, Wilkie, *Hide and Seek*, 3 vols (London: Bentley, 1854).

Collins, Wilkie, 'The Diary of Anne Rodway', *Household Words*, 19 July 1856; reprinted in *Wilkie Collins: The Complete Shorter Fiction*, ed. J. Thompson (London: Robinson, 1995).

Collins, Wilkie, 'A Stolen Letter', originally 'The Fourth Poor Traveller' in *Household Words*, Extra Christmas Issue, 1854, reprinted in *Wilkie Collins: The Complete Shorter Fiction*, ed. J. Thompson (London: Robinson, 1995).

Collins, Wilkie, *The Woman in White*, 3 vols (London: Sampson Low, 1860).

Collins, Wilkie, *No Name*, 3 vols (London: Sampson Low, 1862).

Collins, Wilkie, *Armadale*, 3 vols (London: Smith Elder, 1866).

Collins, Wilkie, *The Moonstone*, 3 vols (London: Tinsley, 1868).

Collins, Wilkie, *The Law and the Lady*, 3 vols (London: Chatto, 1875).

Colquhoun, Patrick, *A Treatise on the Police of the Metropolis* (London: Dilly, 1796).

Crowe, Catherine, *The Adventures of Susan Hopley, or Circumstantial Evidence*, 3 vols (London: Saunders and Otley, 1841).

Curtis, Robert, *The Irish Police Officer* (London: Ward Lock, 1861).

Defoe, Daniel, *Moll Flanders* (London: Chetwood and Ealing, 1722).

Defoe, Daniel, *Colonel Jaque* (London: Brotherton, 1723).

Defoe, Daniel, *The Life of Jonathan Wild* (London: Warner, 1725).

De Quincey, Thomas, 'Confessions of an Opium Eater', *The London Magazine*, September–October 1823.

De Quincey, Thomas, 'On Murder Considered as One of the Fine Arts', *Blackwood's Magazine*, February 1827.

Dickens, Charles, *Oliver Twist* (London: Bentley, 1838).

Dickens, Charles, *Barnaby Rudge* (London: Chapman and Hall, 1841).

Dickens, Charles, *Martin Chuzzlewit* (London: Chapman and Hall, 1844).

Dickens, Charles, *Bleak House* (London: Bradbury and Evans, 1853).

Dickens, Charles, *The Mystery of Edwin Drood* (London: Chapman and Evans, 1870).

Dickens, Charles, *Hunted Down: The Detective Stories of Charles Dickens*, ed. Peter Haining (London: Owen, 1996).

Doyle, Arthur Conan, *A Study in Scarlet* in *Beeton's Christmas Annual 1887* (London: Ward Lock, 1887).

Doyle, Arthur Conan, *Micah Clark* (London: Longman, 1889).

Doyle, Arthur Conan, *The Sign of Four* (London: Blackett, 1890).

Doyle, Arthur Conan, *The White Company* (London: Smith and Elder, 1891).

Doyle, Arthur Conan, *The Adventures of Sherlock Holmes* (London: Newnes, 1892).

Doyle, Arthur Conan, *The Memoirs of Sherlock Holmes* (London: Newnes, 1894).

Doyle, Arthur Conan, *The Hound of the Baskervilles* (London: Newnes, 1902).

Doyle, Arthur Conan, *The Return of Sherlock Holmes* (London: Newnes, 1905).

Doyle, Arthur Conan, *The Valley of Fear* (London: Murray, 1914).

Doyle, Arthur Conan, *His Last Bow* (London: Murray, 1917).

Doyle, Arthur Conan, *Memories and Adventures* (London: Murray, 1924).

Doyle, Arthur Conan, *The Case Book of Sherlock Holmes* (London: Murray, 1927).

Doyle, Arthur Conan, *The Complete Sherlock Holmes Short Stories* (London: Murray, 1928).

Doyle, Arthur Conan, *The Complete Sherlock Holmes Long Stories* (London: Murray, 1929).

Dumas, Alexandre, *Les Mohicans de Paris*, 16 parts (Paris: Cadot, 1856–7), trans. John Lately as *The Mohicans of Paris* (London: Routledge, 1875).

'Felix, Charles', *The Notting Hill Mystery* (London: Saunders and Otley, 1865).

Forrester, Andrew, Jr, *Revelations of a Private Detective* (London: Ward Lock, 1863).

Forrester, Andrew, Jr, *Secret Service* (London: Ward Lock, 1864).

Forrester, Andrew, Jr, *The Female Detective* (London: Ward Lock, 1864).

Forrester, Mrs, *Fair Women*, 3 vols (London: Hurst and Blackett, 1868).

Forrester, Mrs, *From Olympus to Hades*, 3 vols (London: Hurst and Blackett, 1868).

Forrester, Mrs, *My Hero*, 3 vols (London: Hurst and Blackett, 1870).

Gaboriau, Emile, *L'Affaire Lerouge* (Paris: Dentu, 1866), trans. as *The Widow Lerouge* (Boston: Osgood, 1873) and as *The Lerouge Case* (London: Vizetelly, 1881).

Gaboriau, Emile, *L'Argent des Autres* (Paris: Evènement, n.d. [187]), trans. as *Other People's Money* (Boston: Estes and Lauriat, 1874).

Gaboriau, Emile, *Monsieur Lecoq*, 2 vols (Paris: Cassigneul, 1868), trans. as *Monsieur Lecoq* (New York: Munro, 1879), and as 2 vols (London: Vizetelly, 1881); reprinted in separate volumes as *M. Lecoq* (London: Hodder and Stoughton, 1920) and *The Honour of the Name* (London: Hodder and Stoughton, 1920).

Gaboriau, Emile, *La Corde au Cou* (Paris: Dentu, 1873); trans. as *In Peril of His Life* (London: Vizetelly, 1881).

Gaboriau, Emile, *Le Crime d'Orcival* (Paris: Dentu, 1867), trans. as *The Mystery of Orcival* (New York: Holt and Williams, 1871).

Gaboriau, Emile, *Le Dossier no. 113* (Paris: Denton, 1867), trans. as *File no. 113* (New York: Burt, 1875).

Gaspey, Thomas, *The History of George Godfrey*, 3 vols (London: Colburn, 1828).

Gaspey, Thomas, *Richmond: Scenes from the Life of a Bow Street Runner, Drawn up from his Private Memoranda*, 3 vols (London: Colburn, 1827).

Godwin, William, *Things as They Are, or Caleb Williams*, 3 vols. (London: Crosby, 1794); reprinted, ed. David McCracken (Oxford: Oxford University Press, 1970).

Godwin, William, *An Enquiry Concerning Political Justice*, 2 vols (London: Robinson, 1793).

Green, Anna Katherine, *The Leavenworth Case* (New York: Putnam, 1878).

[Hayward, William S.], *Revelations of a Lady Detective* (London: Vickers, 1864).

Hoffmann, E. T. A., *Das Fraülein von Scuderi* (Frankfurt: Wilmans, 1820), trans. Mary Dickins as *Mademoiselle de Scudéry* (London: Gowans Gray, 1908).

Hugo, Victor de, *La dernière journée d'un condamné à mort* (Paris: Gosselin, 1829), trans. Sir P. Hesketh Fleetwood as *The Last Days of a Condemned Man* (London: Smith Elder, 1840).

Hume, Fergus, *The Mystery of a Hansom Cab* (Melbourne: Kemp and Boyce, 1886).

James, G. P. R., *Delaware*, 3 vols (London: Whittaker, 1833).

Knapp, Andrew and Baldwin, William (eds), *Criminal Chronology or The Newgate Calendar*, 4 vols (London: Nuttall, Fisher and Dixon, 1809).

Knapp, Andrew and Baldwin, William (eds), *The New Newgate Calendar*, 5 vols (London: Robins, 1826).

Le Fanu, Sheridan, *Uncle Silas*, 3 vols (London: Bentley, 1864).

Le Fanu, Sheridan, *Wylder's Hand*, 3 vols (London: Bentley, 1869).

Le Fanu, Sheridan, *Checkmate*, 3 vols (London: Hurst and Blackett, 1871).

Marshburn, Joseph E. and Velie, Alan R., *Blood and Knavery: A Collection of English Renaissance Pamphlets and Ballads of Crime and Sin* (Rutherford: Fairleigh Dickinson University Press, 1973).

'Charles Martel' (= Thomas Delf), *The Detective's Notebook* (London: Ward Lock, 1860).

'Charles Martel' (= Thomas Delf), *The Diary of an Ex-Detective* (London: Ward Lock, 1860).

M'Levy, James, *Curiosities of Crime in Edinburgh* (Edinburgh: Kay, 1861).

Morrison, Robert and Baldick, Chris (eds), *Blackwood's Tales of Terror* (Oxford: Oxford University Press, 1995).

Newgate Calendar (1773) *see under* Anon.

Newgate Calendar (1779) *see under* Anon.

New Newgate Calendar see under Knapp, Andrew and Baldwin, William.

'Pelham, Camden' (ed.), *The Chronicles of Crime, or The New Newgate Calendar*, 2 vols (London: Pelham, 1841).

Pinkerton, Alan, *The Expressman and the Detective* (New York: Kemp and Cooke, 1874).

Pinkerton, Alan, *The Molly Maguires and the Detective* (New York: Carleton, 1877).

Pinkerton, Alan, *The Gypsies and the Detective* (New York: Dillingham, 1879).

Poe, Edgar Allan, 'The Murders in the Rue Morgue', *Graham's Magazine*, April 1841; reprinted in Edgar Allan Poe, *Tales of Mystery and Imagination* (London: Dent, 1908).

Poe, Edgar Allan, 'The Mystery of Marie Rogêt', *Snowden's Ladies' Companion*, November–December–February 1842–3; reprinted in *Tales of Mystery and Imagination*.

Poe, Edgar Allan, 'The Purloined Letter', *The Gift*, January 1845; reprinted in *Tales of Mystery and Imagination*.

Poe, Edgar Allan, 'The Gold Bug', *The Dollar Newspaper*, 21 and 28 June 1843, reprinted in *Tales of Mystery and Imagination*.

Poe, Edgar Allan, 'Thou Art the Man', *Godey's Ladies' Book*, November 1844, reprinted in *Tales of Mystery and Imagination*.

'Regester, Seeley' (= Metta Fuller), *The Dead Letter: An American Romance* (New York: Beadle, 1867).

Reynolds, G. W. M, *The Mysteries of London*, 6 vols (London: Lawson, 1846–50); reprinted, ed. Trefor Thomas (Keele: Keele University Press, 1996).

Russell, William, *Recollections of a Policeman* (New York: Cornish Lamport, 1852).

Russell, William, *The Recollections of a Detective Police-Officer* (London: Ward Lock, 1856).

Russell, William, *Leaves from the Diary of a Law Clerk* (London: Brown, 1857).

Russell, William, *The Experiences of a Real Detective* (London: Ward Lock, 1862).

Schiller, J. C. F., *Die Räuber* (Stuttgart: self-published, 1781), trans. A. F. Tytler as *The Robbers* (London: Robinsons, 1792).

Schiller, J. C. F., *Der Geisterseher, Thalia*, 1786–7, trans. D. Boileau as *The Ghost-seer* (London: Vernor and Hood, 1795).

Shiel, M. P., *Prince Zaleski* (London: Lane, 1895).

Stevenson, Robert Louis and Osbourne, Lloyd, *The Wrecker* (London: Cassell, 1892).

Stevenson, Robert Louis and Stevenson, Fanny, *The Dynamiter* (London: Longmans, 1885).

Thomson, Henry, 'Le Revenant', *Blackwood's Magazine*, 21 (1827), 409–16.

Vidocq, Eugène François, *Mémoires*, 4 vols (Paris: Tenon, 1827–8), trans. G. Borrow as *Memoirs*, 4 vols (London: Whittaker, Treacher and Arnot, 1829).

'W.W' (= Mary Fortune), 'The Dead Witness', *The Australian Journal*, January 1866.

Warren, Samuel, *Passages from the Diary of a Late Physician*, 2 vols (Edinburgh: Blackwood, 1832); vol. 3 (Edinburgh: Blackwood, 1838).

Warren, Samuel, 'The Experiences of a Barrister', *Chambers' Edinburgh Journal*, March 1849.

Williams, John B. (ed.), *Leaves from the Note-Book of a New York Detective* (New York: Dick and Fitzgerald, 1865).

Wood, Ellen, *East Lynne*, 3 vols (London: Bentley, 1861).

Secondary

Alewyn, Richard, 'The Origins of Detective Fiction', in *Probleme und Gestalten* (Frankfurt-am-Main: Insel Verlag, 1974), trans. Glenn W. Most, in Most and Stowe (eds), *The Poetics of Murder* (1983).

Ascari, Maurizio, 'Vidocq, or, the French Jonathan Wild', in *Two Centuries of Detective Fiction: a New Comparative Approach*, ed. M. Ascari (Bologna: Cotepra, 2000), 47–55.

Bell, Ian A., *The Literature of Crime in Augustan England* (Basingstoke: Palgrave Macmillan, 1991).

Belsey, Catherine, 'Deconstructing the Text: Sherlock Holmes', in *Critical Practice* (London: Methuen, 1980), 109–17; reprinted in Hodgson (ed.), *Arthur Conan Doyle* (1994) 381–8.

Benjamin, Walter, 'The Flâneur', in *Charles Baudelaire: A Lyric Poet in the Era of High Capitalism*, trans. Harry Zohn (London: New Left Books, 1973), 35–66.

Bleiler, E. F., 'Introduction' to Thomas Gaspey, *Richmond: Scenes from the Life of a Bow* (New York: Dover, 1976).

Bleiler, E. F., 'Introduction' to *Three Nineteenth-Century Detective Novels* (New York: Dover, 1977).

Bonaparte, Marie, *Edgar Poe: étude analytique* (Paris: Denoel et Steele, 1933).

Brantlinger, Patrick, 'What is "Sensational" and the "Sensation Novel"', *Nineteenth-Century Fiction*, 37 (1982), 1–28; reprinted in Pykett (ed.) (1998: 30–57).

Burke, Thomas, 'The Obsequies of Mr. Williams: New Light on De Quincey's Famous Tale of Murder', *The Bookman*, 68 (1928), 257–63.

Campbell, Duncan, 'The Murd'rous Sublime: De Quincey and the Ratcliffe Highway Killings', in Klaus and Knight (eds), *The Art of Murder* (1998), 26–37.

Cohen, Daniel A., *Pillars of Salt, Monuments of Grace: New England Crime Literature and the Origins of American Popular Culture, 1674–1860* (New York: Oxford University Press, 1993).

Collins, Philip, *Dickens and Crime* (London: Macmillan, 1962).

Corrado, Adriana, 'A New Look at *Caleb Williams*', in Ascari (2000: 29–46).

Derrida, Jacques, 'The Purveyor of Truth', trans. W. Domingo, James Hulbert, Moshe Ron and M.-R. Logan, *Yale French Studies*, 52 (1975), 31–113.

Drexler, Peter, *Literatur, Recht, Kriminalität* (Frankfurt-am-Main: Lang, 1991).

Drexler, Peter, 'Mapping the Gaps: Detectives and Detective Themes in British Novels of the 1870s and 1880s', in Klaus and Knight (eds) (1998: 77–89).

During, Simon, *Foucault and Literature: Towards a Genealogy of Writing* (London: Routledge, 1992).

Edwards, Gavin, 'William Godwin's Foreign Language: Stories and Families in *Caleb Williams* and *Political Justice*', *Studies in Romanticism*, 39 (2000), 533–51.

Eliot, T. S., 'Wilkie Collins and Charles Dickens', in *Selected Essays, 1917–32* (London: Faber, 1932).

Emsley, Clive, *Crime and Society in England, 1750–1900*, 2nd edn. (London: Longman, 1996).

Foucault, Michel, *Discipline and Punish*, trans. Alan Sheridan (London: Lane, 1977).

Halttunen, Karen, *Murder Most Foul: The Killer and the American Gothic Imagination* (Cambridge, MA: Harvard University Press, 1998).

Haycraft, Howard, *Murder for Pleasure* (London: Davies, 1942).

Hennessy, Rosemary and Mohan, Rajeswari, ' "The Speckled Band": the Constitution of Women in a Popular Text of Empire', part of 'The Constitution of Women in Three Popular Texts of Empire: Towards a Critique of Materialist Feminism', *Textual Practice*, 3 (1989), 323–59; reprinted in abbreviated form in Hodgson (ed.), *Arthur Conan Doyle* (1994: 89–401).

Herbert, Rosemary (ed.), *The Oxford Companion to Crime and Mystery Writing* (New York: Oxford University Press, 1999).

Hodgson, John (ed.), *Arthur Conan Doyle: Sherlock Holmes: the Major Stories with Contemporary Critical Essays* (Boston, MA: Bedford, 1994).

Hollingworth, Keith, *The Newgate Novel* (Detroit, MI: Wayne State University Press, 1963).

Hoppenstand, Gary, *The Dime Novel Detective* (Bowling Green, OH: Popular Press, 1982).

Hutter, Alfred D., 'Dreams, Transformations and Literature: the Implications of Detective Fiction', *Victorian Studies*, 19 (1975), 181–209.

Irwin, John T., *The Mystery to a Solution: Poe, Borges and the Analytic Detective Story* (Baltimore, MD: Johns Hopkins University Press, 1994).

James, Henry, 'Miss Braddon', *Nation*, 9 November 1865, 593–4; reprinted in *Notes and Reviews* (Cambridge: Dunster House, 1921), 103–16.

James, P. D. and Critchley, T. A., *The Maul and the Pear Tree: The Ratcliffe Highway Killings, 1811* (London: Constable, 1971).

Johnson, Barbara, 'The Frame of Reference: Poe, Lacan, Derrida', in *The Critical Difference* (Baltimore, MD: Johns Hopkins University Press, 1980), 110–46.

Kayman, Martin A., *From Bow Street to Baker Street: Mystery, Detection and Narrative* (Basingstoke: Palgrave Macmillan, 1992).

Kayman, Martin A., 'The Short Story from Poe to Chesterton', in Priestman (2003).

Klaus, H. Gustav and Knight, Stephen (eds), *The Art of Murder* (Tubingen: Stauffenburg, 1998).

Knight, Stephen, *Form and Ideology in Crime Fiction* (London: Macmillan: 1980).

Knight, Stephen, 'Introduction' to Fergus Hume, *The Mystery of a Hansom Cab*, reprint edn (London: Hogarth, 1986).

Knight, Stephen, 'The Case of the Great Detective', *Meanjin* (40), 1981, 175–85; reprinted in Hodgson (ed.), *Arthur Conan Doyle* (1994), 368–80.

Knight, Stephen, *Continent of Mystery: A Thematic History of Australian Crime Fiction* (Melbourne: Melbourne University Press, 1997).

Lacan, Jacques, 'Le séminaire sur "La lettre volée" ', in *Écrits* (Paris: Seuil, 1966), 11–61, trans. Jeffrey Mehlman as 'Seminar on "The Purloined Letter" ', in *Yale French Studies*, 48 (1973), 39–72; reprinted in Most and Stowe (eds), *The Poetics of Murder* (1983).

Landrum, Larry, Jr, *American Mystery and Detective Novels: A Reference Guide* (Westport, CT: Greenwood, 1999).

Lavine, Sigmund A., *Allen Pinkerton: America's First Private Eye* (New York: Dodd Mead, 1967).

Maida, Patricia D., *Mother of Detective Fiction: The Life and Works of Anna Katharine Green* (Bowling Green: Popular Press, 1989).

Mandel, Ernest, *Delightful Murder* (London: Pluto, 1984).

Messac, Régis, *Le 'Detective Novel' et l'Influence de la Pensée Scientifique* (Paris: Champion, 1929).

Miller, D. A., *The Novel and the Police* (Berkeley, CA: University of California Press, 1988).

Morrison, Robert and Baldick, Chris, 'Introduction' to *Blackwood's Tales of Terror* (Oxford: Oxford University Press, 1995).

Most, Glenn and Stowe, William W. (eds), *The Poetics of Murder* (New York: Harcourt, Brace Jovanovich, 1983).

Muller, John P. and Richardson, Will J., *The Purloined Poe: Lacan, Derrida and Psychoanalytic Reading* (Baltimore, MD: Johns Hopkins University Press, 1988).

Nordon, Pierre, *Conan Doyle*, trans. Frances Partridge (London: Murray, 1966).

Osborne, Eric (ed.), *Victorian Detective Fiction: A Catalogue of the Collection made by Dorothy Glover and Graham Greene* (London: Bodley Head, 1966).

Ousby, Ian, *Bloodhounds of Heaven: The Detective in English Fiction from Godwin to Doyle* (Cambridge, MA: Harvard University Press, 1976).

Pederson, Jay P. (ed.), *St James Guide to Mystery Writers*, 4th edn (Detroit, MI: St James, 1996).

Peterson, Audrey, *Victorian Studies of Mystery: From Wilkie Collins to Conan Doyle* (New York: Ungar, 1984).

Priestman, Martin, *Detective Fiction and Literature: The Figure on the Carpet* (London: Macmillan, 1990).

Priestman, Martin, *The Cambridge Companion to Crime Fiction* (Cambridge: Cambridge University Press, 2003).

Pykett, Lyn (ed.), *Wilkie Collins: Contemporary Critical Essays* (Basingstoke: Palgrave Macmillan, 1998).

Rahn, B. J., 'Seeley Regester: America's First Detective Novelist', in *The Sleuth and the Scholar*, ed. Barbara Rader and Howard Zettler (New York: Greenwood, 1988), 47–61.

Reilly, John M. (ed.), *Twentieth Century Crime and Mystery Writers* (New York: St Martin's, 1980).

Rignall, John, 'From City Streets to Country Houses: the Detective as Flâneur', in Klaus and Knight, *The Art of Murder* (1998), 67–76.

Sayers, Dorothy, 'Introduction' to *Great Stories of Detection, Mystery and Horror* (London: Gollancz, 1928).

Schivelbusch, Wolfgang, *The Railway Journey* (Oxford: Blackwell, 1977).

Schutt, Sita, 'Rivalry and Influence: Nineteenth-Century French Detective Narratives', in Klaus and Knight (eds), *The Art of Murder* (1998), 38–49.

Showalter, Elaine, 'Family Secrets and Domestic Subversion: Rebellion in the Novels of the Eighteen-Sixties', in A. Wold (ed.), *The Victorian Family: Structure and Stresses* (London: Croom Helm, 1978).

Sinclair, Struan, 'Attribution of Blame in Detective Fiction: From the Newgate Calendar to the Whodunit', unpublished PhD thesis, Cardiff University, 2000.

Stewart, R. F., *... And Always a Detective* (Newton Abbot: David and Charles, 1980).

Sussex, Lucy, *The Fortunes of Mrs Fortune* (Melbourne: Penguin, 1989).

Sussex, Lucy and Burrows, John, 'Whodunit: Literary Forensics and the Crime Writing of James Skipp Borlase and Mary Fortune',

Bibliographical Society of Australia and New Zealand Bulletin, 21 (1997), 73–93.

Sussex, Lucy and Burrows, John, 'The Detective Maidservant: Catherine Crowe's *Susan Hopley*', htttp:www.mgc.peachnet.edu/bayres/Scholarship/Silent/Silent.html, 2003.

Symons, Julian, *Bloody Murder*, 3rd edn (London: Penguin, 1992).

Trodd, Anthea, *Domestic Crime and the Victorian Novel* (Basingstoke: Palgrave Macmillan, 1989).

Walsh, John, *Poe the Detective* (Rutgers: Rutgers University Press, 1968).

Worthington, Heather, 'Criminality and Criminography: Textual Representations of Crime and Detection, 1820–1850', unpublished PhD thesis, Cardiff University, 2003.

PART II DEATH

Primary

Allingham, Margery, *Mystery Mile* (London: Jarrolds, 1930).

Allingham, Margery, *Police at the Funeral* (London: Heinemann, 1931).

Allingham, Margery, *Look to the Lady* (London: Jarrolds, 1931).

Allingham, Margery, *Sweet Danger* (London: Heinemann, 1933).

Allingham, Margery, *The Fashion in Shrouds* (London: Heinemann, 1938).

Anderson, Edward, *Thieves Like Us* (New York: Mercury, 1937).

'Ashdown, Clifford' (= R. A. Freeman and J. J. Pitcairn), *The Adventures of Romney Pringle* (London: Ward Lock, 1902).

Bailey, H. C., *Call Mr Fortune* (London: Methuen, 1920).

Bailey, H. C., *The Great Game* (London: Gollancz, 1939).

Barr, Robert, *The Triumphs of Eugène Valmont* (London: Hurst and Blackett, 1906); reprinted, ed. Stephen Knight (Oxford: Oxford University Press, 1997).

Bell, Josephine, *The Port of London Murders* (London: Longman, 1938).

Bentley, E. C., *Trent's Last Case* (London: Nelson, 1913).

'Berkeley, Anthony' (= Anthony Berkeley Cox), *The Layton Court Mystery* (London: Jenkins, 1925).

'Berkeley, Anthony' (= Anthony Berkeley Cox), *The Poisoned Chocolates Case* (London: Collins, 1929).

'Berkeley, Anthony' (= Anthony Berkeley Cox), *The Second Shot* (London: Hodder and Stoughton, 1930).

'Berkeley, Anthony' (= Anthony Berkeley Cox), *Trial and Error* (London: Hodder and Stoughton, 1937).

Biggers, Earl Derr, *The House without a Key* (Indianapolis, IN: Bobbs Merrill, 1925).

Biggers, Earl Derr, *The Chinese Parrot* (Indianapolis, IN: Bobbs Merrill, 1926).

'Blake, Nicholas' (= C. Day Lewis), *A Question of Proof* (London: Collins, 1935).

'Blake, Nicholas' (= C. Day Lewis), *The Smiler with the Knife* (London: Collins, 1939).

Bodkin, M. McDonnell, *Paul Beck: The Rule-of-Thumb Detective* (London: Pearson, 1898).

Bodkin, M. McDonnell, *Dora Myrl, the Lady Detective* (London: Chatto and Windus, 1900).

Bodkin, M. McDonnell, *Young Beck: A Chip of the Old Block* (London: Unwin, 1911).

Brackett, Leigh, *No Good from a Corpse* (New York: Coward McCann, 1944).

Brackett, Leigh, *The Tiger among Us* (New York: Doubleday, 1957).

Braddon, Mary, *Lady Audley's Secret*, 3 vols (London: Tinsley, 1862).

'Brown, Carter' (= Alan G. Yates), *Strip without Tease* (Sydney: Transport, 1953).

'Brown, Carter' (= Alan G. Yates), *Homicide Hoyden* (Sydney: Horwitz, 1954).

Burnett, W. R., *Little Caesar* (New York: Dial, 1929).

Burnett, W. R., *High Sierra* (New York: Knopf, 1940).

Burnett, W. R., *The Asphalt Jungle* (New York: Knopf, 1950).

Cain, James M., *The Postman Always Rings Twice* (New York: Knopf, 1934).

Cain, James M., *Double Indemnity* (New York: *Liberty*, 1936).

Carr, John Dickson, *It Walks by Night* (New York: Harper, 1930).

Carr, John Dickson, *Poison in Jest* (New York: Harper, 1932).

Carr, John Dickson, *The Hollow Man* (London: Hamilton, 1935).

Carr, John Dickson, *The Burning Court* (London: Hamilton, 1937).

Chandler, Raymond, *The Big Sleep* (New York: Knopf, 1939).

Chandler, Raymond, *Farewell My Lovely* (New York: Knopf, 1940).

Chandler, Raymond, *The High Window* (New York: Knopf, 1943).

Chandler, Raymond, *The Lady in the Lake* (New York: Knopf, 1944).

Chandler, Raymond, *The Little Sister* (Boston, MA: Houghton Mifflin, 1949).

Chandler, Raymond, *Trouble is my Business* (London: Penguin, 1950).

Chandler, Raymond, *Pearls are a Nuisance* (London: Hamilton, 1953).

Chandler, Raymond, *The Long Goodbye* (London: Hamilton, 1953).

Chandler, Raymond, *Playback* (Boston, MA: Houghton Mifflin, 1958).

Chandler, Raymond, *Killer in the Rain*, ed. Philip Durham (Boston, MA: Houghton Mifflin, 1964).

Chandler, Raymond, *Raymond Chandler Speaking*, ed. Dorothy Gardiner and Katherine Sorley Walker (Boston, MA: Houghton Mifflin, 1962).

Chandler, Raymond, *Chandler before Marlowe*, ed. Matthew J. Bruccoli (Columbia: University of South Carolina Press, 1973).

Chandler, Raymond, *Raymond Chandler's Unknown Thriller: The Screenplay of Playback* (New York: The Mysterious Press, 1985).

'Chase, James Hadley' (= René B. Raymond), *No Orchids for Miss Blandish* (London: Jarrold, 1939).

Chesterton, G. K., *The Man Who Was Thursday* (Bristol: Arrowsmith, 1908).

Chesterton, G. K., *The Innocence of Father Brown* (London: Cassell, 1911).

Cheyney, Peter, *This Man is Dangerous* (London: Collins, 1936).

Cheyney, Peter, *The Urgent Hangman* (London: Collins, 1938).

Cheyney, Peter, *Dark Duet* (London: Collins, 1942).

Christie, Agatha, *The Mysterious Affair at Styles* (London: Lane, 1920).

Christie, Agatha, *The Secret Adversary* (London: Lane, 1922).

Christie, Agatha, *The Murder on the Links* (London: Lane, 1923).

Christie, Agatha, *The Murder of Roger Ackroyd* (London: Collins, 1926).

Christie, Agatha, *Partners in Crime* (London: Collins, 1929).

Christie, Agatha, *Murder at the Vicarage* (London: Collins, 1930).

Christie, Agatha, *Murder on the Orient Express* (London: Collins, 1934).

Christie, Agatha, *Cards on the Table* (London: Collins, 1936).

Christie, Agatha, *Hercule Poirot's Christmas* (London: Collins, 1938).

Christie, Agatha, *Ten Little Niggers* (London: Collins, 1939).

Christie, Agatha, *The Body in the Library* (London: Collins, 1942).

Christie, Agatha, *The Moving Finger* (London: Collins, 1942).

Christie, Agatha, *Crooked House* (London: Collins, 1949).

Christie, Agatha, *Hickory Dickory Dock* (London: Collins, 1955).

Christie, Agatha, *Ordeal by Innocence* (London: Collins, 1958).

Christie, Agatha, *The Mirror Crack'd from Side to Side* (London: Collins, 1962).

Christie, Agatha, *Endless Night* (London: Collins, 1967).

Christie, Agatha, *Postern of Fate* (London: Collins, 1973).

Clurman, Robert (ed.), *Nick Carter, Detective: Fiction's Most Celebrated Detective – Six Astonishing Adventures* (New York: Macmillan, 1963).

Collins, Wilkie, *The Law and the Lady* (London: Chatto and Windus, 1875).

Crofts, Freeman Wills, *The Cask* (London: Collins, 1920).

Crofts, Freeman Wills, *Inspector French's Greatest Case* (London: Collins, 1925).

Detection Club, The, *The Floating Admiral* (London: Hodder and Stoughton, 1931).

Detection Club, The, *Ask a Policeman* (London: Barker, 1933).

'Donovan, Dick' (= Joyce R. Preston Muddock), *Caught At Last! Leaves from the Notebook of a Detective* (London: Chatto and Windus, 1889).

'Donovan, Dick' (= Joyce R. Preston Muddock), *The Fatal Ring* (London: Hurst and Blackett, 1905).

'Donovan, Dick' (= Joyce R. Preston Muddock), *The Knutsford Mystery* (London: White, 1906).

Doyle, Arthur Conan, *A Study in Scarlet*, in *Beeton's Christmas Annual* (London: Ward Lock, 1887).

Doyle, Arthur Conan, *The Sign of Four* (London: Blackett, 1890).

Doyle, Arthur Conan, *The Hound of the Baskervilles* (London: Newnes, 1902).

Eberhart, Mignon, *The Patient in Room 18* (New York: Doubleday, 1929).

Eberhart, Mignon, *The Dark Garden* (New York: Doubleday, 1937).

Evans, Gwyn, 'The Plague of Onion Men', *Union Jack*, 1493 (28 May 1932), 2–25.

Faulkner, William, *Sanctuary* (New York: Cape and Smith, 1930).

Fletcher, J. S., *The Adventures of Arthur Dawe (Sleuth Hound)* (London: Digby Long, 1909).

Fletcher, J. S., *The Middle Temple Murder* (London: Ward Lock, 1919).

Flynn, Errol, *Showdown* (Sydney: Invincible, 1946).

Freeman, R. Austin, *The Red Thumb Mark* (London: Collingwood, 1907).

Freeman, R. Austin, *John Thorndyke's Cases* (London: Chatto and Windus, 1909).

Freeman, R. Austin, *The Singing Bone* (London: Hodder and Stoughton, 1912).

Freeman, R. Austin, *The D'Arblay Mystery* (London: Hodder and Stoughton, 1926).

Futrelle, Jacques, *The Thinking Machine* (New York: Dodd, Mead, 1907).

Futrelle, Jacques, *The Thinking Machine on the Case* (New York: Appleton, 1908).

Futrelle, Jacques, *The Diamond Master* (Indianapolis, IN: Bobbs Merril, 1909).

Gaboriau, Émile, *The Lerouge Case* (London: Vizetelly, 1881).

Gardner, Erle Stanley, *The Case of the Velvet Claws* (New York: Morrow, 1933).

Goodis, David, *Dark Passage* (New York: Messner, 1946).

Goodis, David, *Nightfall* (New York: Messner, 1947).

Goodis, David, *Cassidy's Girl* (New York: Fawcett, 1951).

Goodis, David, *Down There* (New York: Fawcett, 1956).

Greene, Graham, *A Gun for Sale* (London: Heinemann, 1936).

Greene, Graham, *Brighton Rock* (London: Heinemann, 1938).

Greene, Hugh (ed.), *The Rivals of Sherlock Holmes* (London: Bodley Head, 1970).

Greene, Hugh, *Further Rivals of Sherlock Holmes: The Crooked Counties* (London: Bodley Head, 1973).

Greene, Hugh, *The American Rivals of Sherlock Holmes* (London: Bodley Head, 1976).

Hamilton, Patrick, *Hangover Square* (London: Constable, 1941).

Hammett, Dashiell, *Red Harvest* (New York: Knopf, 1929).

Hammett, Dashiell, *The Maltese Falcon* (New York: Knopf, 1930).

Hammett, Dashiell, *The Glass Key* (New York: Knopf, 1931).

Hammett, Dashiell, *The Thin Man* (New York: Knopf, 1934).

Hammett, Dashiell, *The Big Knockover*, ed. Lilian Hellman (New York: Random House, 1966).

Hammett, Dashiell, *The Continental Op*, ed. Steven Marcus (London: Macmillan, 1975).

Heyer, Georgette, *Why Shoot a Butler?* (London: Longman, 1933).

Hitchens, Dolores, *Sleep with Strangers* (New York: Doubleday, 1955).

Hornung, E. W., *The Rogue's March* (London: Cassell, 1896).

Hornung, E. W., *The Amateur Cracksman* (London: Methuen, 1899).

Hughes, Dorothy B., *The So Blue Marble* (New York: Duell, 1940).

Hughes, Dorothy B., *In a Lonely Place* (New York: Duell, 1947).

'Iles, Francis' (= Anthony Berkeley Cox), *Malice Aforethought* (London: Gollancz, 1931).

'Iles, Francis' (= Anthony Berkeley Cox), *Before the Fact* (London: Gollancz, 1932).

'Keene, Carolyn', *The Secret of the Old Clock* (New York: Grosset and Dunlop, 1930).

King, C. Daly, *Obelists at Sea* (London: Heritage, 1932).

King, C. Daly, *Obelists En Route* (London: Collins, 1934).

Leblanc, Maurice, *Arsène Lupin: gentleman-cambrioleur* (Paris: Lafitte, 1907), trans. as *The Exploits of Arsène Lupin* (New York: Harper, 1909).

Leroux, Gaston, *Le Mystère de la Chambre Jaune* (Paris: L'Illustration, 1907), trans. as *The Mystery of the Yellow Room* (New York: Brentano, 1908).

Lowndes, Maria Belloc, *The Lodger* (London: Methuen, 1913).

'Macdonald, Ross' (as 'John Macdonald') (= Kenneth Millar), *The Moving Target* (New York: Knopf, 1949).

'Macdonald, Ross' (= Kenneth Millar), *The Wycherley Woman* (New York: Knopf, 1961).

'Macdonald, Ross' (= Kenneth Millar), *The Underground Man* (New York: Knopf, 1971).

'Macdonald, Ross' (= Kenneth Millar), *The Blue Hammer* (New York: Knopf, 1976).

Marsh, Ngaio, *A Man Lay Dead* (London: Bles, 1934).

Marsh, Ngaio, *The Nursing Home Murder* (London: Bles, 1935).

'Marshall, Raymond' (= René B. Raymond), *Trusted Like the Fox* (London: Jarrolds, 1948).

Mason, A. E. W., *At the Villa Rose* (London: Hodder and Stoughton, 1910).

Mason, A. E. W., *The House of the Arrow* (London: Hodder and Stoughton, 1924).

McCoy, Horace, *No Pockets in a Shroud* (London: Barker, 1937).

McCoy, Horace, *I Should have Stayed Home* (New York: Knopf, 1938).

Mitchell, Gladys, *Speedy Death* (London: Gollancz, 1929).

Mitchell, Gladys, *The Saltmarsh Murders* (London: Gollancz, 1932).

Mitchell, Gladys, *The Rising of the Moon* (London: Joseph, 1945).

Mitchell, Gladys, *The Mudflats of the Dead* (London: Joseph, 1979).

Morrison, Arthur, *Tales of Mean Streets* (London: Methuen, 1894).

Morrison, Arthur, *Martin Hewitt, Investigator* (London: Ward Lock, 1894).

Morrison, Arthur, *The Dorrington Deed-Box* (London: Ward Lock, 1897).

'Olsen, D. B.' (= Dolores Hitchens), *The Cat Saw Murder* (New York: Doubleday, 1939).

Orczy, Baroness, *The Old Man in the Corner* (London: Greening, 1909).

Orczy, Baroness, *Lady Molly of Scotland Yard* (London: Cassell, 1910).

Pirkis, C. L., *The Experiences of Loveday Brooke* (London: Hutchinson, 1894).

Pitcairn, J. J., *see under* 'Ashdown, Clifford'.

Post, Melville Davisson, *The Strange Schemes of Randolph Mason* (New York: Putnam, 1896).

Post, Melville Davisson, *The Man of Last Resort, or, The Clients of Randolph Mason* (New York: Putnam, 1897).

Post, Melville Davisson, *The Corrector of Destinies* (New York: Clode, 1908).

Post, Melville Davisson, *Uncle Abner: Master of Mysteries* (New York: Appleton, 1918).

Punshon, E. R., *Crossword Mystery* (London: Gollancz, 1934).

'Queen, Ellery' (= Frederick Dannay and Manfred B. Lee), *The Roman Hat Mystery* (New York: Stokes, 1929).

'Queen, Ellery' (= Frederick Dannay and Manfred B. Lee), *The American Gun Mystery* (New York: Stokes, 1933).

'Queen, Ellery' (= Frederick Dannay and Manfred B. Lee), *The Chinese Orange Mystery* (New York: Stokes, 1934).

'Queen, Ellery' (= Frederick Dannay and Manfred B. Lee), *The Spanish Cape Mystery* (New York: Stokes, 1935).

Reeve, Arthur B., *The Silent Bullet* (New York: Dodd, Mead, 1912).

Reeve, Arthur B., *The Dream Doctor* (New York: Hearst, 1914).

'Rhode, John' (= Cecil Street), *The Paddington Mystery* (London: Bles, 1925).

'Rice, Craig' (= Georgiana Randolph), *8 Faces at 3* (New York: Simon and Schuster, 1939).

'Rice, Craig' (= Georgiana Randolph), *The Corpse Steps Out* (New York: Simon and Schuster, 1940).

'Rice, Craig', *My Kingdom for a Hearse* (New York: Simon and Schuster, 1957).

Rinehart, Mary Roberts, *The Circular Staircase* (Indianapolis, IN: Bobbs Merrill, 1908).

Rinehart, Mary Roberts, *The Door* (New York: Farrar and Rinehart, 1930).

'Ross, Barnaby' (= Frederick Dannay and Manfred B. Lee), *The Tragedy of X* (New York: Viking, 1932).

Sayers, Dorothy L., *Whose Body?* (London: Unwin, 1923).

Sayers, Dorothy L., *Strong Poison* (London: Gollancz, 1930).

Sayers, Dorothy L., *The Five Red Herrings* (London: Gollancz, 1931).

Sayers, Dorothy L., *Have His Carcase* (London: Gollancz, 1932).

Sayers, Dorothy L., *Murder Must Advertise* (London: Gollancz, 1933).

Sayers, Dorothy L., *The Nine Tailors* (London: Gollancz, 1934).

Sayers, Dorothy L., *Gaudy Night* (London: Gollancz, 1935).

Sayers, Dorothy L., *Busman's Honeymoon* (London: Gollancz, 1937).

Shiel, M. P., *Prince Zaleski* (London: Lane, 1895).

Sims, George, *Dorcas Dene, Detective: Her Adventures* (London: White, 1897).

Spillane, Mickey, *I, The Jury* (New York: Dutton, 1947).

Spillane, Mickey, *Vengeance is Mine* (New York: Dutton, 1950).

Spillane, Mickey, *One Lonely Night* (New York: Dutton, 1951).

Steinbeck, John, *The Grapes of Wrath* (New York: Viking, 1939).

Stout, Rex, *Fer de Lance* (New York: Farrar and Rinehart, 1934).

'Tey, Josephine' (as 'Gordon Daviot') (= Elizabeth Mackintosh), *The Man in the Queue* (London: Methuen, 1929).

'Tey, Josephine' (= Elizabeth Mackintosh), *Miss Pym Disposes* (London: Davies, 1946).

'Tey, Josephine' (= Elizabeth Mackintosh), *The Franchise Affair* (London: Davies, 1948).

'Tey, Josephine' (= Elizabeth Mackintosh), *The Daughter of Time* (London: Davies, 1951).

Thompson, Jim, *Nothing More than Murder* (New York: Harper, 1949).

Thompson, Jim, *The Killer Inside Me* (New York: Lion, 1952).

Thompson, Jim, *The Getaway* (New York: New American Library, 1959).

Upfield, Arthur, *Wings above the Diamantina* (Sydney: Angus and Robertson, 1936).

'Van Dine. S. S.' (= Willard Huntington Wright), *The Benson Murder Case* (New York: Scribner, 1926).

Wallace, Edgar, *The Four Just Men* (London: Tallis, 1906).

Wallace, Edgar, *The Ringer* (London: Hodder and Stoughton, 1927).

Wallace, Edgar, *The Mind of Mr J. G. Reeder* (London: Hodder and Stoughton, 1925).

Wallace, Edgar, *When the Gangs Came to London* (London: Long, 1932).
Wells, Carolyn, *The Clue* (Philadelphia, PA: Lippincott, 1909).
Wentworth, Patricia, *Grey Mask* (London: Hodder and Stoughton, 1928).
Wentworth, Patricia, *Lonesome Road* (London: Hodder and Stoughton, 1939).
Woolrich, Cornell, *The Bride Wore Black* (New York: Simon and Schuster, 1940).
Woolrich, Cornell, (as 'William Irish'), *Phantom Lady* (Philadelphia, PA: Lippincott, 1942).
Zangwill, Israel, *The Big Bow Mystery* (London: Henry, 1892).

Secondary

Auden, W. H., 'The Guilty Vicarage', in *The Dyer's Hand and Other Essays* (London: Faber, 1948); reprinted in Winks (ed.), *Detective Fiction* (1988), 15–24.
Bachelder, Frances H., *Mary Roberts Rinehart: Mistress of Mystery* (*Brownstone Mystery Guides*, 15 (San Bernardino, 1994)).
Bargainnier, Earl F., *10 Women of Mystery* (Bowling Green, OH: Popular Press, 1981).
Barnard, Robert, *A Talent to Deceive: An Appreciation of Agatha Christie* (London: Collins, 1980).
Barzun, Jacques, 'Detection and the Literary Art', in *The Delights of Detection* (New York: Criterion, 1961), 9–23; reprinted in abbreviated form in Winks (ed.), *Detective Fiction* (1988), 144–53.
Bellak, Leopold, 'Psychology of Detective Stories and Related Problems', *Psychoanalytic Review*, 32 (1945), 403–7.
Benstock, Bernard (ed.), *Essays on Detective Fiction* (Basingstoke: Palgrave Macmillan, 1983).
Bentley, E. C., *Those Days* (London: Constable, 1940).
Berkeley, Anthony, 'Preface', *The Second Shot* (London: Hodder and Stoughton, 1930).
'Blake, Nicholas' (= C. Day Lewis), 'Introduction' to Haycraft, *Murder for Pleasure*, xv–xxvii; reprinted in abbreviated form in Haycraft (ed.), *The Art of the Mystery Story* (1974), 398–405.
Bleiler, E. F. 'Introduction' to Martin Hewitt, *Tales of Mean Streets* (New York: Dover, 1976).
Bleiler, E. F. 'Introduction' to Jacques Futrelle, *Best 'Thinking Machine' Stories* (New York: Dover, 1973).

Bonaparte, Marie, *Edgar Poe: étude analytique* (Paris: Denoel et Steele, 1933).

Breen, Jon L. and Greenberg, Martin Harry, *Murder off the Rack* (Metuchen, NJ: Scarecrow, 1989).

Cawelti, John, *Adventure, Mystery, and Romance: Formula Stories as Art and Popular Culture* (Chicago, IN: University of Chicago Press, 1976).

Chandler, Raymond, 'The Simple Art of Murder', *Atlantic Monthly*, December 1944; reprinted in *The Simple Art of Murder* (Boston, MA: Houghton Mifflin, 1950), in *Pearls are a Nuisance* (London: Hamilton, 1964) and in Haycraft (ed.), *The Art of the Mystery Story* (1974), 222–37.

Chesterton, G. K., 'A Defence of Detective Stories', in *The Defendant* (London: Johnson, 1902); reprinted in Haycraft (ed.), *The Art of the Mystery Story* (1974), 3–6.

Christie, Agatha, *An Autobiography* (London: Collins, 1972).

Clurman, Robert, 'Introduction' to *Nick Carter: Detective Fiction's Most Celebrated Detective* (New York: Macmillan, 1963).

Cohn, Jan, 'Mary Roberts Rinehart' in Bargainnier (ed.), *10 Women in Mystery* (1981), 180–220.

Cohn, Jan, *Improbable Fiction: Mary Roberts Rinehart* (Pittsburgh, PA: University of Pittsburgh Press, 1980).

Collins, Max Allan, 'Jim Thompson: the Killer Inside Him', in Breen and Greenberg (ed.), *Murder of the Rack* (1989), 35–54.

Collins, Max Allan and Traylor, James L., *One Lonely Knight: Mickey Spillane's Mike Hammer* (Bowling Green, OH: Popular Press, 1984).

Craig, Patricia and Cadogan, Mary, *The Lady Investigates: Woman Detectives and Spies in Fiction* (London: Gollancz, 1981).

Croft, Andy, 'Worlds without End Foisted upon the Future – Some Antecedents of *Nineteen Eighty Four*', in *Inside the Myth*, ed. C. Norris (London: Lawrence and Wishart, 1984), 183–216.

Danielsson, Karen Molander, *The Dynamic Detective: Special Interest and Seriality in Contemporary Detective Series* (Uppsala: Studia Anglistica Upsaliensa 121, 2002).

Davis, Mike, *City of Quartz* (London: Verso, 1990).

de Marr, Mary Jean (ed.), *In the Beginning: First Novels in Mystery Series* (Bowling Green, OH: Popular Press, 1995).

Donaldson, Norman, *In Quest of Dr Thorndyke* (Bowling Green, OH: Popular Press, 1971).

Durham, Philip, *Down These Mean Streets a Man Must Go: Raymond Chandler's Knight* (Chapel Hill: University of North Carolina Press, 1963).

Dyer, Carolyn Stewart and Romalov, Nancy Tillman (eds), *Rediscovering Nancy Drew* (Iowa City: University of Iowa Press, 1995).

Eliot, T. S. *Selected Essays, 1917–32* (London: Faber, 1932).

Fiedler, Leslie, *Love and Death in the American Novel* (Cleveland, OH: World Publicity, 1960).

Freeman, R. Austin, 'The Art of the Detective Story', *Nineteenth Century and After* (May 1924), reprinted in Haycraft (ed.), *The Art of the Mystery Story* (1974), 7–17.

Freier, Mary P., 'The Decline of Hilda Adams', in Kathleen G. Klein (ed.), *Woman Times Three* (Bowling Green, OH: Popular Press, 1995), 129–41.

Gill, Gillian, *Agatha Christie: The Woman and Her Mysteries* (London: Robson, 1991).

Glover, David, 'The Stuff that Dreams are Made of', in Derek Longhurst (ed.), *Gender, Genre and Narrative Pleasure* (London: Unwin Hyman, 1989), 67–83.

Glover, David, 'Introduction' to Edgar Wallace, *the Four Just Men*, ed. David Glover ([1906] Oxford: Oxford University Press, 1995).

Glover, David, 'Thrillers', in Martin Priestman (ed.), *The Cambridge Companion to Crime Fiction* (Cambridge: Cambridge University Press, 2003).

Grella, George, 'Murder and the Mean Streets: The Hard-Boiled Detective Novel', in *Detective Fiction: Crime and Compromise*, ed. Dick Allen and David Chacko (New York: Harcourt Brace Jovanovich, 1974), 411–28; reprinted in Winks (ed.), *Detective Fiction* (1988), 103–20.

Grella, George, 'Murder and Manners: the Formal Detective Novel', in Larry N. Landrum, Pat Browne and Ray B. Browne (eds), *Dimensions of Detective Fiction* (Bowling Green, OH: Popular Press, 1976), 37–57; reprinted in Winks (ed.), *Detective Fiction* (1988), 84–102.

Hammett, Dashiell, review of S. S. Van Dine, *The Benson Murder Case*, *Saturday Review of Literature*, New York, 15 January 1927; reprinted in Haycraft (ed.), *The Art of the Mystery Story* (1974), 382–3.

Harrison, Michael, *Peter Cheyney: Prince of Hokum* (London: Spearman, 1954).

Haut, Woody, *Pulp Culture, Hardboiled Fiction and the Cold War* (London: Serpent's Tail, 1994).

Haut, Woody, *Neon Noir: Contemporary American Crime Fiction* (London: Serpent's Tail, 1999).

Haycraft, Howard, *Murder for Pleasure: The Life and Times of the Detective Story* (London: Davies, 1942).

Haycraft, Howard (ed.), *The Art of the Mystery Story: A Collection of Critical Essays,* reprint edn ([1946] New York: Carroll and Graf, 1974).

Herbert, Rosemary (ed.), *The Oxford Companion to Crime and Mystery* (New York: Oxford University Press, 1999).

Hilfer, Tony, *The Crime Novel: A Deviant Genre* (Austin: University of Texas Press, 1990).

Horsley, Lee, *The Noir Thriller* (London: Palgrave, 2001).

Irons, Glenwood (ed.), *Feminism in Women's Detective Fiction* (Toronto: University of Toronto Press, 1995).

Isaac, Frederick, 'Enter the Fat man', in de Marr (ed.), *In the Beginning* (1995), 59–68.

Jameson, Fredric, 'On Raymond Chandler', *Southern Review,* 6 (1970), 624–50; reprinted in Most and Stowe (eds), *The Poetics of Murder* (1983), 122–38.

Joshi, S. T., *John Dickson Carr: A Critical Study* (Bowling Green, OH: Popular Press, 1990).

Knight, Stephen, *Form and Ideology in Crime Fiction* (London: Macmillan, 1980).

Knight, Stephen, 'The Case of the Missing Dragon: Simile, Style and Symbolism in *The Big Sleep*', *Q/W/E/RT/Y,* 5 (1995), 259–66.

Knight, Stephen, *Continent of Mystery: A Thematic History of Australian Crime Fiction* (Melbourne: University of Melbourne Press, 1977).

Landrum, Larry N., *American Mystery and Detective Novels: A Reference Guide* (Westport, CT: Greenwood, 1999).

Lane, Margaret, *Edgar Wallace* (London: Heinemann, 1938).

Lewis, Margaret, *Ngaio Marsh: A Life* (London: Chatto and Windus, 1991).

Light, Alison, *Forever England: Femininity, Literature and Conservatism between the Wars* (London: Routledge, 1991).

Madden, David, *James M. Cain* (New York: Twayne, 1970).

Malmgren, Carl D., *Anatomy of a Murder: Mystery Detection and Crime Fiction* (Bowling Green, OH: Popular Press, 2001).

Mandel, Ernest, *Delightful Murder: A Social History of the Crime Story* (London: Pluto, 1984).

Mann, Jessica, *Deadlier than the Male: An Investigation into Feminine Crime Writing* (Newton Abbot: David and Charles, 1981).

Mason, Bobbie Ann, 'Nancy Drew: the Once and Future Prom Queen', Chapter 4 of *The Girl Sleuths* (Old Westbury: Feminist Press, 1975); reprinted in Irons (ed.), *Feminism in Women's Detective Fiction* (1995), 74–93.

Messac, Régis, *Le 'Detective Novel' et l'influence de la pensée scientifique* (Paris: Champion, 1929).

Most, Glenn W. and Stowe, William W. (eds), *The Poetics of Murder: Detective Fiction and Literary Theory* (New York: Harcourt Brace Jovanovich, 1983).

Mottram, Eric, 'Ross Macdonald and the Past of a Formula', in Benstock (ed.), *Essays on Detective Fiction* (1983), 97–118.

Munt, Sally R., *Murder by the Book? Feminism and the Crime Novel* (London: Routledge, 1994).

Narremore, James, 'Dashiell Hammett and the Poetics of Hard-Boiled Detection', in Benstock (ed.), *Essays on Detective Fiction* (1983), 49–72.

Nevins, Francis M., *Royal Bloodline: Ellery Queen, Author and Detective* (Bowling Green, OH: Popular Press, 1974).

Norton, Charles A., *Melville Davisson Post: Man of Many Mysteries* (Bowling Green, OH: Popular Press, 1973).

Orwell, George, 'The Ethics of the Detective Story from Raffles to Miss Blandish', *Horizon*, October 1944, reprinted as 'Introductory Essay' in E. W. Hornung, *The Complete Short Stories of Raffles* (London: Penguin, 1985), 25–38.

Panek, Leroy Lad, *Watteau's Shepherds: The Detective Novel in Britain, 1914–1940* (Bowling Green, OH: Popular Press, 1979).

Panek, Leroy Lad, *Probable Cause: Crime Fiction in America* (Bowling Green, OH: Popular Press, 1990).

Pederson, Jay P. (ed.), *St James Guide to Crime and Mystery Writers*, 4th edn (Detroit, MI: St James Press, 1996).

Pederson-Krag, Geraldine, 'Detective Stories and the Primal Scene', *Psychoanalytic Quarterly*, 18 (1949), 207–14; reprinted in Most and Stowe (eds), *The Poetics of Murder* (1983), 14–20.

Plain, Gill, *Women's Fiction of the Second World War: Gender, Power, Resistance* (Edinburgh: Edinburgh University Press, 1996).

Porter, Dennis, *The Pursuit of Crime: Art and Ideology in Crime Fiction* (New Haven, CT: Yale University Press, 1981).

Priestman, Martin, *Detective Fiction and Literature: The Figure on the Carpet* (Basingstoke: Palgrave Macmillan, 1990).

Priestman, Martin, *Crime Fiction* (Plymouth: Northcote House, 1998).

Rabinowicz, Peter J., *Before Reading: Narrative Conventions and the Politics of Interpretation* (Columbus: Ohio State University Press, 1987).

Raskin, Richard, 'The Pleasures and Politics of Detective Fiction', *Clues*, 13 (1992), 71–113.

Reilly, John M. (ed.), *Encyclopedia of Mystery and Detection* (New York: St Martin's, 1980).

Reilly, John M. (ed.), 'Margaret Millar', in Bargainnier (ed.), *10 Women of Mystery* (1981), 223–46.

Roberts, Jeanne Addison, 'Feminist Murder: Amanda Cross Reinvents Womanhood', in Irons (ed.), *Feminism in Women's Detective Fiction* (1995), 94–111.

Roth, Marty, *Foul and Fair Play: Reading Genre in Classic Detective Fiction* (Athens: University of Georgia Press, 1995).

Rowland, Susan, *From Agatha Christie to Ruth Rendell: British Women Writers in Detective Crime Fiction* (Basingstoke: Palgrave Macmillan, 2001).

Ruehlmann, William, *Saint with a Gun* (New York: New York University Press, 1974).

Rycroft, Charles, 'Analysis of a Detective Story', in *Imagination and Reality* (London: Hogarth, 1968).

Sayers, Dorothy, 'Introduction' to *The Omnibus of Crime* (London: Gollancz, 1928); reprinted in Haycraft (ed.), *That Art of the Mystery Story* (1974), 71–109.

Sayers, Dorothy, '*Gaudy Night*', in *Titles to Fame*, ed. Denys K. Roberts (London: Nelson, 1937); reprinted in Haycraft (ed.), *The Art of the Mystery Story* (1974), 208–21.

Shaw, Marion and Vanacker, Sabine, *Reflecting on Miss Marple* (London: Routledge, 1991).

Symons, Julian, *Bloody Murder: From the Detective Story to the Crime Novel*, 3rd edn (London: Penguin, 1992).

Talburt, Susan, 'Josephine Tey', in Bargainnier (ed.), *10 Women of Mystery* (1981), 40–76.

Thomas, Donald, 'The Dangerous Edge of Things: the Novels of Patrick Hamilton', *Encounter*, 49 (1987), 32–40.

Todorov, Tzvetan, 'The Typology of Detective Fiction', in *The Poetics of Prose*, trans. R. Howard (Oxford: Blackwell, 1977).

Traylor, James A. *see under* Collins, Max Allan.

Turnbull, Malcolm J., *Elusion Aforethought: The Life and Work of Anthony Berkeley Cox* (Bowling Green, OH: Popular Press, 1996).

Tuska, Jon, *Philo Vance: The Life and Times of S. S. Van Dine* (Bowling Green, OH: Popular Press, 1971).

Van Dine, S. S., 'Twenty Rules for Writing Detective Stories', *American Magazine*, September 1928; reprinted in Haycraft (ed.), *The Art of the Mystery Story* (1974), 189–93.

Watson, Colin, *Snobbery with Violence: English Crime Stories and Their Audience* (London: Eyre and Spottiswoode, 1971).

Wells, Carolyn, *The Technique of the Mystery Story* (Springfield, IL: The Home Correspondence School, 1913).

Williams, Raymond, *The Country and the City* (London: Chatto and Windus, 1973).

Wilson, Edmund, 'Who Cares Who Killed Roger Ackroyd?' *New Yorker*, 20 January 1945; reprinted in Haycraft (ed.), *The Art of the Mystery Story* (1974), 390–97 and in Winks (ed.), *Detective Fiction* (1988), 35–40.

Winks, Robin (ed.), *Detective Fiction: A Collection of Critical Essays*, 2nd edn (Woodstock: Countryman, 1988).

Zizek, Slavoj, 'The Detective and the Analyst', *Literature and Psychology*, 36 (1990), 27–46.

Zizek, Slavoj, 'Two Ways to Avoid the Real of Desire', in *Looking Awry: An Introduction to Jacques Lacan through Popular Culture* (Cambridge, MA: MIT Press, 1992).

PART III   DIVERSITY

Primary

Abella, Alex, *The Killing of the Saints* (New York: Crown, 1990).

'Aldyne Nathan' (= Michael McDowell and Dennis Schuetz), *Vermilion* (New York: Avon, 1980).

Allingham, Margery, *The Tiger in the Smoke* (London: Chatto and Windus, 1952).

Arnott, Jake, *The Long Firm* (London: Hodder and Stoughton, 1999).

Auster, Paul, *City of Glass* (Los Angeles: Sun and Moon Press, 1985).

Auster, Paul, *Ghosts* (Los Angeles: Sun and Moon Press, 1986).

Auster, Paul, *The Locked Room* (Los Angeles: Sun and Moon Press, 1986).

Baker, Nikki, *In the Game* (Tallahassee, FL: Naiad, 1991).

Baker, Nikki, *The Lavender House Murder* (Tallahassee, FL: Naiad, 1992).

Baker, Nikki, *Long Goodbyes* (Tallahassee, FL: Naiad, 1993).

Ball, John, *In the Heat of the Night* (New York: Harper, 1965).

Ball, John, *Johnny Get Your Gun* (Boston, MA: Little, Brown, 1969).

Barnes, Linda, *A Trouble of Fools* (New York: St Martin's, 1987).

Barnes, Linda, *Coyote* (New York: Dell, 1990).

Barrett, Robert G., *You Wouldn't Be Dead for Quids* (Sydney: Waratah, 1985).

Baxt, George, *A Queer Kind of Death* (New York: Simon and Schuster, 1966).

Baxt, George, *A Queer Kind of Love* (New York: Penzler, 1994).

Beecham, Rose, *Introducing Amanda Valentine* (Tallahassee, FL: Naiad, 1992).

Beadle, Jeremy, *Dead Scene* (London: GMP, 1988).

Beadle, Jeremy, *Doing Business* (London: GMP, 1990).

Beal, M. F., *Angel Dead* (New York: Daughters, 1977).

Bell, Josephine, *To Let, Furnished* (London: Methuen, 1952).

Bergman, Andrew, *The Big Kiss-Off of 1944* (New York: Holt, Rinehart, 1974).

Bergman, Andrew, *Hollywood and Levine* (New York: Holt, Rinehart, 1975).

Bland, Eleanor Taylor, *Dead Time* (New York: St Martin's, 1992).

Block, Lawrence, *In the Midst of Death* (New York: Dell, 1976).

Block, Lawrence, *A Dance at the Slaughterhouse* (New York: Morrow, 1991).

Bruce, John Edward, *The Black Sleuth, McGirt's Magazine* (1907–9), reprinted in John E. Bruce Collection, Reel 3, Schomburg Center for Research in Black Culture, New York.

Burke, James Lee, *The Neon Rain* (New York: Holt, 1987).

Burke, James Lee, *In the Electric Mist with Confederate Dead* (New York: Hyperion, 1993).

Carlon, Patricia, *Circle of Fear* (London: Ward Lock, 1961).

Carlon, Patricia, *The Whispering Wall* (London: Hodder and Stoughton, 1969).

Carter, Charlotte, *Rhode Island Red* (London: Serpent's Tail, 1997).

'Caudwell, Sarah' (= Sarah Cockburn), *Thus was Adonis Murdered* (London: Collins, 1981).

Charyn, Jerome, *The Good Policeman* (New York: Mysterious Press, 1990).

Christie, Agatha, *The ABC Murders* (London: Collins, 1936).

Christie, Agatha, *Death Comes as the End* (London: Collins, 1945).

Christie, Agatha, *Hickory Dickory Dock* (London: Collins, 1955).

Christie, Agatha, *The Mirror Crack'd from Side to Side* (London: Collins, 1962).

Cody, Liza, *Dupe* (London: Collins, 1980).

Cody, Liza, *Stalker* (Basingstoke: Palgrave Macmillan, 1984).

'Coe, Tucker' (= Donald Westlake), *Kinds of Love, Kinds of Death* (New York: Random House, 1966).

Cohen, Gustavas Roy, *Florian Slappey Goes Abroad* (1928).

'Collins, Hunt' (= Salvatore Lombino), *Cut Me In* (New York: Abelard Schuman, 1954).

Connelly, Michael, *The Black Echo* (New York: St Martin's, 1992).

'Constantine, K. C.', *The Rocksburg Railroad Murders* (New York: Saturday Review Press, 1972).

'Constantine, K. C.', *Good Sons* (New York: Mysterious Press, 1996).

Cornwell, Patricia, *Post-Mortem* (New York: Scribner, 1990).

Cornwell, Patricia, *The Body Farm: A Novel* (New York: Scribner, 1994).

Corris, Peter, *The Dying Trade* (Sydney: McGraw-Hill, 1980).

Corpi, Lucha, *Eulogy for a Brown Angel* (Houston, TX: Arte Publico Press, 1992).

Corpi, Lucha, *Cactus Blood* (Houston, TX: Arte Publico Press, 1995).

'Craig, David' (= Jim Tucker), *Bay City* (London: Constable, 2000).

Crais, Robert, *The Monkey's Raincoat* (New York: Bantam, 1987).

Crais, Robert, *L.A. Requiem* (New York: Doubleday, 1991).

'Crispin, Edmund' (= Bruce Montgomery), *The Case of the Gilded Fly* (London: Gollancz, 1944).

'Cross, Amanda' (= Carolyn Heilbrun), *In the Last Analysis* (New York: Macmillan, 1964).

'Cross, Amanda' (= Carolyn Heilbrun), *Death in a Tenured Position* (New York: Dutton, 1981).

'Cross, Amanda' (= Carolyn Heilbrun), *No Word from Winifred* (New York: Dutton, 1986).

Crumley, James, *The Wrong Case* (New York: Random House, 1975).

Crumley, James, *The Last Good Kiss* (New York: Random House, 1978).

'Cunningham, E. V.' (= Howard Fast), *Samantha* (New York: Morrow, 1967).

Dale, John, *Dark Angel* (Sydney: HarperCollins, 1995).

Davidson, Lionel, *The Night of Wenceslas* (London: Gollancz, 1960).

Davidson, Lionel, *A Long Way to Shiloh* (London: Gollancz, 1966).

Davis, Lindsey, *The Silver Pigs* (London: Sidgwick, 1989).

Day, Marele, *The Last Tango of Dolores Delgado* (Sydney: Allen and Unwin, 1992).

'de la Torre, Lillian' (= Lillian McCue), *Dr Sam: Johnson, Detector* (New York: Knopf, 1946).

Doberman, Stephen, *Saratoga Longshot* (New York: Atheneum, 1976).

Doody, Margaret, *Aristotle Detective* (London: The Bodley Head, 1978).

Douglas, Lauren Wright, *The Always Anonymous Beast* (Tallahassee, FL: Naiad, 1983).
Dreher, Sarah, *Stoner McTavish* (Lebanon, NH: New Victoria, 1985).
Dreher, Sarah, *Gray Magic* (Norwich, VT: New Victoria, 1987).
Drummond, June, *Farewell Party* (London: Gollancz, 1971).
Duffy, Stella, *Calendar Girl* (London: Serpent's Tail, 1994).
Duffy, Stella, *Fresh Flesh* (London: Serpent's Tail, 1999).
Duffy, Stella and Henderson, Lauren (eds), *Tart Noir: Twenty Shocking New Crime Stories* (London: Pan, 2002).
'Dunant, Peter' (= Sarah Dunant and Peter Busby), *Exterminating Angels* (London: Deutsch, 1983).
Dunant, Sarah, *Birth Marks* (London: Joseph, 1992).
Dunant, Sarah, *Under my Skin* (London: Hamilton, 1995).
Dunlap, Susan, *Karma* (New York: Paperjacks, 1984).
Ellis, Brett Easton, *American Psycho* (New York: Vintage, 1991).
Ellroy, James, *The Black Dahlia* (New York: Mysterious Press, 1987).
Ellroy, James, *The Big Nowhere* (New York: Mysterious Press, 1988).
Ellroy, James, *L.A. Confidential* (New York: Mysterious Press, 1990).
Ellroy, James, *White Jazz* (New York: Knopf, 1992).
Engel, Howard, *The Suicide Murders* (Toronto: Clarke Irwin, 1980).
Engel, Howard, *Murder Sees the Light* (Markham: Viking, 1984).
Estleman, Loren D., *Motor City Blues* (Boston, MA: Houghton Mifflin, 1980).
Evanovich, Janet, *One for the Money* (New York: Scribner, 1994).
Fisher, Rudolph, *The Conjure-Man Dies: A Mystery Tale of Dark Harlem* (New York: Covici, Friede, 1932).
Flower, Pat, *Hell for Heather* (London: Hale, 1962).
Flower, Pat, *Hunt the Body* (London: Hale, 1968).
Forrest, Katherine V., *Amateur City* (Tallahassee, FL: Naiad, 1984).
Forrest, Katherine V., *Murder at the Nightwood Bar* (Tallahassee, FL: Naiad, 1987).
Forrest, Katherine V., *Apparition Alley* (New York: Berkley, 1997).
Fremlin, Celia, *The Hours Before Dawn* (London: Gollancz, 1958).
Freney, Dennis, *Larry Death* (Melbourne: Mandarin, 1991).
Friedman, Kinky, *Greenwich Killing Time* (New York: Morrow, 1986).
'Fyfield, Frances' (= Frances Hegarty), *A Question of Guilt* (London: Heinemann, 1988).
'Fyfield, Frances'(= Frances Hegarty), *Shadows on the Mirror* (London: Heinemann, 1989).
Garner, Hugh, *The Sin Sniper* (Toronto: Pocket Books, 1970).
Garner, Hugh, *A Nice Place to Visit* (Toronto: Ryerson, 1970).

'Gilbert, Anthony' (= Lucy Malleson), *And Death Came Too* (London: Collins, 1956).

Gilbert, W. Stephen, *Spiked* (London: GMP, 1991).

Gordon, Alison, *The Dead Pull Hitter* (New York: St Martin's, 1989).

Gordon, Gaelyn, *Above Suspicion* (Auckland: Random House, 1990).

Gores, Joe, *Dead Skip* (New York: Random House, 1972).

Gores, Joe, *Hammett: A Novel* (New York: Putnam, 1975).

Gough, Laurence, *Accidental Deaths* (Toronto: Viking, 1991).

Grafton, Sue, *A is for Alibi* (New York: Holt, 1982).

Grafton, Sue, *K is for Killer* (New York: Holt, 1999).

Grafton, Sue, *Q is for Quarry* (New York: Putnam, 2003).

Greenwood, Kerry, *Cocaine Blues* (Melbourne: McPhee Gribble, 1989).

Grisham, John, *The Firm* (New York: Doubleday, 1991).

Hager, Jean, *Spirit Caller* (New York: Mysterious Press, 1997).

Hall, James, *Under Cover of Daylight* (London: Heinemann, 1987).

Hansen, Joseph, *Fadeout* (New York: Harper and Row, 1970).

Hansen, Joseph, *Death Claims* (New York: Harper and Row, 1973).

Hansen, Joseph, *Early Graves* (New York: Mysterious Press, 1987).

Harris, John Nairn, *The Weird World of Wes Beattie* (Toronto: Macmillan, 1963).

Harris, Thomas, *Black Sunday* (New York: Putnam, 1975).

Harris, Thomas, *Red Dragon* (New York: Putnam, 1981).

Harris, Thomas, *The Silence of the Lambs* (New York: St Martin's, 1988).

Harris, Thomas, *Hannibal* (New York: Delacorte, 1999).

Hayter, Sparkle, *What's a Girl Gotta Do?* (New York: Penguin, 1994).

Haywood, Gar Anthony, *Fear of the Dark* (New York: St Martin's, 1988).

Haywood, Gar Anthony, *Not Long for This World* (New York: St Martin's, 1990).

Headley, Victor, *Yardie* (London: The X Press, 1992).

Hegarty, Frances, *The Playroom* (London: Hamilton, 1991).

Hiaasen, Carl, *Tourist Season* (New York: Putnam, 1986).

Hiaasen, Carl, with Montalbano, William D., *Powder Burns* (New York: Atheneum, 1981).

Higgins, George V., *The Friends of Eddie Coyle* (New York: Knopf, 1972).

Higgins, George V., *Kennedy for the Defence* (New York: Knopf, 1980).

Highsmith, Patricia, *Strangers on a Train* (New York: Harper and Row, 1950).

Highsmith, Patricia, *The Talented Mr Ripley* (New York: Coward McCann, 1955).

Highsmith, Patricia, *Ripley Under Ground* (New York: Doubleday, 1970).

Highsmith, Patricia, *Ripley's Game* (New York: Knopf, 1974).

Highsmith, Patricia, *Edith's Diary* (New York: Simon and Schuster, 1977).

Highsmith, Patricia, *The Boy Who Followed Ripley* (New York: Lippincott, 1980).

Highsmith, Patricia, *Tales of Natural and Unnatural Catastrophes* (London: Bloomsbury, 1987).

Hill, Reginald, *A Clubbable Woman* (London: Collins, 1970).

Hill, Reginald, *Under World* (London: Collins, 1988).

Hill, Reginald, *Born Guilty* (London: HarperCollins, 1995).

Hillerman, Tony, *The Blessing Way* (New York: Harper, 1970).

Hillerman, Tony, *Dance Hall of the Dead* (New York: Harper, 1973).

Hillerman, Tony, *People of Darkness* (New York: Harper, 1980).

Hillerman, Tony, *Coyote Waits* (New York: HarperCollins, 1990).

Himes, Chester, *La reine des pommes* (Paris: Gallimard, 1958), trans. as *For Love of Imabelle* (New York: Fawcett, 1959) and as *A Rage in Harlem* (New York: Avon, 1965).

Himes, Chester, *Cotton Comes to Harlem* (New York: Putnam, 1965).

Himes, Chester, *Blind Man with a Pistol* (New York, Morrow, 1969).

Hogan, Linda, *Mean Spirit* (New York: Ivy, 1990).

Hopkins, Pauline, *Hagar's Daughter: A Story of Southern Caste Prejudice, Colored American* (1901–2); reprinted in *The Magazine Novels of Pauline Hopkins*, The Schomburg Library of Nineteenth-Century Black Women Writers (New York: Oxford University Press, 1988).

Huff, Tanya, *Blood Price* (New York: DAO, 1991).

Hume, Fergus, *Hagar of the Pawnshop* (London: Skeffington, 1898).

'Hunter, Evan' (= Salvatore Lombino), *The Blackboard Jungle* (New York: Simon and Schuster, 1954).

'James, Bill' (= Jim Tucker), *You'd Better Believe It* (London: Constable, 1985).

James, P. D., *Cover her Face* (London: Faber, 1962).

James, P. D., *An Unsuitable Job for a Woman* (London: Faber, 1972).

James, P. D., *Innocent Blood* (London: Faber, 1980).

James, P. D., *The Skull Beneath the Skin* (London: Faber, 1982).

James, P. D., *A Taste for Death* (London: Faber, 1986).

James, P. D., *Devices and Desires* (London: Faber, 1989).

Kaminsky, Stuart, *Bullet for a Star* (New York: St Martin's, 1977).

Keating, H. R. F., *The Perfect Murder* (London: Collins, 1964).

Kellerman, Faye, *The Ritual Bath* (New York: Ballantine, 1986).

Kellerman Jonathan, *When the Bough Breaks* (New York: Atheneum, 1985).

Kemelman, Harry, *Friday the Rabbi Slept Late* (New York: Crown, 1964).

King, Laurie R., *A Grave Talent* (New York: St Martin's, 1995).

King, Laurie R., *Night Work* (New York: Bantam, 2000).

Knight, Stephen (ed.), *Crimes for a Summer Christmas* (Sydney: Allen and Unwin, 1990).

Knight, Stephen (ed.), *Murder at Home* (Sydney: Allen and Unwin, 1993).

Knox, Bill, *Deadline for a Dream* (London: Long, 1957).

Komo, Dolores, *Clio Brown, Private Investigator* (Freedom: Crossing Press, 1988).

Kristeva, Julia, *The Old Man and the Wolves* (New York: Columbia University Press, 1994).

Kristeva, Julia, *Possessions* (New York: Columbia University Press, 1998).

Lafavor, Carol, *Evil Dead Center* (Ithaca, NY: Firebrand, 1997).

'Lathen, Emma' (= Mary J. Latis and Martha Hennissart), *Banking on Death* (New York: Macmillan, 1961).

Lee, Chang-Rae, *Native Speaker* (New York: Riverhead, 1995).

Leonard, Elmore, *City Primeval: High Noon in Detroit* (New York: Arbor House, 1980).

Leonard, Elmore, *Cat Chaser* (New York: Arbor House, 1982).

Leonard, Elmore, *Freaky Deaky* (New York: Arbor House, 1988).

Lewis, Catherine, *Dry Fire* (New York: Norton, 1996).

Lovesey, Peter, *Wobble to Death* (London: Macmillan, 1970).

MacDonald, John D., *The Brass Cupcake* (New York: Fawcett, 1950).

MacDonald, John D., *The Deep Blue Goodbye* (New York: Fawcett, 1964).

MacDonald, John D., *The Dreadful Lemon Sky* (Philadelphia, PA: Lippincott, 1975).

Machin, Barbara, *South of the Border* (London: Women's Press, 1990).

Major, Clarence, *Reflex and Bone Structure* (New York: Fiction Collective, 1975).

Maloney, Shane, *The Brush-Off* (Melbourne: Text Publishing, 1996).

Mantell, Laurie, *Murder and Chips* (London: Gollancz, 1980).

Manthorne, Jackie, *Ghost Motel* (Charlottetown: Gynergy, 1994).

'Marric, J. J.' (= John Creasey), *Gideon's Day* (London: Hodder and Stoughton, 1955).

'McBain, Ed' (= Salvatore Lombino), *Cop Hater* (New York: Simon and Schuster, 1956).

'McBain, Ed' (= Salvatore Lombino), *Lady, Lady, I Did It* (New York: Simon and Schuster, 1961).

'McBain, Ed' (= Salvatore Lombino), *Lightning* (New York: Arbor House, 1984).

'McBain, Ed' (= Salvatore Lombino), *Widows* (New York: Morrow, 1991).

McClure, James, *The Steam Pig* (London: Gollancz, 1971).

McConnell, Vicki P., *Mrs Porter's Letters* (Tallahassee: Naiad, 1982).

McDermid, Val, *Report for Murder* (London: Women's Press, 1987).

McDermid, Val, *Dead Beat* (London: Gollancz, 1992).

McDermid, Val, *Union Jack* (London: Women's Press, 1993).

McDermid, Val, *The Mermaids Singing* (London: HarperCollins, 1995).

McIlvanney, William, *Laidlaw* (London: Hodder and Stoughton, 1973).

McKemmish, Jan, *A Gap in the Records* (Melbourne: Sybylla, 1985).

McLaren, Philip, *Scream Black Murder* (Sydney: HarperCollins, 1995).

Millar, Margaret, *Wall of Eyes* (New York: Random House, 1943).

Millar, Margaret, *The Iron Gates* (New York: Random House, 1945).

Millar, Margaret, *Beast in View* (New York: Random House, 1955).

Millar, Margaret, *A Stranger in My Grave* (New York: Random House, 1960).

Millar, Margaret, *How Like an Angel* (New York: Random House, 1962).

Miner, Val, *Murder in the English Department* (New York: St Martin's, 1982).

Montalbano, William D. *see under* Hiaasen, Carl.

Moody, Susan, *Penny Black* (Basingstoke: Palgrave Macmillan, 1984).

Moorhead, Fiona, *Still Murder* (Melbourne: Penguin, 1991).

Morrell, Mary, *Final Solution* (San Francisco, CA: Spinsters, 1991).

Morse, L. A., *The Old Dick* (New York: Avon, 1981).

Mosley, Walter, *Devil in a Blue Dress* (New York: Norton, 1990).

Mosley, Walter, *Black Betty* (New York: Norton, 1994).

Mosley, Walter, *A Red Death* (New York: Norton, 1991).

Mosley, Walter, *White Butterfly* (New York: Norton, 1992).

Mosley, Walter, *A Little Yellow Dog* (New York: Norton, 1996).

Muller, Marcia, *Edwin of the Iron Shoes* (New York: McKay, 1977).

Muller, Marcia, *Ask the Cards a Question* (New York: St Martin's, 1982).

Muller, Marcia, *The Tree of Death* (New York: Walker, 1983).

Muller, Marcia, *Where Echoes Live* (New York: Mysterious Press, 1991).

Narogin, Mudrooroo, 'Westralian Lead' in *Crimes for a Summer Christmas*, ed. Stephen Knight (1990), 25–47.

Narogin, Mudrooroo, 'Home on the Range' in *Murder at Home*, ed. Stephen Knight (1993), 3–12.

Nava, Michael, *The Little Death* (Boston, MA: Alyson, 1986).

Nava, Michael, *Goldenboy* (Boston, MA: Alyson, 1988).

Neely, Barbara, *Blanche on the Lam* (New York: St Martin's, 1992).

Neely, Barbara, *Blanche among the Talented Tenth* (New York: St Martin's, 1994).

Neely, Barbara, *Blanche Cleans Up* (New York: Viking, 1998).

Neely, Barbara, *Blanche Passes Go* (New York: Viking, 2000).

Newman, G. F., *You Nice Bastard* (London: New English Library, 1972).

O'Donnell, Lillian, *The Phone Calls* (New York: Putnam, 1972).

O'Rourke, Rebecca, *Jumping the Cracks* (London: Virago, 1987).

Owens, Louis, *The Sharpest Sight* (Norman: University of Oklahoma Press, 1992).

Paretsky, Sarah, *Indemnity Only* (New York: Dial, 1982).

Paretsky, Sarah, *Deadlock* (New York: Dial, 1984).

Paretsky, Sarah, *Bitter Medicine* (New York: Morrow, 1987).

Paretsky, Sarah, *Blood Shot* (New York: Delacorte, 1988).

Paretsky, Sarah, *Burn Marks* (New York: Delacorte, 1990).

Paretsky, Sarah, *Tunnel Vision* (New York: Delacorte, 1994).

Parker, Robert B., *The Godwulf Manuscript* (Boston, MA: Houghton Mifflin, 1973).

Parker, Robert B., *Promised Land* (Boston, MA: Houghton Mifflin, 1976).

Parker, Robert B., *Looking for Rachel Wallace* (New York: Delacorte, 1980).

Parker, Robert B., *Perchance to Dream* (New York: Putnam, 1991).

Parker, Robert B., with Raymond Chandler, *Poodle Springs* (New York: Putnam, 1989).

'Peters, Ellis' (= Edith Pargeter), *A Morbid Taste for Bones* (London: Macmillan, 1977).

Phillips, Edward, *Sunday's Child* (Toronto: McClelland and Stewart, 1981).

Phillips, Gary, *Violent Spring* (Portland: West Coast Crime, 1994).

Phillips, Mike, *Point of Darkness* (London: Joseph, 1994).

Phillips, Mike, *An Image to Die For* (London: HarperCollins, 1995).

'Pike, Robert, L.' (= Robert L. Fish), *Mute Witness* (New York: Doubleday, 1963).

'Pike, Robert, L.' (= Robert L. Fish), *Police Blotter* (New York: Doubleday, 1965).

Procter, Maurice, *No Proud Chivalry* (London: Longman, 1946).

Procter, Maurice, *The Chief Inspector's Statement* (London: Hutchinson, 1951).

Procter, Maurice, *Hell is a City* (London: Hutchinson, 1954).

Pryce, Malcolm, *Aberystwyth Mon Amour* (London: Bloomsbury, 2001).

Pynchon, Thomas, *The Crying of Lot 49* (Philadelphia: Lippincott, 1966).

Raftery, Roger, *The Pink Triangle* (Brisbane: Queensland University Press, 1981).

Rankin, Ian, *The Falls* (London: Orion, 2001).

Reed, Ishmael, *Mumbo Jumbo* (New York: Doubleday, 1972).

Reichs, Kathy, *Déjà Dead* (New York: Random House, 1997).

Reilly, Helen, *McKee of Center Street* (New York: Doubleday, 1934).

Rendell, Ruth, *From Doon with Death* (London: Hutchinson, 1964).

Rendell, Ruth, *To Fear a Painted Devil* (London: Long, 1965).

Rendell, Ruth, *No More Dying Then* (London: Hutchinson, 1971).

Rendell, Ruth, *A Demon in my View* (London: Hutchinson, 1976).

Rendell, Ruth, *A Judgement in Stone* (London: Hutchinson, 1977).

Rendell, Ruth, *The Lake of Darkness* (London: Hutchinson, 1980).

Rozan, S. J., *China Trade* (New York: St Martin's, 1994).

Sale, Medora, *Murder in Focus* (New York: Scribner, 1989).

Sallis, James, *The Long-Legged Fly* (New York: Carrol and Graf, 1992).

Sanders, Lawrence, *The Anderson Tapes* (New York: Putnam, 1970).

Sanders, Lawrence, *The First Deadly Sin* (New York: Putnam, 1973).

Sayers, Dorothy L., *Have His Carcase* (London: Gollancz, 1932).

Sayers, Dorothy L., *Gaudy Night* (London: Gollancz, 1935).

Sayers, Dorothy L., with Walsh, Jill Paton, *Thrones, Dominations* (London: Hodder and Stoughton, 1998).

Scoppetone, Sandra, *Everything You have is Mine* (New York: Little Brown, 1991).

Schulman, Sarah, *The Sophie Horowitz Story* (Tallahassee, FL: Naiad, 1984).

'Shannon, Dell' (= Elizabeth Linington), *Case Pending* (New York: Harper and Row, 1960).

Simon, Roger L., *The Big Fix* (New York: Simon and Schuster, 1973).

Slovo, Gillian, *Morbid Symptoms* (London: Pluto, 1984).

Slovo, Gillian, *Death by Analysis* (London: Women's Press, 1986).

Smith, Joan, *A Masculine Ending* (London: Faber, 1987).

Smith, Joan, *Full Stop* (London: Chatto and Windus, 1995).

Stabenow, Dana, *A Cold Day for Murder* (New York: Berkley, 1992).

'Stark, Richard' (= Donald Westlake), *The Hunter* (New York: Pocket Books, 1962).

'Stevenson, Richard' (= Richard Lipez), *Death Trick* (New York: St Martin's, 1981).

Symons, Julian, *The Immaterial Murder Case* (London: Gollancz, 1945).

Symons, Julian, *The Thirty-First of February* (London: Gollancz, 1950).

Symons, Julian, *The Colour of Murder* (London: Collins, 1957).

Symons, Julian, *The End of Solomon Grundy* (London: Collins, 1964).

'Tey, Josephine' (= Elizabeth Mackintosh), *Brat Farrar* (London: Davies, 1949).

'Tey, Josephine' (= Elizabeth Mackintosh), *The Daughter of Time* (London: Davies, 1951).

Thomas, Paul, *Old School Tie* (Auckland: Moa Beckett, 1994).

Thomson, Sir Basil, *P.C. Richardson's First Case* (London: Eldon, 1933).

Thomson, Sir Basil, *Inspector Richardson C.I.D.* (London: Eldon, 1934).

Tidyman, Ernest, *Shaft* (New York: Macmillan, 1970).

Tidyman, Ernest, *The Last Shaft* (London: Weidenfeld and Nicolson, 1975).

Timlin, Mark, *Ashes by Now* (London: Gollancz, 1993).

Treat, Lawrence, *V as in Victim* (New York: Duell, 1945).

Turnbull, Peter, *Deep and Crisp and Even* (London: Collins, 1981).

Turow, Scott, *Presumed Innocent* (New York: Farrar, Strauss, 1987).

Turow, Scott, *Burden of Proof* (New York: Farrar, Strauss, 1990).

Uhnak, Dorothy, *The Bait* (New York: Simon and Schuster, 1968).

Vachss, Andrew H., *Flood* (New York: Fine, 1985).

'Vine, Barbara' (= Ruth Rendell), *A Dark-Adapted Eye* (London: Viking, 1986).

'Vine, Barbara' (= Ruth Rendell), *A Fatal Inversion* (London: Viking, 1987).

'Vine, Barbara' (= Ruth Rendell), *King Solomon's Carpet* (London: Viking, 1991).

'Wade, Henry' (= Henry Lancelot Aubrey-Fletcher), *The Duke of York's Steps* (London: Constable, 1929).

'Wade, Henry' (= Henry Lancelot Aubrey-Fletcher), *Policeman's Lot* (London: Constable, 1933).

'Wade, Henry' (= Henry Lancelot Aubrey-Fletcher), *Constable, Guard Thyself!* (London: Constable, 1934).

'Wakefield, Hannah', *The Price You Pay* (London: Women's Press, 1987).

'Wakefield, Hannah', *A February Mourning* (London: Women's Press, 1990).

Walsh, Jill Paton, *see under* Sayers, Dorothy

Walters, Minette, *The Ice House* (Basingstoke: Palgrave Macmillan, 1992).

Walters, Minette, *The Sculptress* (Basingstoke: Palgrave Macmillan, 1993).

Walters, Minette, *The Scold's Bridle* (Basingstoke: Palgrave Macmillan, 1994).

Walters, Minette, *The Breaker* (Basingstoke: Palgrave Macmillan, 1998).

Waugh, Hilary, *Last Seen Wearing …* (New York: Doubleday, 1952).

Waugh, Hilary, *Sleep Long, My Love* (New York: Doubleday, 1959).

Waugh, Hilary, *'30' Manhattan East* (New York: Doubleday, 1968).

Weller, Archie, 'Songs of the Sea' in *Crimes for a Summer Christmas*, ed. Knight (1990), 119–43.

Weller, Archie, 'All the Pretty Little Horses', in *Murder at Home*, ed. Knight (1993), 171–86.

Wesley, Valerie Wilson, *When Death Comes Stealing* (New York: Putnam, 1994).

Westlake, Donald E., *The Hot Rock* (New York: Simon and Schuster, 1970).

Willeford, Charles, *Cockfighter* (New York: Crown, 1972).

Willeford, Charles, *Miami Blues* (New York: St Martin's, 1984).

Willeford, Charles, *Kiss Your Ass Goodbye* (Toronto: Macmillan, 1987).

Wilson, Barbara, *Murder in the Collective* (Seattle: Seal, 1984).

Wilson, Barbara, *Sisters of the Road* (Seattle: Seal, 1986).

Wilson, Barbara, *The Dog-Collar Murders* (Seattle: Seal, 1989).

Wilson, Barbara, *Gaudí Afternoon* (Seattle: Seal, 1990).

Wings, Mary, *She Came Too Late* (London: Women's Press, 1986).

Wings, Mary, *She Came in a Flash* (New York: New American Library, 1988).

Wright, Eric, *The Night the Gods Smiled* (London: Collins, 1983).

Young, Scott, *Murder in a Cold Climate* (Toronto: Macmillan, 1990).

Zahavi, Helen, *Dirty Weekend* (Basingstoke: Palgrave Macmillan, 1991).
Zaremba, Eve, *A Reason to Kill* (Markham: Paperjacks, 1978).

Secondary

Amos, Thomas L., *Medi-evil Mysteries: A Guide to Detective Fiction Set in the Middle Ages for Collectors, Readers, and Librarians*, Special Supplement, *The Drood Review of Mystery*, May 2001.
Andrews, William C., Foster, Frances Smith and Harris, Trudier, *The Oxford Companion to African-American Literature* (New York: Oxford University Press, 1997).
Ascari, Maurizio (ed.), *Two Centuries of Detective Fiction: A New Comparative Approach* (Bologna: Cotepra, 2000).
Babener, Liahna, 'Uncloseting Ideology in the Novels of Barbara Wilson', in Klein (ed.), *Woman Times Three* (1995) 143–61.
Badmington, Neil (ed.), *Posthumanism* (Basingstoke: Palgrave Macmillan, 2000).
Baker, Diana, *see under* Harris, Anita.
Bakerman, Jane S. (ed.), *10 Women of Mystery* (Bowling Green, OH: Popular Press, 1981).
Barnard, Robert, 'A Talent to Disturb: an Appreciation of Ruth Rendell', *Armchair Detective*, 16 (1983), 146–52.
Bell, Ian A., 'Irony and Justice in Patricia Highsmith' in Bell and Daldry (eds), *Watching the Detectives* (1990), 1–17.
Bell, Ian A., ' "He do the police in different voices": Representations of the Police in Contemporary British Crime Fiction', in Klaus and Knight (eds), *The Art of Murder* (1998), 180–93.
Bell, Ian A. and Daldry, Graham (eds), *Watching the Detectives* (Basingstoke: Palgrave Macmillan, 1990).
Bernstein, Stephen, ' "The Question is the Story Itself": Postmodernism and Intertextuality in Auster's *New York Trilogy*', in Merivale and Sweeney (eds), *Detecting Texts* (1999), 134–53.
Bertens, Hans and D'haen, Theo, *Contemporary American Crime Fiction* (Basingstoke: Palgrave Macmillan, 2001).
Betz, Phyllis, M., 'Playing the Boys' Game' in Gosselin (ed.), *Multicultural Detective Fiction* (1999), 85–103.
Bird, Delys (ed.), *Killing Women: Rewriting Detective Fiction* (Sydney: Angus and Robertson, 1993).
Black, Joel, *The Aesthetics of Murder* (Baltimore, MD: Johns Hopkins University Press, 1991).

252   *References*

Bloom, Clive (ed.), *Twentieth-Century Suspense: The Thriller Comes of Age* (Basingstoke: Palgrave Macmillan, 1990).

Bromley, Roger, 'Rewriting the Masculine Script: the Novels of Joseph Hansen', in Longhurst (ed.), *Gender, Genre and Narrative Pleasure* (1989) 102–17.

Butler, Judith, *Gender Trouble: Feminism and the Subversion of Identity* (New York: Routledge, 1990).

Cadogan, Mary and Craig, Patricia, *The Lady Investigates: Women Detectives and Spies in Fiction* (London: Gollancz, 1981).

Campbell, Sue Ellen, 'The Detective Heroine and the Death of her Hero: Sayers to James', *Modern Fiction Studies*, 29 (1983), 497–10; reprinted in Irons (ed.), *Feminism in Women's Detective Fiction* (1995), 12–28.

Chernaik Warren, Swales Martin and Vilain Robert (eds), *The Art of Detective Fiction* (London: Macmillan, in Association with the Institute for English Studies, School of Advanced Studies, University of London, 2000).

Christianson, Scott, ' "Talkin' Tough and Kickin' Butt": Sue Grafton's Hard-Boiled Feminism', in Irons (ed.), *Feminism in Women's Detective Fiction* (1995), 127–47.

Clover, Carol, 'Her Body, Himself: Gender in the Slasher Film', in *Fantasy and the Cinema*, ed. James Donald (London: British Film Institute, 1989), 91–133.

Cobley, Paul, *The American Thriller: Generic Innovation and Social Change in the 1970s* (Basingstoke: Palgrave Macmillan, 2000).

Cohen, Josh, 'James Ellroy, Los Angeles and the Spectacular Crisis of Masculinity', *Women: A Cultural Review*, 7 (1996), 1–15; reprinted in Messent (ed.), *Criminal Proceedings* (1997), 168–84.

Coward, Rosalind and Semple, Linda, 'Tracking Down the Past: Women and Detective Fiction', in Helen Cross (ed.), *My Guy to Sci Fi: Genre and Women's Writing in the Postmodern World* (London: Pandora, 1989), 39–57.

Cranny-Francis, Anne, *Feminist Fiction* (Cambridge: Polity, 1990).

Daldry, Graham, *see under* Bell, Ian A., 1990.

Danielsson, Karin Molander, *The Dynamic Detective: Special Interest and Seriality in Contemporary Detective Series* (Uppsala: Studia Anglistica Upsaliensa, 2002), 121.

D'haen, Theo, *see under* Bertens, Hans.

Dove, George N., *The Police Procedural* (Bowling Green, OH: Popular Press, 1982).

Dunant, Sarah, 'Body Language: a Study of Death and Gender in Crime Fiction', in W. Chernaik et al. (eds), *The Art of Detective Fiction* (2000), 10–20.

Elmer, Jonathan, *see under* Wolfe, Cary.

Engel, Howard, letter to Stephen Knight, 23 November 1987.

Gair, Christopher, 'Policing the Margins: Barbara Wilson's *Gaudí Afternoon* and *Trouble in Transylvania*', in *Criminal Proceedings*, ed. Messent (1997), 111–26.

Geason, Susan, 'Ain't Misbehavin'', in Bird (ed.), *Killing Women* (1993), 111–23.

Geherin, David, *Sons of Sam Spade* (New York: Ungerer, 1980).

Gorrara, Claire, 'Victors and Victims: the Hard-Boiled Detective and Recent Feminism Crime Fiction', in Klaus and Knight (eds), *The Art of Murder* (1998), 167–79.

Gosselin, Adrienne Johnson, (ed.), *Multicultural Detective Fiction: Murder from the 'Other' Side* (New York: Garland, 1999).

Gosselin, Adrienne Johnson, 'Harlem Heteroglossia: the Voice of Nobody's "Other"', in Gosselin (ed.), *Multicultural Detective Fiction* (1999), 325–49.

Grierson, Thomas, 'An Un-Easy Relationship: Walter Mosley's Signifyin(g) Detective and the Black Community', in Gosselin, *Multicultural Detective Fiction* (1999), 235–55.

Hansen, Joseph, 'Matters Grave and Gay', in Winks, Robin W. (ed.), *Colloquium on Crime*, 111–26.

Harris Anita and Baker, Diana, ' "If I Had a Hammer": Violence as a Feminist Strategy in Helen Zahavi's *Dirty Weekend*', *Women's Studies International Forum*, 18 (1995), 595–601.

Harvey, John, ' "The Last Good Place": James Crumley, the West and the Detective Novel', in Messent (ed.), *Criminal Proceedings* (1997), 150–67.

Haut, Woody, *Pulp Culture: Hardboiled Fiction and the Cold War* (London: Serpent's Tail, 1994).

Haut, Woody, *Neon Noir* (London: Serpent's Tail, 1999).

Heffernan, Nick, 'Law Crimes: the Legal Fictions of John Grisham and Scott Turow', in Messent (ed.), *Criminal Proceedings* (1997), 187–213.

Herbert, Rosemary (ed.), *The Oxford Companion to Crime and Mystery* (New York: Oxford University Press, 1999).

Hilfer, Tony, *The Crime Novel: A Variant Genre* (Austin: University of Texas Press, 1990).

Holquist, Michael, 'Whodunit and Other Questions: Metaphysical Detective Stories in Post-War Fiction', *New Literary History*, 3 (1971), 135–56; reprinted in Most and Stowe (eds), *The Poetics of Murder*, 1983, 149–76.

Horsley, Lee, 'Founding Father: "Genealogies of Violence" in James Ellroy's L.A. Quartet', *Clues*, 19 (1998), 139–65.

Horsley, Lee, *The Noir Thriller* (Basingstoke: Palgrave Macmillan, 2001).

Humm, Maggie, 'Feminist Detective Fiction', in Bloom (ed.), *Twentieth Century Suspense* (1990), 237–54.

Irons, Glenwood (ed.), *Feminism in Women's Detective Fiction* (Toronto: University of Toronto Press, 1995).

Irons, Glenwood (ed.), with Warthly-Roberts, Joan, 'From Spinster to Hipster: the "Suitability" of Miss Marple and Anna Lee', in Irons (ed.), *Feminism in Women's Detective Fiction* (1995), 63–73.

Izzo, Donatella, 'Introduction to Gender and Ethnicity in Contemporary Detective Fiction', in Ascari (ed.), *Two Centuries of Detective Fiction* (2000), 225–31.

Jones, Manina, *see under* Walton, Priscilla L. (1999).

Klaus, H. Gustav and Knight, Stephen (eds), *The Art of Murder: Contemporary Essays on Crime Fiction* (Tübingen: Stauffenburg, 1998).

Klein, Kathleen Gregory (ed.), *Woman Times Three* (Bowling Green, OH: Popular Press, 1995).

Klein, Kathleen Gregory (ed.), 'Patricia Highsmith', in Bakerman (ed.), *And Then There were Nine* (1985) 168–97.

Knight, Stephen, *Form and Ideology in Crime Fiction* (London: Macmillan, 1980).

Knight, Stephen, 'The Knife Beneath the Skin: Crime Writing, Masculinity and Sadism', *Arena*, 97 (1991), 145–56.

Knight, Stephen, *Continent of Mystery: A Thematic History of Australian Crime Fiction* (Melbourne: Melbourne University Press, 1997).

Kristeva, Julia, *Powers of Horror: An Essay on Abjection*, trans. Leon S. Roudiez (New York: Columbia University Press, 1982).

Landrum, Larry N., *American Mystery and Detective Novels: A Reference Guide* (Westport, CT: Greenwood, 1999).

Libretti, Tim, 'Lucha Corpi and the Politics of Detective Fiction', in Gosselin (ed.), *Multicultural Detective Fiction* (1999), 61–81.

Longhurst, Derek (ed.), *Gender, Genre and Narrative Pleasure* (London: Unwin Hyman, 1989).

Maassen, Irmgard, ' "An Unsuitable Job for a Woman": Gender, Genre and the New Detective Heroine', in Klaus and Knight (eds), *The Art of Murder* (1998), 152–66.

Malmgren, Carl D., *Anatomy of a Murder: Mystery, Detection and Crime Fiction* (Bowling Green, OH: Popular Press, 2001).

Mandel, Ernest, *Delightful Murder* (London: Pluto, 1984).

Mann, Jessica, *Deadlier than the Male: An Investigation into Feminine Crime Writing* (Newton Abbot: David and Charles, 1981).

Marchino, Lois A., 'Katherine A. Forrest's Writing', in Klein (ed.), *Woman Times Three* (1995), 65–79.

Merivale, Patricia and Sweeney, Susan Elizabeth, *Detecting Texts: The Metaphysical Detective Story from Poe to Postmodernism* (Philadelphia: University of Pennsylvania Press, 1999).

Messent, Peter (ed.), *Criminal Proceedings: The Contemporary American Crime Novel* (London: Pluto, 1997).

Messent, Peter, 'Introduction: from Private Eye to Police Procedural: the Logic of Contemporary Crime Fiction', in Messent (ed.), *Criminal Proceedings* (1997), 1–21.

Messent, Peter, 'Authority, Social Anxiety and the Body in Crime Fiction: Patricia Cornwell's *Unnatural Exposure*', in Chernaik et al. (eds), *The Art of Detective Fiction* (2000), 124–37.

Most, Glenn and Stowe, William W. (eds), *The Poetics of Murder* (New York: Harcourt, Brace, Jovanovich, 1983).

Munt, Sally, *Murder by the Book: Feminist and the Crime Novel* (London: Routledge, 1994).

Murray, David, 'Reading the Signs: Detection and Anthropology in the Work of Tony Hillerman', in Messent (ed.), *Criminal Proceedings* (1997), 127–49.

Nealon, Jeffrey, T., 'Work of the Detective, Work of the Writer: Auster's *City of Glass*', *Modern Fiction Studies*, 42 (1996), 91–110; reprinted in revised form in Merivale and Sweeney (eds), *Detecting Texts* (1999), 117–33.

Nixon, Nicola, 'Gray Areas: P. D. James's Unsuiting of Cordelia', in Irons (ed.), *Feminism in Women's Detective Fiction* (1995), 29–45.

Oates, Joyce Carol, ' "I Had No Other Thrills or Happiness" ', *New York Review of Books*, 24 March 1994, 52–9.

Palmer, Paulina, 'The Lesbian Thriller: Transgressive Investigations', in Messent, *Criminal Proceedings* (1997), 87–110.

Panek, Leroy Lad Panek, 'PostWar American Police Fiction', in Priestman, *Detective Fiction* (2003).

Paretsky, Sara (ed.), *A Woman's Eye* (New York: Delacorte, 1990).

Pederson, Jay P. (ed.), *St James Guide to Crime and Mystery Writers*, 4th edn (Detroit, MI: St James Press, 1996).

Pepper, Andrew, *The Contemporary American Crime Novel: Race, Ethnicity, Gender, Class* (Edinburgh: Edinburgh University Press, 2000).

Pepper, Andrew, 'Black Crime Fiction', in Priestman, *Detective Fiction* (2003).

Plain, Gill, *Twentieth-Century Crime Fiction: Gender, Sexuality and the Body* (Edinburgh: Edinburgh University Press, 2001).

Priestman, Martin, *Detective Fiction and Literature: The Figure on the Carpet* (Basingstoke: Palgrave Macmillan, 1990).

Priestman, Martin, *Crime Fiction* (Plymouth: Northcote House in Association with the British Council, 1998).

Priestman, Martin (ed.), *The Cambridge Companion to Crime Fiction* (Cambridge: Cambridge University Press, 2003).

Pykett, Lyn, 'Investigating Women: the Female Sleuth after Feminism', in Bell and Daldry (eds), *Watching the Detectives* (1990), 48–67.

Rankin, Ian, 'Heroes Doing it by the Book', *The Times*, 18 May 1998, 9.

Reddy, Maureen, T., *Sisters in Crime: Feminism and the Crime Novel* (New York: Continuum, 1988).

Reddy, Maureen, T., 'Women Detectives', in Priestman, *Detective Fiction* (2003).

Reilly, John M. (ed.), *Twentieth-Century Crime and Mystery Writers* (New York: St Martin's Press, 1980).

Reilly, John M. (ed.), 'Margaret Millar', in Earl R. Bargainnier (ed.), *10 Women of Mystery* (Bowling Green, OH: Popular Press, 1981), 123–66.

Reitz, Caroline, 'Do We Need Another Hero?' in Gosselin (ed.), *Multicultural Detective Fiction* (1999), 213–33.

Roberts, Jeanne Addison, 'Feminist Murder: Amanda Cross Reinvents Womanhood', in Irons (ed.), *Feminism in Women's Detective Fiction* (1995), 94–111.

Roth, Lawrence, 'Unravelling "Intermarriages" in Faye Kellerman's Detective Tradition', in Gosselin (ed.), *Multicultural Detective Fiction* (1999), 185–211.

Roth, Marty, *Foul and Fair Play: Reading Genre in Classic Detective Fiction* (Athens: University of Georgia Press, 1995).

Rowland, Susan, *From Agatha Christie to Ruth Rendell: British Women Writers in Detective and Crime Fiction* (Basingstoke: Palgrave Macmillan, 2001).

Schmid, David, 'Chester Himes and the Institutionalization of Multicultural Detective Fiction', in Gosselin (ed.), *Multicultural Detective Fiction* (1999), 283–302.

Selzer, Mark, 'Serial Killers (1)', *Differences: A Journal of Feminist Cultural Studies*, 5 (1995), 92–128.

Semple, Linda, *see under* Coward, Rosalind.

Skene-Melvin, L. St C. David, *Canadian Crime Fiction* (Shelburne: The Battered Silicon Despatch Box, 1996).

Soitos, Stephen F., *The Blues Detective: A Study of African-American Detective Fiction* (Amherst: University of Massachusetts Press, 1996).

Soitos, Stephen F., 'Crime and Mystery Writing', in Andrews, William L., Foster, Frances Smith and Harris, Trudier (eds), *The Oxford Companion to African-American Literature* (New York: Oxford University Press, 1997), 182–4.

Soitos, Stephen F., 'Queering the "I": Black Lesbian Detective Fiction', in Gosselin (ed.), *Multicultural Detective Fiction* (1999), 105–21.

Sturm, Terry (ed.), *The Oxford History of New Zealand Literature*, 2nd edn (Auckland: Oxford University Press, 1998).

Swales, Martin, *see under* Chernaik, Warren.

Sweeney, Susan Elizabeth, 'Gender-Blending, Genre-Bending and the Rendering of Identity in Barbara Wilson's *Gaudí Afternoon*', in Gosselin (ed.), *Multicultural Detective Fiction* (1999), 123–41.

Symons, Julian, *Bloody Murder*, 3rd edn (London: Penguin, 1992).

Tamaya, Meera, 'Keating's Inspector Ghote: Post-Colonial Detection?' in Gosselin (ed.), *Multicultural Detective Fiction* (1999), 17–36.

Tani, Stefano, *The Doomed Detective: The Contribution of the Detective Novel to Postmodern American and Italian Fiction* (Carbondale: Southern Illinois University Press, 1984).

Templeton, Wayne, '*Xojo* and Homicide: the Postcolonial Murder Mysteries of Tony Hillerman', in Gosselin (ed.), *Multicultural Detective Fiction* (1999), 37–59.

Tomara, Edward, 'James McLure's Mickey Zondi: the Partner of Apartheid', in Gosselin (ed.), *Multicultural Detective Fiction* (1999), 37–54.

Tomc, Sandra, 'Questing Women: the Feminist Mystery after Feminism', in Irons (ed.), *Feminism in Women's Detective Fiction* (1995), 46–63.

Vanacker, Sabine, 'V. I. Warshawsi, Kinsey Millhone and Kay Scarpetta: Creating a Feminist Detective Hero', in Messent (ed.), *Criminal Proceedings* (1997), 62–88.

Vilain, Robert, *see under* Chernaik, Warren.

Walker, Ronald G. and June M. (eds), *The Cunning Craft: Original Essays on Detective Fiction and Contemporary Literary Theory* (Urbana: University of Illinois Press, 1990).

Walton, Priscilla L., ' "E" is for Engendering Readers: Sue Grafton and Kinsey Millhone', in Klein (ed.), *Woman Times Three* (1995), 101–15.

Walton, Priscilla L., 'Business Metaphysics? Feminist Paradigms and Racial Intervention in Mainstream Hardboiled Women's Detective Fiction', in Gosselin (ed.), *Multicultural Detective Fiction* (1999), 257–79.

Walton, Priscilla L., and Jones, Manina, *Detective Agency: Women Rewriting the Hard-Boiled Tradition* (Berkeley: University of California Press, 1999).

Watson, Colin, *Snobbery with Violence* (London: Eyre and Spottiswoode, 1971).

Willett, Ralph, *Hardboiled Detective Fiction* (Keele: British Association for American Studies, 1992).

Willett, Ralph, *The Naked City: Urban Crime Fiction in the USA* (Manchester: Manchester University Press, 1996).

Winks, Robin W., 'Afterword' to K. C. Constantine, *The Rocksburg Railroad Mystery*, reprint edn (Boston, MA: Godine, 1982).

Winks, Robin W. (ed.), *Colloquium on Crime: Eleven Renowned Mystery Writers Discuss Their Work* (New York: Scribner, 1986).

Winks, Robin W. (ed.), *Mystery and Suspense Writers: The Literature of Crime, Detection and Espionage*, 2 vols (New York: Scribner, 1998).

Winston, Robert P., and Mellerski, Nancy C., *The Public Eye: Ideology and the Police Procedural* (New York: St Martin's, 1992).

Wolf, Naomi, 'The Animals Speak', *New Statesman and Nation*, 12 April, 1991, 33–4.

Wolfe, Cary and Elmer, Jonathan, ' "Subject to Sacrifice": Ideology, Psychoanalysis and the Discourse of Species in Jonathan Demme's *The Silence of the Lambs*', *boundary 2*, 22 (1995), 141–70.

Woods, Paula L., *Spooks, Spies and Private Eyes: Black Mystery, Crime and Suspense Fiction of the 20th Century* (New York: Doubleday, 1995).

Index

Titles of works published under pseudonyms are entered under authors' real names when known, with cross-references from the pseudonym.

DATE DUE

SEP 2 2			